INTENTIONAL MANHOOD

A COACH'S PERSPECTIVE

BY COACH MIKE STANLEY

Book design and production by Columbus Publishing Lab
www.ColumbusPublishingLab.com

Paperback ISBN: 978-1-63337-389-1
E-book ISBN: 978-1-63337-390-7

Printed in the United States of America
1 3 5 7 9 10 8 6 4 2

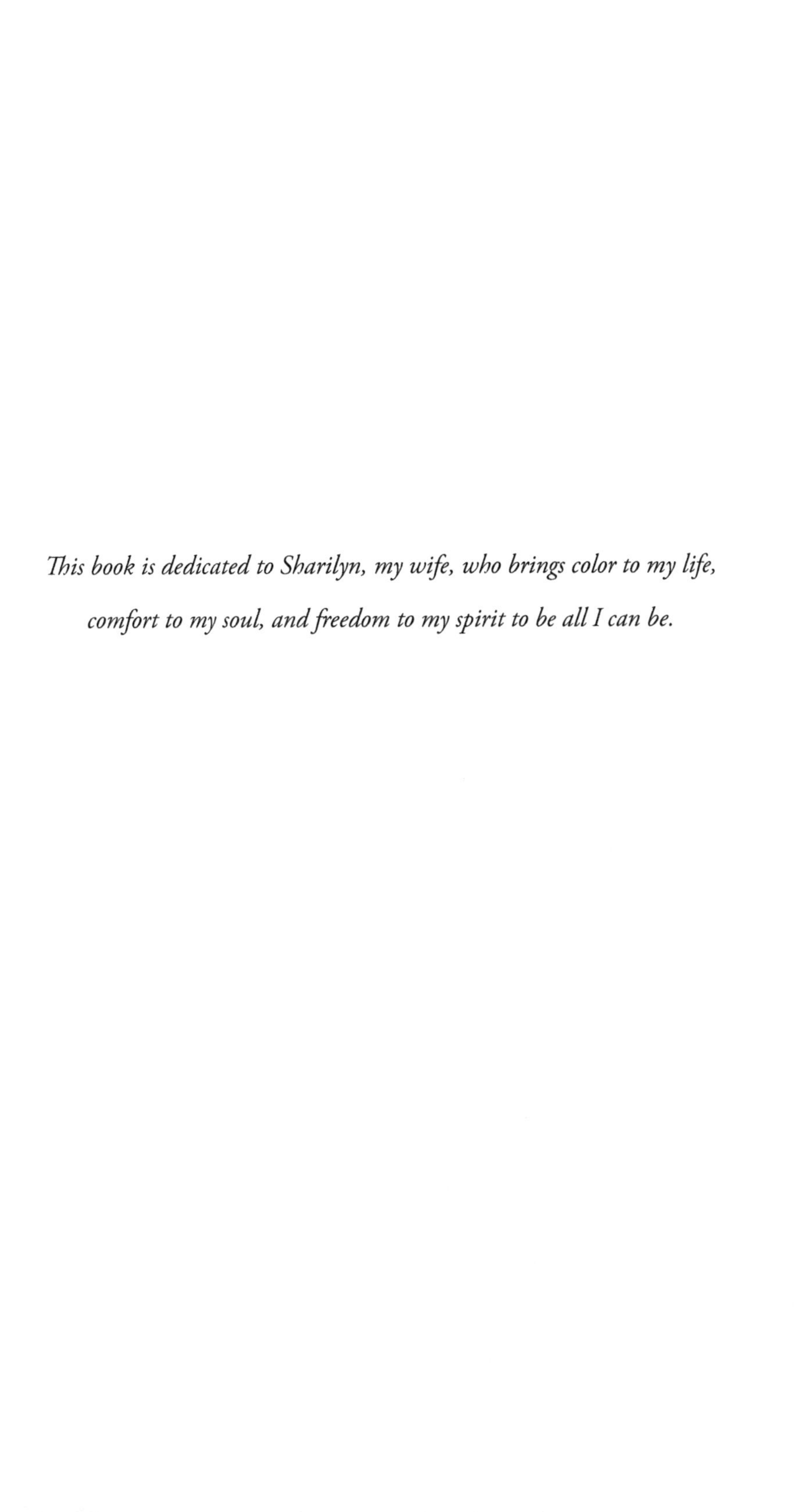

This book is dedicated to Sharilyn, my wife, who brings color to my life, comfort to my soul, and freedom to my spirit to be all I can be.

CONTENTS

FOREWORD

MIKE CHEESEMAN,
FOUNDER OF THE COLUMBUS CRUSADERS

I HAVE KNOWN COACH MIKE STANLEY for many years. I met him when he was a new believer in Christ, long before there was a Columbus Crusaders program. A few years after I met Mike, we asked him to be the head coach for our team. Thankfully, he accepted. During his first year of coaching, Mike was challenged by a football player named Ben Barlow to explain the lack of spiritual direction within the program. Mike did not cower from the challenge. He was grieved, yet he was also passionate about seeking God's direction. While working through this challenge, God graciously empowered Mike to lead our football program to its transformation into a ministry where manhood is taught and Jesus is honored.

Throughout this process, I observed how God truly empowered Mike with the wisdom, skill, and heart to exceed what we had imagined and hoped for. I believe that God changed Mike as He equipped him to lead our team spiritually, and that the Crusader ministry would not be what it is today had Mike not been involved.

Mike's leadership and dependence upon Christ have taught me and others to learn and embrace the same biblical truths that he is now sharing with you in this book.

The stories and catchphrases in this book will stick with you. Mike's lessons are easy to read, yet also powerful. This combination brings clarity to biblical principles through practical application, sure to resonate with men of all ages and in all life stages.

FOREWORD

I tend to get lost in the formal academics of teaching, but Mike's conversational style of writing spoke to me in a way that was profound. The themes of this book are universal and applicable, while also effectively personal. Many others have written books about leadership, manhood, etc., but this book really hits home, where you live, and where the rubber meets the road.

Sitting under Mike's coaching and teaching for so many years has given me first-hand knowledge of how the ideas in this book can impact your life. Mike's influence has changed my life in ways for which I am deeply grateful.

I am a building contractor by trade, so I recognize the importance of laying a solid foundation. Mike has built this book on the solid foundation that is the name of Christ, presented within these pages as the acrostic: C. H. R. I. S. T. As I move throughout my day-to-day life, dealing with different situations that arise, I think frequently of this acrostic and it reminds me moment by moment to be Committed, be Honorable, be Responsible, take Initiative, be a Servant, and speak Truth. Mike uses each letter of the name of Christ as his foundation, from which he builds and develops practical examples of men in the Bible who God used to reveal their purpose and plan. God has that same plan for men today. It's a timeless message, and one that can be found in *Intentional Manhood* if you'll listen.

Mike is the real deal, and I am blessed to have coached with him for many years. I am doubly blessed to have Mike as a brother in Christ and to consider him my very good friend.

Mike Cheeseman
Founder of The Columbus Crusaders

PREFACE

IT SEEMS LIKE YESTERDAY when Tom Ensign asked me if I would meet with him and Mike Cheeseman. Certainly, this was an innocent request as I know both men well. I had a great deal of respect for them and their ministry, the Columbus Crusaders, which they had started first as the Central Ohio Crusaders in 1996. The concept was truly unique. They had formed a football program for young men attending private schools with no football programs, plus homeschoolers and a few public-school youngsters. They also included young ladies as cheerleaders.

The real impetus for this endeavor began one Sunday morning when Mike's pastor, Jim Custer of Grace Polaris Church, gave a sermon on who among us is called to full-time Christian ministry. As you might imagine, his assertion was that we are all called to full-time Christian service; it's just that some of us are cleverly disguised as doctors, plumbers, teachers, and homemakers. Mike's wife, Betsy, had been earnestly trying to get Mike to teach Sunday school with her, but Mike, one of the finest remodeling contractors I know, felt he was not gifted to be a teacher and public speaker. So God made a way to put a round peg in a round hole and not force a square peg into a round hole.

In the sermon that morning, Pastor Jim contended that each professing Christian could combine his love for Jesus with his passion in life. Mike considered this challenge and decided he could combine his love for Jesus and his love for football. Living in Columbus, Ohio, following The Ohio

State Buckeyes, and having a young son about the age of a beginning football player convinced Mike to start a football ministry with Tom's help. Because the school where the young men attended did not have a football program, Mike was concerned his son and others would never get to experience "Friday Night Football" as other young men did.

The two men combined forces and started a sixth-grade team and seventh-grade team. They were very successful in football and character development using biblical discipleship, and three years later the program had grown to a high school team, a middle school team, a fifth-grade team, and a sixth-grade team.

Now, for some reason they wanted to meet with me. I remember telling my wife as I was leaving for the meeting that they were probably going to ask me to coach. However, I was only going to meet with them out of respect for who they were; I certainly was not going to coach. Two hours later, I returned home with a stack of playbooks under my arm, and my wife looked at me and chuckled. "Guess you changed your mind," she said.

That day, I started on a journey God had planned for me before the beginning of the world, unbeknownst to me. I realized I was in a unique situation where I had the time, talent, and treasure for this calling because God had provided them in advance of the need. In fact, I realized that my whole life up to that point had been orchestrated by the Lord to give me the skills I would need to be the director of the ministry. During my journey, the Lord has revealed some amazing insights to me. For example, athletics is useful for teaching lessons about life: teamwork, sacrifice for the team, playing within the rules, and the joy of achieving a goal that you never thought you could achieve. Football teaches you how to get back up after being knocked down, and that there is always someone better than you, which teaches humility.

IN THIS DAY AND AGE, ONE OF THE MOST CRITICAL LESSONS YOU CAN LEARN IS HOW TO PROPERLY SUBMIT TO CRITICISM AND HOW TO REACT WHEN YOU ARE HANDED A SETBACK.

ACKNOWLEDGMENTS

AS I BEGIN THIS BOOK, I have a few very special people I want to thank. First, my wife, Sharilyn, who inspires me to be "intentional" about growing more like Christ every day.

My sons, Beau and Stephen, have grown up to be terrific young men fully committed to being men of C. H. R. I. S. T. Fellows, you make your old father proud.

As you can imagine, growing requires you to have men around you who will tell you when you fall short. As a coach, I have been fired up and shared things with officials in a poor way at times. Mike Cheeseman and Jim Bauman have been friends I trust for the truth. Sometimes that requires me to ask for the forgiveness of players, officials, and even my own coaches.

I will never be able to say thank you enough to Rick Nuzum, the human instrument God used to save my soul. Thanks, Rick, for mentoring me and becoming my dear friend.

Pastor Jim Custer has poured spiritual insights and wisdom into me in Sunday morning sermons and chats at McDonald's for thirty-plus years. I respect you immensely.

Robert Lewis deserves my deep gratitude because his book *Raising a Modern-Day Knight* changed my life and the spiritual direction of the Columbus Crusaders.

This book would not be as clear and concise as it is without the help of Jennifer Edwards, my editor. Jennifer has made me appear to be a good writer, and I'm grateful.

My publisher, Columbus Publishing Lab, led by Emily Hitchcock, has polished my thinking and guided me through a very difficult journey as a new author. You guys are the best.

I want to thank the men and women of the Crusaders—coaches, parents, and volunteers—who have sharpened me with their insights and have cared about me so much that I never wanted to let them down.

Lastly, I want to thank the young men who have allowed me to play a part in shaping their lives. In so doing, you have enriched mine. I am not worried about the next generation. If you knew the men I do, you wouldn't be worried either.

INTRODUCTION

MEN, WE ARE GIVEN A *HEROIC CALLING* by God Himself. However, much of our society, TV, and Hollywood have maligned men repeatedly. Many of us have forgotten, or perhaps never knew, just how important a man's calling is to a healthy and well-functioning society. The common wisdom of the day about men and manhood is wrong.

BEING A MAN IS A SPECIAL GIFT.

The first time I read the assertion that men are less emotionally stable than women, I was completely caught off guard and didn't buy the idea. Nevertheless, I reflected on the young men I have coached over the last forty years and the men with whom I have coached. I was stunned to realize that most men really are not as secure and confident as most women are. Oftentimes, we mistake the "public persona" of men as their real personality, but truly it is their very "private persona" that drives most of us. The English writer Samuel Johnson put it clearly and concisely when he said, "Every man knows that of himself which he dare not tell his dearest friend."[1] God said much the same thing when He spoke through

---

1 David White, "Starting Over… *Again,*" BBN Bible Institute, published January 10, 2014, http://www.bbnradio.org/wcm4/bbnbienglish/BiblebrInstitute/tabid/257/ArticleID/15306/Default.aspx.

the Prophet Jeremiah saying, "The heart is desperately wicked who can know it" (Jeremiah 17:9 NASB).[2]

This self-awareness leads to poor self-esteem and often leads men to seek approval in addictive, harmful, or unacceptable ways. Men begin to put on the "public persona" of toughness, control, and insensitivity, while often feeling alone and unsure in their "private persona." I have found there to be a disconnect between the inward and the outward man, which leads to false bravado and gang thinking. As Fred Smith, Zig Ziglar's mentor, has said to me, "Men begin to confuse being respected with being feared." What a travesty for them and society.

I believe in "Intentional Manhood." I have written this book to give men a clear, organized, and concise definition of biblical manhood—the only *true* manhood there is. With this clear definition, men can be *intentional* about striving to achieve all that God has called them to be. When we can see the target clearly, we can then move boldly to become the men society needs.

Much of the recent writings in Christian circles, as well as some secular writings, call all men to be involved in *manly* activities. I believe, and Manhood in Action Ministries, my ministry, teaches, that music, theater, and art are as much manly activities as hunting, rafting, and climbing mountains. Manhood isn't about the activity; it is about your inner strength in whatever honorable activity you pursue. All you have to do is listen to Handel's *Messiah* and you can hear the very spirit of manhood bursting out. Therefore, Manhood in Action exists to challenge and inspire men to follow and honor Jesus Christ with their lives.

When the Bible tells us to "train up a child in the way he should go," it refers to encouraging the child to follow his God-given bent for life. When I was a young man, my father, who was a true academic, would have far preferred I be admitted to Phi Beta Kappa (a national honorary academic

---

2 Ken Boa & Larry Moody, *I'm Glad You Asked: In-Depth Answers To Difficult Questions About Christianity,* (Colorado Springs: David C Cook Publishing, 1995), 181.

club) than to be a great football player. Yet he knew my desire was to excel in athletics, so he read books and researched other resources to help me reach my dreams. He encouraged me in the way I should go, even though it was not his preference, and I am truly grateful to him.

When we prepare for a journey, very few of us would ever consider hiking in the wilderness areas of Canada without a guide or a map. So why do so many of us try to go through the maze of life with its obstacles and pitfalls without direction? One definition for guide is an "outline of conduct." What could be a better outline of our conduct as men than Jesus Christ Himself? Psalm 48:14 says, "For such is God, Our God forever and ever; He will guide us until death." So, in this book, we will use an outline of conduct for Intentional Manhood that calls men toward the traits of C. H. R. I. S. T.: Commitment, Honor, Responsibility, Initiative, Service, (the) Truth. Many folks from many religions, even atheists, wish to be true men, but they can never achieve their goal because it takes the Holy Spirit to be able to live a life of Christ, as opposed to simply being a man of *chris* (notice the absence of the *T*, for *truth*). It takes all six of these traits to be a God-honoring, biblical man.

Fred Smith also said as a guest on my radio show, "You are the way you are because that's the way you want to be. If you really wanted to be any different, you would be in the process of changing right now." Just by reading and embracing the concepts in this book, you are beginning the process of change. Most men like formulas with specifics, and *Intentional Manhood* will present a clear, detailed game plan to pursue true manhood. However, never lose sight of the fact that formulas or methods only work when a true desire to "seek first His kingdom and His righteousness" exists (Matthew 6:33).

To paraphrase E. M. Bounds, "Men are God's method. Society is looking for better methods. God is looking for better men."[3] However, I

---

3 Andrew Webb, "E.M. Bounds on the Kind of Man Preachers Need to Be," published December 13, 2008, https://biblebased.wordpress.com/2008/12/13/em-bounds-on-the-kind-of-man-preachers-need-to-be/.

would add that sometimes men need better methods to become better men. My prayer is that this formula, this method, this game plan, will help us all become better men.

Our game plan for raising boys and sharpening men has been successful; it has changed men's lives for the better. As a coach, I believe in the KISS concept: Keep It Simple, Stupid. This concept reminds me that I need to keep it simple so we can all reach this worthy goal. My sons, our coaches, and our players use Manhood Language on a day-to-day basis to be able to exhort, encourage, and correct one another. If you apply the ideas in this book intentionally, they will change your life and the lives of those around you in a positive way.

In the movie *Facing the Giants*, the coach admits to Mr. Bridges, a man who walks the halls and prays for the students, that he is struggling with the season; he is praying, but he just isn't seeing God at work. Mr. Bridges then tells him this story:

"There were two farmers who desperately needed rain. Both of them prayed for rain, but only one of them went out and prepared his fields to receive it. Which one do you think really trusted God to send the rain?"[4]

MEN, WE NEED TO BE ABOUT PREPARING THE FIELDS RIGHT NOW!

As you read this book, my hope for you is that, first and foremost, you will have a definition of what biblical manhood really looks like. With this definition and a copy of the Manhood Language, you will be able to examine your life through the filter of Intentional Manhood. But the journey only starts there. I hope you will share this with your sons, grandsons, sons-in-law, and friends, maybe even your kids' coaches, so they can begin to implement Intentional Manhood principles in their families and teams.

If you want to have a different definition of manhood, that's fine, but at least have one! I highly encourage you to make sure it is based in biblical Truth.

---

4 *Facing the Giants*, directed by Alex Kendrick (Albany, GA: Sherwood Pictures, 2006).

Allow me to pray this prayer for you and all of us as we begin this journey toward true manhood:

> *Father God, You are so awesome. We stand in amazement that You would call us friends if we know You as Lord and Savior. Lord Jesus, may our lives honor You in all we do. Holy Spirit, we can only live the life we want to live which glorifies You, as You give us the power to do so. Fill us and let us be warriors for You in a darkened world. We have hope because we have read the final chapter of the Bible and we know You love us.*
>
> *May all the men who read this book and put it into action stand before You someday, and may You say "well done" to them and to me. It is with gratitude that we acknowledge what You have done for us at such a terrible cost to You. May our lives honor You as we live intentionally for You.*
>
> *I pray this in Your name and for Your glory, Jesus. Amen!*

CHAPTER ONE

SEE IT CLEARLY

I HAVE SPENT MY LIFE coaching and working with men of all ages. I am not a Bible scholar, but I am very serious about the Word of God. I try as much as humanly possible to accurately reflect God's call to men as He chronicled in the Bible.

Until I was thirty-nine, I didn't care about God's thoughts; I only tried to please myself. From a worldly perspective I had it all. I was a McDonald's franchise owner; I had a beautiful, fit, and caring wife, and two great boys. From the outside appearance of my life, I should have been happy and satisfied. But I wasn't. I was miserable.

All my life, I busted my tail to achieve, either in athletics or making money. As an athlete, I was All-League in football, wrestling, and baseball, and I placed third in the state of Ohio in wrestling and was honorable mention All-State in football. Some could say I achieved a lot of notoriety in sports. Even though I achieved my goal of making lots of money, by August 1, 1986, I was terribly unhappy with life. How did I have so much and feel completely empty? I kept asking myself, *Is this all there is to life?* I was at the top, but I was so low. My marriage was falling apart (and would have ended if it were not for my wife's toughness and determination), and things were spiraling out of control. I didn't know what else to do but turn in the only direction I never had before. I asked God to show Himself to me. Incredibly, He did.

Today, I serve Jesus Christ from appreciation not obligation; not from the "must I?" of duty, but the "may I?" of love. He took me from a boy who was always seeking approval from others to a man who understood that my intrinsic worth was due to the God of Creation, the God of the Universe. As a result, I no longer need a steady diet of the approval of others. God is showing me what true love really is. By God's grace and my decision to believe and receive Christ, Sharilyn and I celebrated our fiftieth wedding anniversary in June of 2019. It was a wonderful celebration with family and friends who walked with us and stood by us all these years. You see, I am convinced that had I not turned to God, we would have been divorced and my children's lives would have been much harder. I also know beyond a doubt that had I not changed I would have likely died from heart problems or obesity.

Over the past fifty years I have coached seven state wrestling champions, an All-American at Miami University, and multiple All-League football players. I coached with some terrific young coaches, such as Jim Tressel, the former head football coach at The Ohio State University, and Jim Bollman, a coach who is at Michigan State University at the time of this writing. My teams won a State Championship and had two Runners-Up in wrestling. I learned early on in coaching that Woody Hayes was right: "You win with people." Sometimes I had them, and sometimes I didn't. However, the most critical thing I ever did from a coaching perspective was to coach for the Columbus Crusaders, where we say, "Manhood is taught, and Jesus is honored."

When I became a Christian, Jesus changed my entire focus of coaching. My reasons and goals for coaching, which used to be self-serving and self-seeking, are now focused on honoring Jesus in every way—both in my own life and by building true manhood into the lives of those God has entrusted to me. As the apostle Paul said in 2 Corinthians 3:2, "You are our letter, written in our hearts, known and read by all men." That's a paraphrase of how I feel as a coach about the players and men I have coached over the years.

Every day is an adventure serving the King of Kings, and I am happy to be walking with you on this quest, this journey toward intentional manhood.

As an athlete, I have had many coaches and men in my life, and I learned a great deal from them. My high school coach, Marv Moorehead, was one of the winningest coaches in Ohio high school football. One of his favorite sayings was "See it clearly." He recognized that if we didn't have a clear picture of what we wanted to accomplish, then we would hesitate at critical times. Great men, like great athletes, must be willing, able, and prepared to act properly on a moment's notice. We must know in advance what our *goal* is so that we can intentionally press on toward that goal.

"WE MUST KNOW IN ADVANCE WHAT OUR GOAL IS SO THAT WE CAN INTENTIONALLY PRESS ON TOWARD THAT GOAL."

When I speak to young men, I often ask for two helpers. I'll ask one of the young men to find a person they know, and I'll ask the other young man to find a person, but I don't tell him whom. When I say *go,* the first young man makes a straight line to his target, while the other young man stands confused, unable to go anywhere because he has no clear goal. I believe many men live their lives that way. They get up in the morning and life happens to them. Billy Graham was once asked what surprised him most about life, and he answered, "The brevity of it." No matter how much life you have left, use it wisely or it will pass you by. An old cliché says that "failing to plan is planning to fail," and every plan should start with the goal, the target, the end result in mind.

In the Bible, Jesus asks the people in the crowd who want to follow him:

> For which one of you, when he wants to build a tower, does not first sit down and calculate the cost to see if he has enough to complete it? Otherwise, when he has laid a foundation and is not

> able to finish, all who observe it begin to ridicule him, saying, "This man began to build and was not able to finish." Or what king, when he sets out to meet another king in battle, will not first sit down and consider whether he is strong enough with ten thousand men to encounter the one coming against him with twenty thousand? Or else, while the other is still far away, he sends a delegation and asks for terms of peace (Luke 14:28–32).

Jesus knows planning is critical to success, but you can't plan if you aren't sure of what your goal is. Personally, my goal in life is simple! I wish to stand before the Lord Jesus Christ and hear Him say, "Well done, good and faithful servant; you were faithful with a few things, I will put you in charge of many things, enter into the joy of your master" (Matthew 25:21). I know men who have a list of goals for family, personal growth, ministry, and many other aspects of their lives. That's too many goals for me! A goal must be short, specific, and at the top of your mind to have any real value. To be effective, your goal must be able to help you with decision-making every day, whether the decision is small or big. How can I know what I do will cause Jesus to say, "Well done"? I test all my behavior by thinking, *Will it honor Jesus?*

1. Is it beneficial?
2. Is it enslaving?
3. Will it hinder the spiritual growth of a brother?
4. Does it edify?

Many ask themselves the question, "What would Jesus do?" Unfortunately, sometimes I don't know, but I almost always know what would Honor Jesus.

"IF EVERY DECISION I MAKE HONORS JESUS, I WILL REACH MY GOAL."

One of the great missionaries in Egypt, a man named Douglas Thornton, had the qualities of a man who sees the goal not the obstacles. A colleague of Thornton's once said to him, "You are different than anyone else I know. You are always looking at the end of things. Most people, me included, find it better to do the next thing." Thornton responded, "I find the constant inspiration gained by looking at the goal is the chief thing that helps me persevere."[1]

You and I need to "fix our eyes on Jesus, the author and perfecter of faith" (Hebrews 12:2). And like Peter, we must get out of the boat to meet the heroic calling Christ has for men. But unlike Peter, we must not take our eyes off of Christ, so we can complete our mission, our goal (Matthew 14:28–30).

Whatever your goal is, be aware that only what is done for Christ will count at the believers' judgment, commonly called the Bema Seat. In 2 Corinthians 5:9–10, Paul says, "Therefore we also have as our ambition whether at home or absent, to be pleasing to Him. For we must all appear before the judgment seat of Christ [Bema Seat] so that each one may be recompensed for his *deeds* in the body according to what he has done, whether good or bad." 1 Corinthians 3:12–15 expands on what happens at the judgment seat: "Now if any man builds on the foundation (saving faith) with gold, silver, precious stones, wood hay, straw, each man's *work* will become evident; for the day will show it to be revealed with fire, and the fire itself will test the quality of each man's work. If any man's work is burned up, he will suffer loss; but he himself will be saved yet so as through fire." I have emphasized the words "deeds" and "work" to make this clear—Jesus cares about how we live and will reward us in heaven when we honor Him.

I like how author and missionary Dr. J. Herbert Kane defines the criteria for what will be rewarded at the Bema Seat:

---

1 J. Oswald Sanders, *Spiritual Leadership: Principles of Excellence for Every Believer* (Chicago: The Moody Bible Institute, 2007), 56.

1. Did you do it for the glory of God?
2. Did you do it because you love Jesus Christ?
3. Did you do it in the power of the Holy Spirit?

When our actions are done "heartily as unto the Lord," we will be rewarded by having Jesus say, "Well done" (Matthew 25:21). Certainly, this is a worthy goal for life! Remember, "Only one life 'twill soon be passed, only what's done for Christ will last."[2]

Since this book is about working toward intentional manhood—our clear, concise goal—and we know Jesus is our guide, it's time for the game plan. How will we get there? We need to be careful that our game plan reflects God's will for our lives and not our own selfish desires. Isaiah 30:1 makes this very clear when God says, "Woe to the rebellious children, who execute a plan but not Mine." H. Stanley Judd once said, "A good plan is like a road map; it shows the final destination and usually the best way to get there."[3] No coach or general would ever go to battle without clear, specific strategies for how the team can know the enemy and exploit his weakness. "If you know the enemy and you know yourself, you need not fear the results of 100 battles. If you know yourself and not the enemy, for every victory gained you will also suffer a defeat. If you know neither your enemy nor yourself, you will succumb."[4] Victory is the only acceptable outcome.

We need to know exactly what true manhood means...and since our guide is Christ, then we're after a higher form of manhood—a biblical manhood, which Christ Himself defines. He's the one with the game plan. Let's find out what it is.

---

2 C.T. Studd, *Only One Life, Twill Soon Be Past, Poetry About Jesus & Salvation*, http://cavaliersonly.com/poetry_by_christian_poets_of_the_past/only_one_life_twill_soon_be_past_-_poem_by_ct_studd.

3 H. Stanley Judd, Personal communication.

4 Sun Tzu, *The Art of War* (New York: Dover Ixia Press, 2019).

CHAPTER TWO

GAME PLAN FOR INTENTIONAL MANHOOD

IN CRUSADER FOOTBALL, we work hard to provide our players with a quality football experience. Who would want to play football and not truly compete in order to really test our manhood? In our politically correct society, the name "Crusader" sometimes carries a negative connotation. A true crusader is one who engages in a vigorous, concerted action to achieve a significant goal or mission. No goal is more significant than sharing the good news of Jesus Christ to keep another soul from spending eternity in hell. Like Jesus, and unlike the early crusaders, we must never force a person to follow Christ; we must simply be available to be used by the Holy Spirit so the person's life can be transformed. Nevertheless, we balance football with strong discipleship and character building.

The mission statement for Crusader Football is "Guiding Young Men to Biblical Manhood through Excellence in Football." This two-pronged objective demands serious commitment to balancing athletics and discipleship. This is truly an "adventure to live," as John Eldridge describes in his book *Wild at Heart,* one far beyond the mundane, common adventures of life.[1]

Our ministry and my life changed forever in the off-season coaches' Bible study in 2001. One of our coaches, Bob Natale, came to us and recommended we read Robert Lewis's book *Raising a Modern-Day Knight.*

---

1 John Eldridge, *Wild at Heart: Discovering the Secret of a Man's Soul* (Nashville: Thomas Nelson, 2001).

Lewis challenges fathers to consider raising young men in the same manner that men of old developed knights. In the knight tradition, a young man of a certain age became a page first, then a squire, and finally a knight. When he became a knight, he never had to wonder if he had met the definition of a knight because he was officially dubbed a knight in a special, visible, and moving ceremony.[2]

In our society today, many men wonder if they truly measure up to manhood. To begin with, they are not entirely sure what the title "Man" means, and secondly, no one has ever conferred the title "Man" upon them. Our society doesn't confer manhood clearly or publicly. Manhood in Action Ministries is deeply committed to helping men know for sure what it means to be a man and how to go about achieving that goal. Many men reading this are old enough to know they are a man by age but aren't absolutely sure they measure up to manhood in the eyes of those around them. Part of the reason why they're not sure is that no one ever conferred manhood upon them. The knight was clearly and publicly proclaimed a knight. Some men have a void in their lives, a confusion—something needing immediate resolution because they do not know whether or not they measure up as a man.

Imagine your dad saying, "Be a man," and thinking to yourself, *What does that mean exactly? Am I not to cry; am I to fight at any slight? Am I to drink and carouse and seduce lots of women? What does "being a man" mean?* To achieve success, we must know the goal and see the target. Try playing darts sometime with the target covered by a cloth. Trying to become a man with no idea of the target creates an unattainable quest. Personally, I was struck by the fact that I hadn't given my sons a road map for life; I had not given the Crusader football players a road map for life, either. I had not given them a *specific, clear,* and *concise* definition. As a coach, when you realize you need to correct something, you correct it.

---

2 Robert Lewis, *Raising a Modern-Day Knight* (Carol Stream: Tyndale House Publishers, 2007).

"TRYING TO BECOME A MAN WITH NO IDEA OF THE TARGET CREATES AN UNATTAINABLE QUEST."

USING MANHOOD LANGUAGE

As our coaching staff studied Lewis's book, I felt that the definition of manhood he gave was excellent; however, I wanted a definition that directed our focus to Jesus Christ. That is why I chose to use an acrostic as our game plan to define what a true man is—C. H. R. I. S. T. Over the years, I have added some sub-acrostic words as I have sought to flesh out the skeleton even more completely. Here's what that looks like:

COMMITMENT	HONOR	RESPONSIBILITY	INITIATIVE	SERVICE	TRUTH
JUDICIOUSLY CHOOSES; THEN FINISHES THE COURSE	PURE IN MIND	TRUTH IS ABSOLUTE	PROACTIVE	JOYFUL HEART	JUSTIFIED
OBEDIENT TO CHRIST	PURE IN ACTION	ILLUSTRATES FORGIVENESS	ELITE FORCE	OTHERS FIRST	EXPECTS A HEAVENLY REWARD
STRONG AND COURAGEOUS	ACCOUNT-ABLE TO CHRIST	MATURE DISCERNMENT	TEACHER	SPIRIT CONTROLLED = SELF-CONTROL	STANDS FIRM AGAINST THE DEVIL
HABITS OF A CHAMPION	UNPRETEN-TIOUS	OVERCOMER, NOT A VICTIM	ENCOUR-AGER	EFFECTIVE LISTENER	UNIQUE CALLING
UNWAVERING	LAUDABLE	TEAMMATE	REJECTS PASSIVITY	PRAYER	SACRED MISSION
ACTION		HATES EVIL		HOPE	
		YES IS YES			

A true, biblical man is a man of Commitment, Honor, Responsibility, Initiative, Service, and (the) Truth. Each of the six major qualities has a sub-acrostic associated with it to expand on the trait and give you a memory trigger. You can then more easily recall the quality and what comprises them. These acrostics make up the "Manhood Language," our game plan for victory.

Testing our behavior against this format will help us successfully raise boys and sharpen men. Our players, coaches, and parents in the Crusader football program have embraced this definition and we see results every day. I have had parents say to me, "We had a discussion around the kitchen table and my son told us that a man of commitment would complete his task." That's the value of this acrostic—it gives everyone a common definition, a clear goal, and it sets the standard through which all of our actions get filtered.

Manhood Language is a way to talk to your children and to other men about how a biblical man would conduct himself. We tell our players that we won't really know how well we have done as their mentors for another ten to fifteen years. When we see how they treat their wives and how they treat their children, then we'll know. We cling to the promise that if we "Train up a child in the way he should go, / Even when he is old, he will not depart from it" (Proverbs 22:6). Our job is to ensure the boys have a clear *goal, guide,* and *game plan.* Only after these parameters are in place can we work on specifics. Working with young men is "sowing forward," and we believe this will have an impact for generations to come if the Lord doesn't return soon.

DISCERNING GUILT VERSUS CONVICTION

Before we get too deeply engrossed into the acrostic itself, I want to address a concern I have. As we discuss the traits of a biblical man, each of us will and should reflect on how well we stack up against that definition. I expect that to happen. I also expect that each of us will reflect on how well we are doing. There is a danger in such reflection. Our introspection may lead to guilt from past failures or a conviction of not measuring up. Guilt is bad; it is unnecessary for a Christian. 1 John 1:9 says, "If we confess our sins, He is faithful and righteous to forgive us our sins and to cleanse us from all unrighteousness."

Some of you believe God could never forgive you because your past is too bad. Because we only know our own sins, we tend to believe no one else has sinned—certainly not like we have. Romans 3:23 makes it very clear that "all have sinned and fall short of the glory of God." But if you are still having difficulty believing that we all offend God, and that God can still use us, allow my story to influence you. I asked my spiritual mentor once how I could ever be used by God. I said to him, "I know you have sinned, but my life seems to be much worse than yours." His response was classic and vividly showed me why my perspective and emphasis were wrong. He said, "Your bag of crap may be bigger than my bag of crap, but to God, they both smell the same." Don't use your past failure as an excuse not to serve God now!

"YOUR BAG OF CRAP MAY BE BIGGER THAN MY BAG OF CRAP, BUT TO GOD, THEY BOTH SMELL THE SAME."

If it is an issue of guilt, it is simply a choice to confess it and trust in God's promise to forgive. Guilt wallows in the past. It's from Satan. Satan wants you to live in the past. He doesn't want liberated, vigorous men living in the present. Imagine trying to play a game while thinking about the past; you will be very ineffective. There is a biblical way to deal with guilt. Confess it, thank God for His mercy, accept His promise of forgiveness, and move on. Do as Paul said to do in Philippians 13:13–14: "Forgetting what lies behind and reaching forward to what lies ahead, I press on toward the goal for the prize of the upward call of God in Christ Jesus."

Conviction, on the other hand, is a good thing, because it is from the Holy Spirit. If you are convicted about something and you see your need for change, then change. Our focus should be how we can do better going forward, not living and wallowing in the past. Conviction is designed to help us improve. It is useful for growth.

As we study the traits of a biblical man, if guilt bothers you, confess it and move on. If you feel convicted, then listen to the Holy Spirit. Make positive, intentional changes and press on.

Now let's get to the first letter of the C. H. R. I. S. T. acrostic: "C" for Commitment.

A MAN OF CHRIST

COMMITMENT = A PROMISE COMPLETED

HONOR = CHARACTER ABOVE REPROACH; LIVING BY A BIBLICAL STANDARD

RESPONSIBILITY = TRUSTWORTHINESS DEMONSTRATED OVER TIME

INITIATIVE = BOLDNESS WITH INTEGRITY

SERVICE = INTENTIONALLY PUTTING THE NEEDS OF OTHERS FIRST, EXPECTING NOTHING IN RETURN

TRUTH = A STATEMENT OR PRINCIPLE THAT APPLIES TO ALL PEOPLE, IN ALL PLACES, AT ALL TIMES

C. H. R. I. S. T.

A MAN OF COMMITMENT

J. O. S. H. U. A.

JUDICIOUSLY CHOOSES,
THEN FINISHES THE COURSE

OBEDIENT TO CHRIST

STRONG AND COURAGEOUS

HABITS OF A CHAMPION

UNWAVERING

ACTION

CHAPTER THREE

A MAN OF COMMITMENT

J.O.S.H.U.A.

COMMITMENT IS DEFINED as "a promise completed." In our manhood language, we use this term to communicate the idea of keeping promises as a real man should. For example, one of my sons had promised a man with whom he was delivering furniture that he would pick him up at 5:45 in the morning. My son, Stephen, got sick the night before he was to pick him up. Nevertheless, he got up early, went and picked the man up, took him to work, then came home and took the rest of the day off sick. He had made a commitment and needed to complete his promise. I was able to compliment him using manhood language by saying, "You did what a man of commitment would do."

I had a different situation with a young man who called me to say, "I had an appointment this morning for breakfast and I blew it. I didn't get up on time, and I didn't go." Referring to the common vocabulary of the manhood language, I was able to say to him, "Well, you're right. A man of commitment would have made that meeting. No question about it. But now the issue is 'What do you do now?'" He said, "I need to call up the man I had the appointment with and ask for his forgiveness. Then if he wants to, I can reschedule the meeting." Great answer!

This vocabulary allows you to talk about good things and bad things in a less volatile way. When men have a common language based around biblical truth, they can more easily sharpen, encourage, and challenge each other.

A man of Commitment is a man like Joshua, who famously said, "Choose today whom you will serve…as for me and my house, we will serve the Lord" (Joshua 24:15). He essentially made a commitment to God, saying, "There is a way I will go and a way I will not go. I will serve the Lord" (paraphrase mine). We can use the acrostic J. O. S. H. U. A. to define for us what a man of commitment exemplifies, just like Joshua did.

J. O. S. H. U. A.

A MAN OF COMMITMENT IS ONE WHO JUDICIOUSLY CHOOSES, THEN FINISHES THE COURSE

It has been said that the next generation sees broken promises as the defining attribute of their generation. Can you imagine that? The defining attribute for the next generation is how many times they have been let down because of people who broke promises to them. No wonder young people don't trust. How sad! Promise Keepers had it right, men. Biblical manhood is about keeping your promises. To do so, we must choose carefully what we commit to, then complete our commitment.

Some people would probably follow through on their commitments if they were wiser about making them in the first place. We all know people who never say no to anything. They agree to every request. They can't possibly do all the things they commit to doing. Therefore, a key component to making commitments is to Judiciously Choose what you commit to. A man of commitment realizes he can't do everything, even if they are all good things.

When I talk about making too many commitments, I'm not assuming these are bad things to commit to. It is very possible to commit to too many things, all of which might be good. Nevertheless, overcommitting will cause you to fail in the final analysis. You should commit only to your life's best options. Nothing else!

How do you do that? You make an intentional decision to commit to fewer opportunities. Pray seriously about your options and commit only to those which enhance what the Lord has called you to do. For example, I know a man who would like me to become involved in a counseling ministry. It is a wonderful project and is changing lives for the better all the time. I realize, however, that God has not called me to that ministry. I don't have the time to do that ministry and to properly care for the opportunities I know God has clearly called me to care for in another work already. A fellow I coached with talked about the "test of time." Many people can do one task well one time, but they can't do it well over time because they are overcommitted.

I have observed people who live their lives based on what I call the "open-door philosophy." If the door is open, they assume God opened it and they can go through it. But sometimes we fail to remember that God has also given Satan certain rights in this world and that an open door is often what I call the "open elevator shaft." You go running through the open door and find out there's no floor. Down you go! Anytime you are faced with a serious commitment, make sure you have godly counsel. Make sure you have time to analyze the situation. God will not ask you to give an immediate answer to something He doesn't give you the time to be prepared for. He just does not operate that way. People should never be fooled by get-rich-quick schemes. Great ideas are like buses; one comes along every hour. And if someone pushes you to decide quickly, it's probably something you should avoid. That's not the way God works. So, beware—open door or open floor?

BIG AND SMALL COMMITMENTS

Marriage is a big commitment, of course. In life, no commitment is more important than your marriage vows, except your commitment to Jesus Christ as your Savior. Our children need to be able to trust in us and depend upon us. How can they if we break such a critical commitment? It isn't always easy; in fact, it is seldom ever easy. The national divorce rate is about 50 percent. That's a lot of marriages, meaning that many parents have broken trust with their children and each other. It is critical to stay married—to stay committed to the woman you promised to love and cherish until death.

There does appear to be some good news among church-going people, however. Shaunti Feldhahn, a Harvard-trained researcher and best-selling author on relationships, found that 72 percent of church-going Christians remain married to their original spouse.[1] That's great news, but we can do better. As Christians, we should be the role models for the rest of society. Do we really believe what God says? If so, we will act on our belief by staying married. God says, "I hate divorce" (Malachi 2:16). God says stay committed, so we should (Genesis 2:24). Was God giving commandments or suggestions? Is God serious or is He not serious? Of course He is serious!

I have a friend who illustrates commitment with his wife this way. I think he makes a profound point. Every once in a while, he and his wife have a discussion that goes something like this:

Buzz: "Debbie, do you love me?"

Debbie: "Yes."

Buzz: "Why?"

Debbie: "Because I choose to!"

You see, love is more than a feeling. Marriage is more than a ceremony. Feelings and emotions come and go, but our commitments are the foundation of our honor, our character, and our reputations. A commitment is a choice you promise to complete; and in the case of marriage, that means forever.

Some of you may be saying, "I am already divorced." That's a fact of life in our society. I could be divorced too if it weren't for my wife and for God.

---

1 Shaunti Feldhahn, *The Good News about Marriage* (Colorado Springs: Multnomah Books, 2014).

So what do you do about it now? If you marry again, fulfill the promise you made—stay committed.

Small commitments are just as important. A lot of small commitments made over time tell others you are a man of your word. If you tell me you'll be on time for lunch, I should be able to expect you to fulfill your promise. This is a small commitment, but a commitment nonetheless. When you tell me you'll do something, I should be able to take it to the bank as a pledge. A biblical man of commitment follows through on the commitments he makes.

GUIDELINES FOR STAYING COMMITTED

How can we learn to stick with our commitments? Here are some guidelines I live by: first, commit to the best. Second, never make a commitment unless you're prepared to complete the promise. And if you do make a commitment, be sure to follow through on it. I would also add that it is helpful to think through all of the possible ramifications as you decide to commit to something. Who will be affected by your commitment? What things will you have to give up? Are there negative consequences?

Here's another area of tension: never make a commitment unless you have the authority to make it. Children often make plans without their parents' permission and then get upset when the parents won't help them complete their promises. The same thing can be said of husbands who don't consult their wives when making a commitment that obligates both of them. Big mistake! Consider who will be affected by the commitments you make.

INVOLVEMENT VS. COMMITMENT

In our society, sometimes we make "promises" and then discard them when a better option comes along. We seem to be unable to tell the difference between *commitment* and *involvement.* I think we can learn a lesson from an unlikely source—the pig and the chicken. True commitment is like a breakfast of ham and eggs. The chicken is involved, but the pig is committed.

The pig will give his life for the project, but the chicken only gives what is convenient to give.

One of the greatest compliments I ever received was when one of the players in the Crusader football ministry wrote a paper in English class and he called me "the pig of the Columbus Crusaders!" I thought that was very special. I knew what he meant. The teacher wasn't really sure, but that is exactly how I want to be seen.

We had a young man that Coach Cheeseman and I used to watch all the time; we talked about the fact that he was the pig of the weightlifting program. He came in religiously, day after day, and he always worked hard. His improvement was tremendous because he was committed. He wasn't just involved.

I had a father ask me once if his son could play on our football team and also play for his traveling soccer team. He assured me that his son would be at all of the games and he was smart so he could keep up. My answer was "no," because his son was not committed, just involved. A crucial part of any team is being at all the practices, hanging out with the players and coaches. I was sad for the son because the father was teaching him a terrible life lesson.

COACHING COMMITMENT

A commitment is also a matter of *conviction* not *convenience*. One of my biggest challenges as a coach is dealing with parents who want their son to play but don't want to be committed parents and do what's required of them. As parents and coaches, it's our job to teach the young men that commitment is a matter of doing what you said you would do, not bailing out for something else that sounds better. Many times, we have appointments with a person, yet somebody else comes along whom we would frankly rather meet with, so we say to the first appointment, "I need to cancel our meeting; something has come up." That's garbage! If you made a commitment to meet with someone, then that's the commitment; you're not released from it just because it is less convenient or appealing now. That's the whole concept of *judiciously choosing*.

All of us need to learn early that we can't do everything just because we want to. Here is a great illustration that my wife saw on a sitcom TV show: a teenager asked his dad for permission to join the tennis team, and the father said *no*. The teenager pitched a fit saying, "Why not? Why can't I do this?" Silently, the father went to the hall closet and he pulled out a football and he said, "Two weeks." Then he pulled out a baseball glove and he said, "Three weeks." Next, he pulled out a trumpet and he said, "One month." He was making the point about how long the youngster, who *really* wanted to do those things, had stayed with them, which wasn't very long at all. This youngster did not understand true commitment. But maybe more importantly, his father didn't know how to teach it!

You've probably heard the rule of commitment, which goes something like this: "If you start it, you finish it." That is a good rule to remind your son. Tell him, "If you start football, you finish it. I don't care if you're unhappy about it midway through. You made a commitment; finish it." There is a lot at stake here if you think about it. For example, if you teach your children that it's okay to quit things when times are tough, one of the things they may someday quit is their marriage. Don't miss that. If they learn to quit when boredom or adversity arrives, they may later walk out on the important things in life, such as their marriage, school, a good-paying job, or even their faith. Teach them how to judiciously choose a commitment, and then how critical it is to finish the course.

TWO EXAMPLES OF COMMITMENT

In the fifty-plus years I've coached, a number of young men stood out in remarkable ways. One such young man was Shawn, a captain for us. He suffered his third concussion in the last scrimmage of his junior year. His doctors felt that because it was a third concussion, Shawn should no longer play football. He had just been elected captain for the third time, but no one could blame him if he quit the team. In fact, many people asked if he was going to hang up his cleats. They said, "Shawn, you're going to be out there every single day and you can't play. Are you going to quit?" And his response was, "No way! This is my team. I am committed to this team." He stayed with the team for the next two years, never expecting to play. He was finally cleared to punt, but he made and maintained his commitment without ever expecting to play. That is what I mean by biblical commitment.

There was another young man who played for the Columbus Crusaders in 2002 named Jonathan. This young man was six foot five, 260 pounds, and moved very, very well. He had never played football before and was going out as a senior, but he was going to be a great football player. While playing basketball over the summer, he had broken a bone in his foot. At first, he was on crutches with a cast. Periodically, he would go to the doctor to see what his progress was, expecting to be released to play. However, the doctor kept saying, "It's just not knitting properly."

During that time, Jonathan never missed a practice. He was trying to be prepared. I can recall a vision of him sitting on a stationary bike with his helmet and shoulder pads on, riding the bike, preparing for the day when he got cleared so that he would be ready to play.

About three-quarters of the way through the season, the doctors came to him and said his foot hadn't healed. He was never going to be cleared to play a single snap. Jonathan was a great student, and he felt pressure from people questioning why he was going to football practice since it was just going to be a waste of two or three hours. People told him he should go home and study. Jonathan refused. He was committed to the program and he would not quit. He felt there were other things he could do to help the team even though he wasn't playing.

Jonathan's contribution to the Crusaders wasn't as the great player he hoped to be; however, he served as a godly model of commitment that still has a lasting impact on our program. His story is one of the most remarkable things I have ever witnessed. The young man never played a snap in a practice or a game, yet he never quit. Such is true commitment. At the year-end banquet, Jonathan won the Coaches Award because of his special example. This young man was, and is, an incredible man.

Once you commit, quitting is not an option unless God's laws are being violated. We should model ourselves after the apostle Paul and be able to say, "I have fought the good fight, I have finished the course, I have kept the faith" (2 Timothy 4:7). When you make a commitment, finish the course, keep the faith.

For many years, I believed I was a poor finisher. The truth is, I was committing to too many things and didn't have the energy or the time to do it all. Learn early to say no. Teach your children to say no. Learn early to *judiciously choose, then finish the course* for all of your commitments.

J. **O.** S. H. U. A.

A MAN OF COMMITMENT IS ONE WHO IS:
OBEDIENT TO CHRIST

The second letter in J. O. S. H. U. A., "O," stands for being Obedient to Christ. Right off the bat, if you're not a Christian, you can't even begin to be obedient to Christ. Search yourself, search your heart, and recognize that without the help of the Holy Spirit, you couldn't possibly be obedient to Christ. You could not live as the Lord wants you to.

Being a Christian is like being pregnant. You either are or you aren't. You can't be sort of pregnant. It's the same with being a Christian. If you're not absolutely sure that you're a Christian, then you probably aren't. The Bible says in 2 Corinthians 13:5, "Test yourselves *to see* if you are in the faith; examine yourselves! Or do you not recognize this about yourselves, that Jesus Christ is in you—unless indeed you fail the test?" (emphasis mine).

In 1 John 5:13, John says that what he has written is so that you might *know* you have eternal life. So many people flounder in life and wonder if they are really going to heaven and if they really have a relationship with Jesus Christ. You don't have to wonder if you've made that commitment; you've driven a stake in the ground. At that point, salvation depends on Jesus. He said, "My sheep hear My voice, and I know them, and they follow Me; and I give eternal life to them, and they will never perish; and no one will snatch them out of My hand. My Father, who has given *them* to Me, is greater than all; and no one is able to snatch *them* out of the Father's hand. I and the Father are one" (John 10:27–30). When you put your trust in Jesus Christ as your Lord and Savior, that ends the wondering.

THE ABCs OF SALVATION

A - AGREE WITH GOD THAT YOU HAVE SINNED.

B - BELIEVE JESUS DIED FOR YOUR SINS AND HAS RISEN FROM THE DEAD JUST AS THE BIBLE TELLS US.

C - CHOOSE TO ACCEPT JESUS AS YOUR LORD AND SAVIOR BECAUSE HE DIED TO PAY THE PENALTY FOR YOUR SINS.

TALK TO JESUS THROUGH PRAYER EXPRESSING YOUR TRUST IN HIM:

"GOD, I KNOW I AM A SINNER. I BELIEVE JESUS CHRIST DIED FOR MY SINS. I TURN TO YOU, GOD, BELIEVING JESUS CHRIST ROSE FROM THE DEAD TO OFFER ETERNAL LIFE. THANK YOU, JESUS. I ACCEPT YOUR GIFT OF SALVATION."

Once we are committed to Christ, we should be all in, surrendered to Christ as a matter of obedience.

Adrian Rogers, a famous twentieth-century Baptist preacher, once went on a mission trip to Romania. Over the course of two weeks, he bonded with his interpreter but hadn't learned much about his thoughts. So, toward the end of the trip he asked, "Tell me, what do you think of American Christians?"

> "I don't want to talk about it," came the strange reply. This of course only made Dr. Rogers more curious, so he began to press him for an answer.
>
> Finally, the interpreter capitulated. "Well, okay then, but you are not going to like my answer. I don't think you Americans understand what Christianity is all about. Back in the 1960s, you started to use the word 'commitment' to describe your relationship with Christ. However, any time a word comes into use, another goes into disuse."
>
> He continued, "Until the 1960s, you Americans talked about 'surrender' to Christ. Surrender means giving up control, turning over all to the Master, Jesus. By changing the word to 'commitment,' your relationship has become something you do; therefore, you are able to keep control. Surrender means giving up all rights to oneself. You Americans don't like to do that, so instead you make a commitment."

MOVING TOWARD OBEDIENCE

If you know you're a Christian, there are at least four ways to become obedient: 1) read the Bible, 2) get baptized, 3) go to church, 4) live holy. These are all actions Jesus has instructed us to do. In Acts 5:29, Peter says, "We must obey

God rather than men." So often, we're put in positions where society wants or expects us to behave a certain way, but Christ calls us to behave differently. Balaam's words in Numbers 22:18 should inspire us to obedience: "Balaam replied to the servants of Balak, 'Though Balak were to give me his house full of silver and gold, I could not do anything, either small or great, contrary to the command of the Lord my God.'"

You and I must see Jesus's instructions as commandments, not suggestions. Let's look at each of these in more depth.

READ THE BIBLE

One way to be obedient is to read and study God's Word to deepen your relationship with Him and keep from harm. In Psalm 119:11, the psalmist says, "Your word I have treasured in my heart, that I may not sin against You." God wrote the Bible, His love letter to us. He wants to speak with us daily. I am often amazed that it seems so difficult to read the Bible every day. I shouldn't be surprised. Satan doesn't want us to be comforted by reading God's promises. The further we are from our source of power, the greater is Satan's ability to get us off course. John 15:5 says, "I am the vine, you are the branches; he who abides in Me and I in him, he bears much fruit, for apart from Me you can do nothing." We must be plugged in to Jesus, our power source, to finish the course well. In fact, 2 Timothy 2:15 gives us another critical reason to study the Bible. It says, "Be diligent to present yourself approved to God as a workman who does not need to be ashamed, accurately handling the word of truth."

Sometimes not reading the Bible creates guilt. Then Satan says, "You're a failure because you didn't read God's Word yesterday." So, you don't read God's Word today because you're feeling so bad that you didn't read it yesterday. Such are Satan's lies! If you didn't read it yesterday, read it today. If you didn't read it last week at all, and you read it twice this week, that's two times more than you read it last week. That's success! Not failure.

GET BAPTIZED

Another way to be obedient is to be baptized. The Bible clearly calls Christians to be baptized as a matter of obedience. Sometimes people come to me and say, "I don't want to be baptized because I might be embarrassed." Jesus said, "Therefore, everyone, who confesses Me before man, I will also confess him before My Father who is in heaven, but whoever denies Me before men, I will also deny him before My Father who is in heaven" (Matthew 10:32–33). That's a strong statement. Baptism is one way to proclaim and confess Jesus before men. It is a command not a suggestion, as Matthew 28:19 spells out very clearly what Jesus expects of us: "Go therefore and make disciples of all the nations, baptizing them in the name of the Father, and the Son, and the Holy Spirit." However, we must never lose sight of the fact that "grace alone, through faith alone, in Christ alone" is what saves us, as the 16th century reformers said. Without the presence of the Holy Spirit we cannot live this way.

"GRACE ALONE, THROUGH FAITH ALONE, IN CHRIST ALONE IS WHAT SAVES US."

When a person is baptized with no heart change driven by the Holy Spirit, it is no more valuable than taking a bath. When I was twelve years old, my mother sent me to church even though my dad never went. While I was there, I decided to get baptized. I wanted to please my mother whom I loved very much. The problem was that I didn't know Jesus from Fred. My baptism had no power because I didn't have Christ as my Savior, and by extension, I didn't have the Holy Spirit as my teacher and guide. Praise God that I came to really join His team on August 1, 1986. What about you? Do you remember the day you were baptized? If you haven't yet been baptized, but believe you committed your life to Jesus, make this a priority for the upcoming month. You'll be glad you did.

GO TO CHURCH

We can obey Jesus by going to church. Every now and then, someone tells me, "I do go to church. I am at St. Mattress of the Springs every Sunday morning visiting with Pastor Sheets." That doesn't count. I have other people tell me that they commune with God while walking through nature. That's fine, but there is a need to get to church because the Bible tells us to. Hebrews 10:24–25 says, "Let us consider how to stimulate one another to love and good deeds, not forsaking our own assembling together, as is the habit of some, but encouraging one another." Church serves a purpose beyond just singing songs, listening to a sermon, and taking communion. It is the place where other Christians gather who may need encouragement and can also encourage you. We all need positive fellowship after a tough week. We live and work in a society that snubs and dismisses Christians. We're fortunate they aren't killing Christians as they do in some other places, but society can sure make you feel like your beliefs are naïve or intolerant. Get in church where other folks can recharge your batteries and encourage or serve you, and you can do the same for them.

We need churches that are filled with the Holy Spirit. If you go to a dead church, meaning one that isn't teaching the whole counsel of the Bible, serving others, or reaching out with the gospel message, and you have tried to infuse life there, leave. I am not advocating church hopping, but staying in a church because your grandparents founded it doesn't help you or your family grow if the Holy Spirit has left.

Let me also make it very clear that you and I should not go to church only for what we get. We should be going to church expecting to give encouragement, care, and concern to others. Sometimes we will get more than we give, but every week someone in church could use a kind, caring word from you or a warm hug. Some days we just need "Jesus with skin on." We must obey Christ, not out of obligation, but out of appreciation for what He has done for us. Every day of my life, I realize how blessed I am. What

God has done to change me and my life is fabulous, so when I do things for Jesus Christ, it's like breathing for me—it's natural. I serve Him not because I'm such a good guy, but because I'm so indebted to Him. It's not a hardship; it's an honor to do the work of the King of Kings. I'm so appreciative of what He has done for me.

LIVE HOLY

Obedience is a 24/7 thing, not a sometimes thing. I want to share a story with you about what God sometimes wants from us in terms of obedience.

> A man was awakened in his cabin by the voice of the Lord. The Lord told the man he had work for him to do and showed him a large rock in front of his cabin. The Lord explained that the man was to push against the rock with all his might. This the man did, day after day. He toiled from sunup to sundown, his shoulders set squarely against the cold, massive surface of the unmoving rock, pushing with all his might. Each night the man returned to his cabin sore and worn out, feeling that his whole day had been spent in vain.
>
> Seeing that the man was showing signs of discouragement, Satan decided to enter the picture, placing thoughts into the man's mind, such as: "You have been pushing against that rock for a long time, and it hasn't budged. Why kill yourself over this? You are never going to move it." These thoughts discouraged and disheartened the man even more. *Why kill myself over this?* he thought. *I'll just put in my time, giving just the minimum effort, and that will be good enough.*
>
> And he planned to do just that until one day he decided to make it a matter of prayer and take his troubled thoughts to the Lord.

> "Lord," he said, "I have labored long and hard in Your service, putting all my strength to do that which You have asked. Yet after all this time, I have not even budged that rock by half a millimeter. What is wrong? Why am I failing?" To this the Lord responded compassionately, "My son, when I asked you to serve me and you accepted, I told you that your task was to push against the rock with all your strength, which you have done. Never once did I mention to you that I expected you to move it. Your task was to push. And now you come to me, with your strength spent, thinking that you have failed. Through opposition you have grown much. Yet you haven't moved the rock. Your calling was to be obedient and to push and to exercise your Faith and trust in My wisdom. This you have done. Now, my son, I will move the rock."[2]

Most of us don't like this story because we are success driven. We want to see results. We want to handle all of life's problems ourselves; God simply calls us to do only what He asks us to do. Often God gives us a task and we leave it to ourselves to decipher what end result He wants—what God considers success. Sometimes, He simply wants our faith and our obedience. We need to demonstrate the depth of faith that can move mountains, but we also need to remember that it is He who moves the mountains. Don't be so concerned with the results that you get, but rather be concerned with what you learned from the task and how you furthered His kingdom by obeying Him.

"WE NEED TO DEMONSTRATE THE DEPTH OF FAITH THAT CAN MOVE MOUNTAINS, BUT WE ALSO NEED TO REMEMBER THAT IT IS HE WHO MOVES THE MOUNTAINS."

---

2 Cindy Lu, "I Will Move The Rock," Inspirational Christian Stories & Poems, accessed July 30, 2019, http://www.inspirationalarchive.com/1647/i-will-move-the-rock/.

Patrick Morley wrote a book called *The Man in the Mirror*. It's a tremendous book. Morley said in regard to obeying God: "The turning point in our lives is when we stop seeking the God we want and start seeking the God who is."[3] Many times we use God as a rabbit's foot. We use God as a candy store, saying, "Give me this and give me that." Sometimes we even think we can manipulate God using the "name-it-and-claim-it" doctrine that is so pervasive in our culture today. How silly it is for us to believe we can obligate God to give us something simply because we want it and believe God should give it to us. God can do anything that He wants to do, but He will never violate His character or His plan. God is sovereign and we need to remember that.

"THE TURNING POINT IN OUR LIVES IS WHEN WE STOP SEEKING THE GOD WE WANT AND START SEEKING THE GOD WHO IS."

—PATRICK MORLEY, *THE MAN IN THE MIRROR*

Notice not one of the ones I mentioned before says, "Stop doing this or stop doing that." I think too often we teach Christianity as a bunch of "don'ts" only. Christianity is just like a football game. Sometimes we are on offense, and sometimes we are on defense. We need to be careful, however, that we don't play defense so much that we miss great kingdom opportunities. In wrestling, if your opponent is being pinned, his first concern is with getting off his back, not about getting away or scoring. Satan knows that and tries to keep us focused on simply getting off our backs. That way he can keep us from living the abundant life Jesus planned for us.

Many people say, "I can't read the Bible; I don't understand it." If the Holy Spirit doesn't live inside you, that is true on the deepest level—you won't understand what it's saying. However, the reality is that for most people

3 Patrick M. Morley, *The Man in the Mirror* (Grand Rapids: Zondervan, 1997).

when they say they don't understand the Bible, it's more a function of not liking what it says. Mark Twain, one of the great American humorists, said, "It's not the parts of the Bible I don't understand that bother me, it's the parts I do understand." For the most part, you and I know exactly what God wants us to do, but in our own selfishness, we just don't want to obey. A true man obeys anyway.

If you are a parent or a coach, I have one note of caution. Be biblically honest with yourself and your children. Don't try to make the Bible say something that it doesn't. If you warn your children later and haven't been accurate and honest before, they may not believe you. For example, we don't have alcohol in our home. But it is not because the Bible says, "Thou shalt not drink." That's not true. I hate to break this to some of you, but that isn't true. The Bible says don't get drunk. We don't have alcohol in our home because we have seen the devastation of what alcohol can do to you. We've seen what happens with drunk driving, so we said early on to our children, "We want you to understand. We don't have alcohol in our home, not because the Bible says you can't drink, but because we don't think it's wise." We have tried to be biblically honest.

However, in relation to pre-marital sex, we said, "We want you to understand very clearly that God says you should not be out having sex since you are not married. That would be defined as fornication and that is wrong." It violates God's word. You and I have to be careful that when we give our children advice, we tell them the truth—biblically. Let's commit to being faithful, obedient followers of Christ, not situational followers.

In some churches, there has been terrible legalism; there is no grace, no love. That is true, but it is also true that in some churches, God has become at best a rabbit's foot, and at worst, a God who only loves and never holds anyone accountable for their sins.

The true God is not one or the other—He is both. God forgives our sin, but He must, by His nature, punish disobedience. God's grace isn't cheap;

Jesus gave His life to cleanse our sins and forgive us of all unrighteousness. Why would we spit in His face when He has done so much for us?

J. O. **S.** H. U. A.
A MAN OF COMMITMENT IS:
STRONG AND COURAGEOUS

The S in Joshua stands for Strong and Courageous. God made man to be strong and courageous, willing to step up and put his very being on the line. In Joshua 1, the Lord commands Joshua to be strong and courageous at least three different times. In 1 Kings 2:2, David tells Solomon, "Be strong, therefore, and show yourself a man." God is interested in strength of character. In fact, God told Joshua to be strong and *very* courageous (Joshua 1:7). By this, God was telling Joshua to believe in the fact that He would be with him to guide him through. Joshua was to then follow God's directions. When a difficult challenge arises, strong and courageous men have such confidence in God that they will do the right thing and do it immediately.

To better explain the overall concept behind the "Strong and Courageous" language, I would like to give you the following definitions and examples. Strength is often confused with "guts." A man with "guts" charges ahead to conquer the obstacle with very little thought to his actions. As my friend Dr. Duke Heller says, "It's like painting a fence in 110-degree heat in order to beat a time limit." For me, it's like charging into battle with no thought about the overwhelming odds you are fighting. That's guts.

Strength and courage, on the other hand, are "controlled power"—a thoughtful decision as to the best course of action in a difficult circumstance. An example is purposely going to a loved one who has hurt you over many years to attempt to rebuild that relationship. Deep courage is persistently overcoming difficult situations in our life that keep repeating themselves; usually not seeing acceptable results.

As God told Joshua to be "strong and courageous," He realized that Joshua would encounter difficult people, difficult decisions, and difficult outcomes (think Ai, the place where Joshua sent his spies and Israel was defeated in Joshua chapter 7). To be successful, Joshua could not act without thinking, and he would need to be able to live with his decisions even when others criticized him.

Have you ever heard the term "drop-dead conviction"? A drop-dead conviction is when you have a belief you will not give up on; a value you won't compromise. Ask yourself, *Do I have any drop-dead convictions? Do I have anything in my life that I absolutely will not ever do because it violates God's Word? Is there anything I would stand up for so boldly that I would accept any recrimination that came against me because it's a drop-dead issue for me?* Living out our drop-dead convictions requires great courage. How do you stand up for the Lord when your children come home and say, "Gee, Dad, the Joneses let their kids watch that TV program!" You need to decide *in advance* what things you will or will not compromise on. Single men, have you decided on the answer to this question: "Why not have sex?" Society tells us that everybody else does it. That's a lie—a rationalization for doing something you know is wrong. Have you heard men say this? "It's okay if I pad my expense account because the company has a ton of money, and they don't pay me enough. It doesn't really hurt anyone but the company, and they make too much profit anyway."

The problem is, if you'll cheat your company, you'll cheat others. Many people call in sick for work but really aren't sick. They say they need a mental health day off. But when we lie, we violate God's Word and impede our fellowship with Him.

Have you heard this one? "Since I am two hundred miles from home, I can do anything I wish." I know men who frequent strip clubs, have one-night stands, or become engrossed in pornographic movies all because of the 200-mile rule. The "200-mile rule" is an invention of Satan and a horrible lie.

Without the Holy Spirit, I'm firmly convinced that I could do any evil thing in the entire world. The only reason I haven't done some of them is because the Holy Spirit has kept me under control.

Sometimes we're presented with challenges that are far more subtle than these. For example, one year the Crusaders needed coaching help really badly, and I interviewed four or five men. One man was truly outstanding. Coach Cheeseman and I agreed that the fellow was exceptionally well-qualified. He was an awesome coach. We got all the way through the interview, and as an afterthought, I said, "Where do you go to church?" He said, "I'm a Mormon." I was sick! Why? Because I knew that he did not believe biblically what we believe. Our coaches are Born-Again Christians. I had a huge problem. The man was a great coach. We needed him, but he did not fit spiritually with us. I remember feeling as if God was saying to me, "Do you trust Me? Will you stay true to Me or fill your needs yourself?" I needed to obey and trust God, not myself. So we didn't bring the man on board. You are probably wondering if God honored the outcome. That particular year we never got the other coaches we needed, in my opinion, yet we finished seven and one.

I know it doesn't always happen like that. Mike Cheeseman and I have believed that each year God has confronted us with some issue that requires us to choose Him or the easy way. To the best of our knowledge, we have and will continue to honor Jesus with our choices. It does take strength and courage, but Jesus never claimed that following Him is easy. To paraphrase Martin Luther King in 1965: *Our lives begin to end the day we become silent about things that matter.*[4]

In his book *Wild at Heart*, John Eldridge says that "men were designed

---

4 Emery, David, "Did MLK Say 'Our Lives Begin To End the Day We Become Silent?'" Snopes.com, published January 16, 2017, https://www.snopes.com/fact-check/mlk-our-lives-begin-to-end/.

for a battle to fight and an adventure to live."[5] I believe most men waste their time on battles and adventures that have very little lasting value. Sometimes men make the mistake of believing *the* adventure is the conquest of a young woman. Instinctively, women understand that they want to be a part of an adventure, not the adventure itself. They want a man who will lead, yet partner with them on an exciting adventure—life itself. Women understand that if they are the adventure, once you have captured the target, you'll discard them. They are so right!

Athletics is a great place to allow a young man to develop his courage. He longs to know if he can stack up as a man. That's why I wrestled; I wanted to know if I could go one-on-one with my opponent to see if I was tough enough to handle it. After every single match I wrestled, I came off the mat and threw up. I was so nervous that I would finish the match and have dry heaves. I didn't get sick before the match like most people do. Nevertheless, the key was that I kept coming back, never quitting, battling through the nerves and persevering. Life is full of trying times, and everyone bears fear and anxiety. *Only the courageous stay the course.* Courage is not the absence of fear—it is having the courage to battle through being afraid and finishing the mission. Yes, I kept going back for more. I can't say it was the most fun I ever had, but it made me feel better about myself. I knew I could hang in through difficult situations. That's why guys test their manhood. They want to know they won't fold under pressure.

Dad, you can kill your son's spirit and his manhood by treating him like he never measures up. Moms can kill their son's manhood if they never let him attempt anything with risk. It's sad to me when a father who understands the needs of a young man caves to Mom's fears. We must allow young men to test their manhood. Cole Trickle, the main character in the movie *Days of Thunder*, made a telling comment. He said, "I am more afraid of being nothing than I am of being hurt." Most men would

---

5 Eldridge, John, *Wild at Heart* (Nashville: Thomas Nelson, 2001).

agree with that statement. We must let young men challenge themselves; stop pampering them and trying to make young girls out of them. You will neuter them or kill their spirits. How can a man truly protect his family if he has grown up afraid?

"I AM MORE AFRAID OF BEING NOTHING THAN I AM OF BEING HURT."
—COLE TRICKLE, *DAYS OF THUNDER*

So, let's allow the challenges and adventures as young men, so that when they become older men they're not wimps. They will have the courage to lead their families like they should.

Henry David Thoreau once said, "The mass of men lead lives of quiet desperation."[6] Looking around, that's what we see: simply a bunch of men just hanging on. They're just going through the motions. But as Andrew Jackson is said to have stated, "One man with courage makes a majority."[7] If your dad has killed your spirit, God is waiting to restore it. While it's true that for most children Dad is Jesus with flesh, he's not Jesus. If you had a dad who was a lousy father, don't let that hold you back. Stop using that as an excuse. Your heavenly Father is more than prepared to be your Father with a capital "F." Psalm 68:5 captures this perfectly: "A father of the fatherless and a judge for the widows / Is God in His holy

---

6 Henry David Thoreau, *Walden; or, Life In The Woods* (Overland Park: Digireads, 2009), chap. 1, location 124, https://www.goodreads.com/quotes/401512-the-mass-of-men-lead-lives-of-quiet-desperation-what.

7 Attributed to Jackson by Robert F. Kennedy in his foreword to the Young Readers Memorial Edition of John F. Kennedy's *Profiles in Courage* (New York: Harper & Brothers, 1956) and by Ronald Reagan in nominating Robert Bork to the US Supreme Court. This has never been found in Jackson's writings, and there is no record of him having declared it. Somewhat similar statements are known to have been made by others.

habitation."

Pray God will direct you to a godly surrogate father who can bestow manhood on you. If you have never had a man say to you, "I love you. I'm proud of you," go find one who will. If you are reading this book, you are trying to grow more like Jesus each day. If your father has never blessed you, find a man who will. We need real men in our lives. As Proverbs 27:17 challenges us, "Iron sharpens iron, so one man sharpens another." Never, never buy the lie that you are worthless. That is a lie from Satan; it is from the pit of hell, and it is not true. While it is true that you are *unworthy*, you are not worthless. In fact, according to Jesus and His death on the cross, you are priceless. You're worth *everything* to Him!

I have a group of young men in my life whom I refer to as "Young Champions." These are young men with whom I work to help sharpen them to imitate Christ. All of us need an advocate, a cheerleader in our lives. I try to be that for these young men.

Look at Gideon; the angel of the Lord (probably Jesus) appeared to Gideon in Judges 6:12, and his first words to him were, "The Lord is with you, O valiant warrior." He called him valiant warrior long before he was. Someone is waiting for you to be their coach; ask God to direct you to him.

J. O. S. **H.** U. A.

A MAN OF COMMITMENT HAS:

HABITS OF A CHAMPION

The next letter in Joshua is H, to remind us that men of commitment will have the Habits of a Champion.

As a coach, I've heard people say over and over again, "Practice makes perfect. Practice makes perfect." That's nonsense. Practice makes habits. If you practice poorly, you will make poor habits. Perfect practice makes perfect. That's the key. Perfect practice makes perfect habits, the kind a champion has. How do you develop those? We practice them day after day in a winning way.

READ THE BIBLE

I mentioned Bible reading in the Obedience chapter, but I can't reiterate enough how crucial this habit is for becoming a champion in life. We had a fellow do chapel for us a couple of years ago, who as a seventeen-to-eighteen-year-old young man, made a vow to God. He vowed to read the Bible every day for the rest of his life and he's done so. He's now forty-seven years old. He has developed the "Habits of a Champion."

My pastor Jim Custer's motto is "no Bible, no bread." If he doesn't get up and study the Word of God, he doesn't eat. Perhaps "no Bible, no TV" would be more motivating for some of us. There are any number of methods you can use, but the fact of the matter is that you can become a champion. Do you have a plan for reading the Bible? Be intentional or you won't be consistent in your study.

GIVE TO GOD'S WORK

Another habit of a champion is giving to God's work. People hate hearing about giving, yet God is very serious about our care of His money. One story I read greatly encourages me to know how God uses everyday people to further His plans through money.

> Shortly after Dallas Theological Seminary was founded in 1924, it almost came to the point of bankruptcy. All the creditors were going to foreclose at noon on a particular day. That morning, they met in the president's office with Dr. Chafer for prayer that God would provide. In that prayer meeting was a man by the name of Harry Ironside. When it was his turn to pray, he prayed

> in his characteristic manner: "Lord, we know that the cattle on a thousand hills are Thine. Please sell some of them and send us the money."
>
> While they were praying, a tall Texan with boots on and an open collar stepped up to the business office, and said, "I just sold two carloads of cattle in Ft. Worth. I've been trying to make a business deal, but it fell through, and I feel compelled to give the money to the seminary. I don't know if you need it or not, but here's the check!"
>
> A secretary took the check, and knowing how critical things were financially, went to the door of the prayer meeting and timidly tapped. When she finally got a response, Dr. Chafer took the check out of her hand. It was exactly the amount of the debt! When he looked at the name, he recognized the cattleman in Ft. Worth, and turning to Dr. Ironside, said, "Harry, God sold the cattle!"[8]

Don't you love that? God owns all the cattle on a thousand hills, but He uses you and me to slaughter one, sell it, and give the money to further His plans. People ask me all time, "Should I tithe?" Yes, you should. When they say, "That's an Old Testament command," I tell them, "Realize this. There are only three things that last—God, God's Word, and God's people." So my question to you is: if your church is alive, what are you doing to help them reach people? You can only do that through a few means—your time, your talent, and your treasures. People used to ask Pastor Dick DeArmey if they should tithe off their gross or net income. I love Pastor Dick's answer. He said, "Well, that depends on whether you want a gross or a net blessing."

---

8 James S. Hewitt, *Illustrations Unlimited* (Wheaton: Tyndale House Publishers, 1988), 419.

"WELL, THAT DEPENDS ON WHETHER YOU WANT A GROSS OR A NET BLESSING."
—PASTOR DICK DEARMEY

God owns it all. It's amazing to me how much He lets us keep! We get to keep 90 percent. In the Old Testament, the tithe was a guideline. Malachi 3:8–10 says, "Will a man rob God? Yet you are robbing Me! But you say, 'How have we robbed You?' In tithes and offerings. You are cursed with a curse, for you are robbing Me, the whole nation of you! 'Bring the whole tithe into the storehouse, so that there may be food in My house, and test Me now in this,' says the Lord of hosts, 'if I will not open for you the windows of heaven and pour out for you a blessing until it overflows.'" But 2 Corinthians 9:7 makes it very clear that whatever your guideline is, "God loves a cheerful giver." So if you give out of obligation, and if you give begrudgingly, God will not honor your gift. Often people who quote 2 Corinthians 9:7 try to use this verse to say that God doesn't care about the amount of your giving, only our heart attitude. I believe that is a false teaching. If a millionaire gives ten dollars per week, would God be happy because the fellow gave cheerfully but clearly from his excess? I believe God wants us to tithe cheerfully, expectantly, and gratefully.

If you choose to give over and above a tithe, that's an offering. I think we live in a society where some churches have abused their congregation's giving. The tendency, then, has been for people to say, "You can't trust the church; you can't give." No! You are responsible and I am responsible to get into a church we can trust. We should monitor what they are doing with the money and how it's being used for God's purposes. If it's not being used for God's purposes, you should leave and take your money with you. A friend of mine, Tom Smith, was a McDonald's operator. One of his favorite sayings is, "You don't really believe something until you are willing to act on it." If you and I really believe that all that will remain someday is God, God's Word, and

God's people, then we must use our money as a tool to further the kingdom of God joyfully, willingly, and liberally.

MEMORIZE SCRIPTURE

A champion also memorizes Scripture. Many men tell me, "I can't memorize Scripture." Nonsense! Psalm 119:11 says, "Your Word have I treasured in my heart that I might not sin against You." Why should you memorize Scripture? To help you in life's day-to-day struggles! To help you live. Psalm 119:105 says, "Your Word is a lamp to my feet and a light to my path."

SHARE YOUR FAITH

It has been reported that 90 percent of the Evangelical Christian Church, nine out of ten people, have never been used by God to lead another individual to know Jesus Christ in a personal saving way. That's astonishing to me! Why would you come to church and read the Bible and grow closer to Christ if you don't want to share about His wonder and majesty with others? If you had the cure for cancer and somebody had cancer, wouldn't you tell them about it? Why, sure you would. We don't have the cure for cancer; we have the cure for death! Everyone has that disease.

> **"IF YOU HAD THE CURE FOR CANCER AND SOMEBODY HAD CANCER, WOULDN'T YOU TELL THEM ABOUT IT?"**

Have you gotten your children excited about sharing their faith? Are they motivated to share? "Then He said to His disciples, 'The harvest is plentiful, but the workers are few'" (Matthew 9:37). The laborers really are few. Could you do what Peter said: "Always be ready to make a defense to everyone who asks you to give an account for the hope that is in you yet with gentleness and reverence" (1 Peter 3:15)? Sometimes I don't do well with the gentleness and reverence part, but I'm more than willing to share. I believe in Jesus. I know that my life has been changed. If your life hasn't been changed, you need to ask yourself if you are really saved. God wants you to have abundant life, and He wants you to be joyful. Then He commands, not suggests, that we share the good news with others. Matthew 28:19–20 says, "Go therefore and make disciples of all the nations, baptizing them in the name of the Father and the Son and the Holy Spirit, teaching them to observe all that I commanded you; and lo, I am with you always, even to the end of the age." When was the last time you shared your faith? If you aren't intentional, you won't.

FLEE IMMORALITY

The apostle Paul said, "Flee immorality" (1 Corinthians 6:18). Do you *flee* immorality? I have a friend of mine who prays, "Lord, if I have an adulterous affair, kill me." That's how serious he is about being obedient to God in that area of his life. He has committed to honor his wife. He is committed to not violating God's commandments. He has the habits of a champion.

Sometimes we tell ourselves we don't want to sin, but we don't separate from people and circumstances in our lives we know are dangerous. If you stand by a muddy puddle long enough, you will get some mud on you. Flee immorality!

WORK HARD

Are you the best student you can be? Colossians 3:23 challenges us: "Whatever you do, do your work heartily, as for the Lord rather than for men." Be the best you can be. This exhortation applies to all areas of our lives. Are you working heartily with excellence for the Lord as a husband, employee, volunteer, or father for Jesus? The call from the Lord starts with our attitudes and effort, and it culminates in obedience.

It's important to realize that hard work alone won't get it done. A tire stuck in the snow works very hard, but it doesn't get anything accomplished. Be intentional with your efforts.

WATCH YOUR LANGUAGE

One area that is controversial for men is our language. When I was a college coach, I could hardly say five words without swearing. Though I wasn't a Christian, I knew it was wrong; in fact, my mother had taught me that using bad language was an indication of a poor vocabulary. The Bible tells us in Ephesians 4:29 that we shouldn't use unwholesome words, and Ephesians 5:4 calls out filthy words, silly talk, and coarse jesting. I had to decide when I became a Christian if I was going to follow Jesus wholly or partially. Each of us must make that same decision. I mean, if Jesus is to be the Lord of our lives, shouldn't He also be the Lord of our lips?

GUARD YOUR TESTIMONY

As an athlete or coach, how do you feel about trash talking? Everyone does it, right? Consider this: If you as a Christian are trash talking a non-Christian, you are giving a bad testimony. And if you are trash talking a Christian, you are running a brother in the Lord down. The first time I heard this was from Ray Slagle, the basketball coach at Worthington Christian High School. He's right.

Let me share with you a funny story about that. We had a player, Wes Lowry, who talked to guys all game long. But instead of putting them down, he would ask them what they got for Christmas, what their favorite food was, and anything else he could to divert their attention from their job. Effective but not malicious.

FOSTER A WILL TO WIN

One of the most misunderstood concepts in life revolves around winning and losing. If I ask a group of people, "Do you want to win?" everyone would say, "Yes." That's not the right question. The proper question is, "Do you have the will to prepare to win?" The will to win is not nearly as important as the will to prepare to win. Someday in life you're going to have an off-day and your habits are going to carry you through. That's true of football teams; it's true of individuals; it's true of companies. Consequently, the fact that you trained, that you prepared, that you constantly improved is what is going to ultimately allow you to succeed even on an off-day. The will to win is not as important as the will to prepare to win. Great habits create great results!

"THE WILL TO WIN IS NOT NEARLY AS IMPORTANT AS THE WILL TO PREPARE TO WIN."

On September 11, 2001, we got to see the habits of a real champion in action. Let me share with you the story of Todd Beamer, a common man with an uncommon story.

> Todd Beamer had two sons, David, 4, and Drew, 10 months, and his wife, Lisa, was pregnant with a third child.
>
> The television broke the news about the plane crash in rural Pennsylvania. "At that time, I knew it was Todd's flight. I sensed no hope for survival," Lisa said.
>
> On September 14, Lisa received a call from a crisis counselor at United Airlines. It turns out that Todd had called on the plane's Airfone, but for some reason the call did not go to Lisa. It wound up with an Airfone operator in Chicago named Lisa Jefferson. The next morning, the two Lisas had a tearful conversation by telephone. Jefferson told Lisa that her husband had been calm and matter-of-fact during the call.
>
> The passengers were discussing ways to overpower the hijackers. "It's what we have to do," Todd had said.

> The hijackers, in an apparent effort to thwart these plans, sent the plane diving and swerving to try to knock the passengers off their feet. For a moment, Todd's voice showed fear. "Jesus, we're going down," he said. Then he steadied. "We're coming back up."
>
> Jefferson told Lisa that Todd had talked about his family, and he asked her to call his wife if he did not make it home. "I don't think we're going to get out of this thing," he told Jefferson. "I'm going to have to go out on faith."
>
> Todd asked Jefferson to pray with him, and together over the phone they recited the Lord's Prayer. *"Our Father, who art in heaven… "* He then recited the 23rd Psalm, *"The Lord is my shepherd / I shall not want… "*
>
> "Jesus, help me," Todd said. Then Jefferson heard him say: "Are you guys ready? Let's roll"—a phrase he used often with his boys.
>
> Lisa Beamer made this observation, "Todd lived every day trying to make little decisions that were in line with the big goals he had for his life. The actions he took on September 11 were just one more example of that. Obviously, these were some of the hardest and most courageous decisions he made, but he was able to make them because he was practicing every day before September 11."[9]

Todd Beamer's story is sad and inspiring at the same time. Todd Beamer had prepared all of his life for his moment. Therefore, when he had to "put it all on the line," he was ready. I pray that you are as well.

---

9 Jim McKinnon, "The Phone Line From Flight 93 Was Still Open When A GTE Operator Heard Todd Beamer Say 'Are You Guys Ready? Let's Roll,'" *Pittsburgh Post-Gazette*, September 16, 2001.

HABITS OF A CHAMPION

PRACTICE PRACTICING PERFECTLY
READ THE BIBLE
GIVE TO GOD'S WORK
MEMORIZE SCRIPTURE
FLEE IMMORALITY
SHARE YOUR FAITH
WORK HARD
WATCH YOUR LANGUAGE
GUARD YOUR TESTIMONY
FOSTER A WILL TO WIN

J. O. S. H. **U.** A.

A MAN OF COMMITMENT IS:

UNWAVERING

The U in Joshua stands for Unwavering, which means to hold steady—in your opinion, allegiance, and direction—to never falter. A godly man receives his opinions and allegiance directly from God through the Bible. God's Word tells us what to remain steadfast about. Sometimes, it's hard to stay the course for God because you feel so alone. But remember this: If you try to please both God and society, you will please neither.

Remember Peter? Peter the apostle had a reputation as a hothead. Yes, he was, but he was also a man of action. He was the only disciple who got out of the boat! (Matthew 14:29). Peter had his flaws, but he was a man's man. He made plenty of mistakes, but he never stopped trying. Remember, the only time you fail is the last time you try. Let me share with you a more recent story about a man who was unwavering.

> In 1989, an 8.2 earthquake almost flattened Armenia, killing over 30,000 people in less than four minutes.
>
> In the midst of utter devastation and chaos, a father left his wife securely at home and rushed to the school where his son was supposed to be, only to discover that the building was as flat as a pancake.
>
> After the traumatic initial shock, he remembered the promise he had made to his son: "No matter what, I'll always be there for you!" And tears began to fill his eyes. As he looked at the pile of debris that once was the school, it looked hopeless, but he kept remembering his commitment to his son.
>
> He began to concentrate on where he walked his son to class at school each morning. Remembering his son's classroom would be in the back-right corner of the building, he rushed there and started digging through the rubble.
>
> As he was digging, other forlorn parents arrived, clutching their hearts, saying, "My son!" and, "My daughter!" Other well-meaning parents tried to pull him off of what was left of the school saying:
>
> "It's too late!"

"They're dead!"

"You can't help!"

"Go home!"

"Come on, face reality. There's nothing you can do!"

"You're just going to make things worse!"

To each parent he responded with one line: "Are you going to help me now?" And then he proceeded to dig for his son, stone by stone.

The fire chief showed up and tried to pull him off of the school's debris saying, "Fires are breaking out, explosions are happening everywhere. You're in danger. We'll take care of it. Go home." To which this loving, caring Armenian father asked, "Are you going to help me now?"

The police came and said, "You're angry, distraught, and it's over. You're endangering others. Go home. We'll handle it!" To which he replied, "Are you going to help me now?" No one helped.

Courageously he proceeded alone because he needed to know for himself: "Is my boy alive or is he dead?"

He dug for eight hours…12 hours…24 hours…36 hours…then, in the 38th hour, he pulled back a boulder and heard his son's voice. He screamed his son's name, "ARMAND!" He heard back, "Dad!?! It's me, Dad! I told the other kids not to worry. I told 'em that if you were alive, you'd save me and when you saved me, they'd be saved. You promised, 'No matter what, I'll always be there for you!' You did it, Dad!"

"What's going on in there? How is it?" the father asked.

"There are fourteen of us left out of thirty-three, Dad. We're scared, hungry, and thankful you're here. When the building collapsed, it made a wedge, like a triangle, and it saved us."

"Come on out, boy!"

"No, Dad! Let the other kids out first, 'cuz I know you'll get me! No matter what, I know you'll be there for me!"[10]

Do your kids have that kind of confidence in you? Is that the kind of biblical man you are? That's how I want my wife and children to think about me. I want them to know I am unwavering in my commitment to my family.

"REMEMBER, THE ONLY TIME YOU FAIL IS THE LAST TIME YOU TRY."

Few men in the Bible illustrate this trait of a committed unwavering man more than Daniel. Daniel was an incredible man. He was transported to Babylon by Nebuchadnezzar after God gave Jerusalem to the Chaldeans. Once there, Daniel was commanded to eat the king's choice food, but it violated God's dietary laws. Therefore, "*Daniel purposed in his heart* that he would not defile himself with the portion of the king's delicacies, nor with the wine which he drank; therefore, he requested of the chief of the eunuchs that he might not defile himself" (Daniel 1:8 NKJV, emphasis mine). Daniel and his three buddies, Shadrach, Meshach, and Abednego, with God's help,

10 Mark V. Hansen, "Are You Going to Help Me? From *Chicken Soup For The Soul 20th Anniversary Edition*," Chicken Soup for the Soul, last modified 2020, https://www.chickensoup.com/book-story/36264/are-you-going-to-help-me.

talked the Commander of the officials into allowing them to eat the food God commanded. When Daniel and his friends were tested, not one of the other captives was found to be like Daniel and his friends. God protected them when they obeyed His instructions.

In Daniel 3:17–18, we read, "If it be so, our God whom we serve is able to deliver us from the furnace of blazing fire; and He will deliver us out of your hand, O king. But even if He does not, let it be known to you, O king, that we are not going to serve your gods or worship the golden image that you have set up." These men were prepared to die based on what God had told them. This is a perfect illustration of unwavering commitment while following God's instruction. Inspiring! Challenging!

Notice Daniel had teammates, men who were like encouragers. It is very easy to quit on yourself. I first learned this as a wrestling coach in summer tournaments where my wrestlers did not compete for a team. When they knew they were part of a team score, they would fight hard to win or even not get pinned, but when they represented only themselves, it was easy to quit. Surround yourself with teammates who encourage you to be your best.

My friend Mark Stier, a pastor at Westerville Christian Church in Westerville, Ohio, often talks about two types of people we have in our lives: basement people and balcony people. Basement people drag us down. Basement people don't like when others succeed, as they are jealous. Basement people are always full of discontent and draining.

Balcony people, on the other hand, cheer us on, encourage us, call us to be better. As Transformational Leadership says, basement people would be tank emptiers, while balcony people are tank fillers. To remain unwavering in the important times and events in life, we need to surround ourselves with balcony people.

Who are your top three balcony people? If you don't know, you should be intentional about finding them *now*!

In Manhood in Action, we have a Manhood Creed. I hope this will give you a mantra for living that is easy to memorize.

HOLY SPIRIT HELP ME TO BE:

HONORABLE IN CONDUCT

UNWAVERING IN DUTY

GENTLE IN SPEECH

CALM IN CHAOS

Commit to becoming a man who is *unwavering;* one who purposes in his heart to remain steadfast to God and sure in his opinion, allegiance, and direction, no matter what.

J. O. S. H. U. **A.**

A MAN OF COMMITMENT IS A MAN OF:

ACTION

Lastly, the A in Joshua stands for Action. Manhood in Action Ministries is called this because godly men put the traits of Christ into Action. James tells us that "faith without works is dead" (James 2:26). Talk is cheap. Action shows what you really believe and hold dear. Take a look at what I learned about the great Spanish explorer, Hernando Cortez, that I believe exemplifies this point:

> In 1518, the Spanish sent Hernando Cortez to Mexico to conquer the Aztec Indians. Cortez was one of the most ruthless conquistadors of his time. When Cortez landed on the coast,

> near the city of Vera Cruz he established his base there. In order to subdue the Aztecs, Cortez had to march his troops inland to Mexico City. As they started up the mountain to go inland, the troops turned to see flames coming from the boats on which they had just arrived. To ensure that his men were one hundred percent committed to winning the battle, Cortez burned the ships. With no way to retreat or flee, his men were filled with a passion to finish the mission successfully.

Cortez and his men had to win or die. Retreat was not an option. We must learn to be equally as dedicated to our commitments as they were. The key, however, is that *a man of commitment burns the boats on his own*. It is his choice, and therefore, he will complete his promise.

Sometimes we are not men of action because life has beaten us down, so we stop trying. When I was the head wrestling coach at Miami University, I had a young coach address my team before we went to the National Tournament. That young coach was Jim Tressel, who later went on to lead The Ohio State Buckeye football team to a National Championship. Jim told us the story of a bull elephant who was born to a circus troupe. He was just a little fellow, and as they moved from town to town, the circus would put an iron shackle around his leg which was chained to a large stake. They would drive the stake into the ground. The bull elephant would yank on the shackle to get away, but he wasn't strong enough. This went on for years, and finally, the bull elephant was big enough and strong enough to rip the stake out of the ground, but he stopped trying. He had learned he couldn't succeed so he stopped trying.

Many men I meet are like that; they have learned defeat from their lives so they stop trying. They haven't realized they are stronger and wiser than they once were. With the proper action, they can pull up the stake that holds them back. Intentional reflection is called for to recognize the areas you are holding back in because of previous defeats. You can change your life when you realize you have power to overcome.

Nothing is stronger in your life than God, and as Romans 8:31 says, "What then shall we say to these things? If God is for us, who can be against us?" No one.

The movie *Apollo 13* is an exciting film. The crew was having mechanical problems in space and it looked very dim for their return. Eugene Kranz, a director at the communications center, called a meeting and explained the materials the capsule had available to make the repairs. He then said to the support staff, "Find me a solution." As the people begin to leave the room, he stopped them and said these famous words, "And failure is not an option."[11]

Jesus was a man of Action. When he threw the moneychangers out, it was not an impulsive act on his part. John 2:15 tells us that "He made a scourge of cords." His action was not impulsive; He took the time to make the scourge and then He used it.

William Wallace said, in the movie *Braveheart,* "Every man dies; not every man really lives."[12] Life is most exhilarating when pursuing a cause far greater than ourselves. How sad it must be to be on your deathbed and feel remorse about opportunities lost to serve Jesus.

If you take an inventory right now, how are you doing? The great thing about life is that we can be intentional and change today.

The most inspiring example of commitment and action that I know is when Jesus was in the garden of Gethsemane and his human nature was being tested as He looked toward death on the cross. In fact, it's described in the Bible saying, "His agony was demonstrated by flooding drops of blood," which is a known medical condition only caused under conditions of incredible stress. His heartfelt prayer was offered to His Father, God Almighty, with this plea, "Father, if you're willing, remove this cup from me, yet not my will, but yours

11 *Apollo 13,* directed by Ron Howard (Los Angeles, CA: Universal, 1995).

12 *Braveheart,* directed by Mel Gibson (Los Angeles, CA: Icon Productions, 1995).

be done" (Luke 22:42). He was on a mission; He was committed to fulfilling that mission. Even if it meant His death, even if it required incredible pain, He gladly went through the test. Although the prospects were beyond our imagination, Jesus finished the course. He completed His commitment. He is the best example that we can find of someone who made a commitment, and under extreme conditions, completed that commitment.

Oh, that we would be men of action! Oh, that we would be like Jesus! Let's pledge to ourselves and each other that we will be.

A MAN OF CHRIST

COMMITMENT = A PROMISE COMPLETED

HONOR = CHARACTER ABOVE REPROACH; LIVING BY A BIBLICAL STANDARD

RESPONSIBILITY = TRUSTWORTHINESS DEMONSTRATED OVER TIME

INITIATIVE = BOLDNESS WITH INTEGRITY

SERVICE = INTENTIONALLY PUTTING THE NEEDS OF OTHERS FIRST, EXPECTING NOTHING IN RETURN

TRUTH = A STATEMENT OR PRINCIPLE THAT APPLIES TO ALL PEOPLE, IN ALL PLACES, AT ALL TIMES

C. **H.** R. I. S. T.

A MAN OF HONOR

P. A. U. L.

PURE IN MIND AND ACTION

ACCOUNTABLE TO CHRIST

UNPRETENTIOUS

LAUDABLE

CHAPTER FOUR

A MAN OF HONOR

P.A.U.L.

WE NOW MOVE TO THE NEXT letter in the C. H. R. I. S. T. acrostic. H is for Honor, another critical attribute of a godly man. To honor someone else is to show respect or reverence toward another person. In one sense, honor refers to those whom we revere or respect. However, the honor I am referring to means to have such noble character and integrity that we might deserve the respect of others.

No man wakes up in the morning and says to himself, "I want to be a failure today and in life." When I first address my football players each year, I ask them, "How many of you are as good a football player today as you ever hope to be?" Fortunately, no one has ever raised their hand. At that point I tell them in order to improve they need a coach and they need to accept coaching. It amazes me that many men say they want to improve but they are unwilling to take any coaching. Are you as good a man as you ever hope to be? Can you accept coaching from others to help you get there?

To be a man of honor is to have a deep sense of our obligations and to fulfill them. Manhood in Action defines a man of honor as someone who is "above reproach, living by a biblical standard." 1 Timothy 3:7 NIV challenges us to have a good reputation, especially outside the church. "He must also have a good reputation with outsiders, so that he will not fall into disgrace and into the devil's trap."

I would like to begin this section with two real-life examples. The first shows great honor, while the third shows a tremendous lack of honor. I find it's useful to learn from errors as well as successes. Let's take a look.

In 2002, *Time Magazine* picked three people for their "Person of the Year" award. The three people exemplified what was happening in America at that time. The first was a woman named Cynthia Cooper, who "exploded the bubble that was WorldCom when she informed its board that the company had covered up $3.8 billion in losses through the prestidigitations [sleight of hand] of phony bookkeeping."[1]

The second honoree was Sherron Watkins, the Enron Vice President, who wrote a letter to Chairman Kenneth Lay in the summer of 2001 warning him that the company's methods of accounting were improper. And the third person was Colleen Rowley, the FBI staff attorney who caused a sensation in May with a memo she wrote to FBI Director Robert Mueller about how the bureau brushed off pleas made by her Minneapolis field office to investigate Zacarias Moussaoui. The home office of the FBI blew off her request. Moussaoui was later indicted as a co-conspirator of the terrorist attacks that took place on September 11, 2001.

You have three women: Cynthia Cooper, Sherron Watkins, and Colleen Rowley, who were selected as *Time*'s 2002 Persons of the Year. These women were truly honorable. They were courageous. And they deserve this distinction and our respect. According to the magazine, "Their lives may not have been at stake, but Watkins, Rowley, and Cooper pretty much put everything else on the line, their jobs, their health, their privacy, their sanity, they risked all of them to bring us badly needed word of trouble inside crucial institutions."

These ladies didn't start out to be troublemakers; they simply could not sit idly by and leave these wrongs unrighted. However, my question is this: Where

---

1 Richard Lacayo & Amanda Ripley, "Persons of the Year 2002: The Whistle-Blowers," *Time,* December 30, 2002, http://content.time.com/time/specials/packages/0,28757,2022164,00.html.

were the men? How could you have the problems in Enron, WorldCom, and the FBI, yet not one man stood up? Surely some men knew. Why didn't they stand up and be counted? Honorable men do what is right and necessary, no matter what the cost to them personally. We are called by God to be such men. Yes, it takes guts; it takes courage. But that is what men of honor do.

Not all stories tell tales of honor. In fact, some show great dishonor. Such is the following story printed in the December 10, 2002 edition of *USA Today*:

> Federice Robinson can still see Dennis Franchione sitting in her living room last winter, pressing for the ultimate trust. The Alabama coach didn't just promise to turn her quarterback into a cornerback. He promised to turn her boy into a man.
>
> "He guaranteed he'd be there for Ramzee no matter what, he said, 'believe in me. Don't worry about anything, I'm not going anywhere. I'm recruiting your son, and I'll be there for any problem he has.'"
>
> Ramzee Robinson, a redshirt freshman, woke up today with a problem: His coach's office is as empty as his coach's word.
>
> The team got the news the way a real tough-guy coach should deliver it; through his defensive coordinator.
>
> "Out of simple respect," Ramzee Robinson said, "We should've been the first to know. We deserved that much from Coach Fran. If you preach to us to be a certain type of man and then do the total opposite, you're not being a man."
>
> "Almost every day at practice he would preach loyalty and staying together. Before we got on the plane to Hawaii for our last game, he

> lectured us that the rumors of him leaving were false. Coach Fran didn't even have the decency to face us, so everybody's ticked off."
>
> His website was headlined by the words Accountability, Loyalty, and Trust, virtues he converted into punch lines.
>
> "I committed right when the NCAA penalty was announced," Ramzee said, "and Coach Fran said we'd get through the probation together. I'm Christian, so I'll pray for him to come back and talk to us, because that would help so much."
>
> At 18, Ramzee Robinson is old enough to know he shouldn't hold his breath.[2]

As we look in the newspaper, we see great examples of tremendous honor and many examples of dishonor. We see examples of preaching one thing and then doing the opposite. I'd rather be known as having the honor of the three ladies as opposed to the lack of honor displayed in the Franchione story.

A coaching associate of mine used a pretty brutal statement to describe this type of behavior. He would say,

"REMEMBER, MIKE, NOBODY'S WORTHLESS. THEY CAN ALWAYS BE USED AS A BAD EXAMPLE."

That's a pretty brutal comment, but unfortunately it's correct. Commit right now in your mind and in your heart to live as a man of honor. My grandfather Stanley used to say, "No matter what you say or do, your *tale* will always follow you." The things that we do and the things that we don't do become a matter of our history. One by one, they form our reputation.

It's hard to display honor in our everyday lives. Moment-by-moment

---

2 Ian O'Connor, "Franchione Word is Out With Tide," *USA Today,* December 10, 2002.

issues face us, such as, *Do I cheat on my income tax? Do I tell the truth?* Always! *Do I exaggerate to make myself look more important than I am?* Habits can be good or bad. Some men get into the habit of telling white lies. Of course, there is no such thing as a white lie because a lie is a lie. It's not white or black or green or blue. It's a lie. Unfortunately, in our society, many people think that some lies are okay, and some lies aren't okay. Biblically, that's just not the case. Lying and cheating are not things a man of honor can do.

Most of this section will center on how to personally become a man of honor. However, before we go any further, I think it's important to review some of the people the Bible tells us we need to honor.

WHO DO WE NEED TO HONOR?

1. ***GOD:*** In 1 Samuel 2:30, the Bible says, "Honor God." In fact, God states, "Honor God." And His promise to us is "I will honor those who honor me." It's interesting to me that God is gracious and kind to honor us if we honor Him. We do that by living lives that glorify Him.

2. ***YOUR FATHER AND MOTHER***: Exodus 20:12 says, "Honor your father and your mother so that your days may be prolonged in the land which the Lord gives." That's the fifth of the Ten Commandments, and it is described as the first commandment with a promise. If we honor our parents, our days will be prolonged.

3. ***OUR LEADERS***: 1 Peter 2:17 says, "Honor all men. Honor the King." This is a hard command currently. To Americans, that would refer to the President of the United States, no matter who is in office. Sometimes that's a great deal easier than other times. But God's Word says we should. In fact, He not only says to honor the person, but He says to pray for that person as well. Oftentimes, the President of the United States needs that prayer. Whether you agree or disagree

with the president, recognize that God has put them in control. God allowed Adolf Hitler to be in charge. I can't tell you why. I don't understand why. But you can bet your boots that God knew Hitler's depravity and allowed it. If we want to affect the way our leaders lead, we need to pray for them to help and support them.

4. ***YOUR WIFE***: If you have a wife, she should be honored. 1 Peter 3:7 says, "Grant her [your wife] honor as a fellow heir of the grace of life." And Hebrews 13:4 goes even further by saying, "Marriage is to be held in honor among all and the marriage bed is to be undefiled." This is a strong warning to people who would stray in their vows of the commitment made at their wedding. Very strong language!

5. ***WIDOWS***: 1 Timothy 5:3 says, "Honor widows who are widows indeed." Verse 5:4 explains what a "widow indeed" is. The key is that we know there are ladies we need to honor and take care of as a church body.

6. ***CHURCH ELDERS, PASTORS***: "Let the elders who rule well be considered worthy of a double honor" (1 Timothy 5:17). Imagine the pressure of being an elder. What a tremendous honor, but what tremendous pressure because you are spiritually responsible for the congregation, the flock of the Lord Jesus Christ. God also says if you are an elder and you elder well, that you are worthy of a double honor. What a remarkable thing! Young people, if you want to know how to live your life, one thing is very clear. Paul said, desire to be an elder. "Overseer" is the word he uses, but he is talking about elders. Live your life so that people would observe your behavior and say, "that man should be an elder in our church." "It is a trustworthy statement if any man aspires to the office of overseer, it is fine work he desires to do" (1 Timothy 3:1). Strive

hard to meet the qualifications for God's definition of honorable conduct so you can be an elder.

7. ***JESUS CHRIST:*** In John 5:22b and 23, John says, "He has given all judgment to the Son, so that all will honor the Son even as they honor the Father. He who does not honor the Son does not honor the Father who sent Him." So, we need to honor Jesus Christ Himself. In fact, we need to honor Jesus Christ first, above all.

Sometimes we don't feel like honoring these folks. I understand that, but God tells us to do it. What we need to do is start by honoring people with our actions and the feelings will follow. Most of you know that. Knowing something is right doesn't make it easy. Nevertheless, we as Christians are called to a higher standard than non-Christians. As fathers, I believe we are called to an even higher standard, and it starts with those closest to you—your wife and children. Perhaps your wife offends you or your children really make you angry. The feelings will pass but what you say and do may be remembered forever. You can control your reactions with the Holy Spirit's help.

As we examine how to become men of honor, we're going to use the biblical hero, Paul, who gave us the guide to honor when he said, "Be imitators of me, just as I also am of Christ" (1 Corinthians 11:1). Paul showed us that no matter what our past was, Jesus Christ can use us in a positive way. Paul had ordered the death of Christians, held the coats of men while they stoned Stephen, undoubtedly cheering in his heart. But God chose him to be the man who wrote over half of the New Testament and took the truth of Jesus to non-Jews. He became the greatest missionary the world has ever known. He was simply an ordinary (read sinful) man who served an extraordinary God.

We can use the acrostic P. A. U. L. to define for us what a man of honor is like, just like Paul did—a man who is Pure in mind and action; a man who is Accountable to Christ; a man who is Unpretentious, and a man who is Laudable. These are the traits of a man of honor. Let's start with the first one.

P. A. U. L.

A MAN OF HONOR IS:

PURE IN MIND AND ACTION

The P in Paul stands for Pure in Mind and Action. One of the most important and difficult things to talk about, and we don't do it enough as men, is the issue of purity. Purity is defined as "freedom from anything that contaminates us." Freedom from evil! While most people think of purity as being a physical issue, it starts in your heart and mind. Jesus made it very clear in Matthew 5:28 when He said, "I say to you everyone who looks at a woman with lust for her has already committed adultery with her in his heart." Jesus is both clear and emphatic about this. He also said if you call your brother an idiot, that is akin to the sin of murder (v. 22). Strong words.

The Bible is very clear about the fact that most sin, deep sin, starts in the heart and comes out in some form of action. Many people come across as holier than thou. Some would say, "I would never behave like Ted Bundy. I'm not like Adolf Hitler." However, we all have purity issues. It just comes out differently than it did in Bundy and Hitler because "the heart is more deceitful than all else and is desperately sick" (Jeremiah 17:9). You can spend your entire day thinking about the fact that all you want to be is an NFL quarterback. You can spend your entire day thinking about what you want to do with your money, never once thinking about God. You could never once honor your wife and your children. Your mind is polluted. Absolutely polluted!

Before we get too deeply into purity, let's distinguish between these two terms: sin and temptation. Temptation is not sin. If you're living life and you see a beautiful woman and it pops into your head, "That's a beautiful woman," that is not a sin. That's a fact. She is a beautiful woman. Now what you do with the thought from there may turn it into sin. If you decide that in your mind you're going to undress her, now we're talking sin. And if you begin to plan what it is that you're going to do with her in some clandestine affair, that is absolutely sin.

There's a distinction between temptation and sin. Temptation is something that tries to lead us away from God's best for our lives. In 1 Corinthians 10:13, Paul says, "No temptation has overtaken you but such as is common to man; and God is faithful, who will not allow you to be tempted beyond what you are able, but with the temptation will provide the way of escape also, so that you will be able to endure it." Faithful to what? To take away the temptation? No. He will not allow you to be tempted beyond what you are able but will provide the way of *escape* from the temptation. You must be committed in advance to avoiding temptation because it can easily turn to sin. We need to be careful not to enjoy the "pleasure in sin for a season" (Hebrews 11:25 KJV). Don't be the kind of dad who says to your children, "No, sin is not pleasurable." That's not being biblically honest. The Bible says that you can enjoy sin for a season, but that season ends. You are left with the consequences, and they are not pleasurable and last far longer than the sin did.

If you go out on Saturday night and intentionally look for a quiet place to have sex with the girl you are with, God will still provide the way of escape. You don't have to plan the rendezvous in the first place, or you can leave when you see you are moving from temptation to sin. But you can't expect that God is going to keep you from sinning against your will. Jesus said, "Lead us not into temptation, but deliver us from evil" (Matthew 6:13). Free will isn't free. Use it wisely.

Billy Graham did not allow himself to be alone with a woman anywhere—not an elevator, not a room. He wanted to be so far above reproach that no one could accuse him of an indiscretion. He could still have had a problem in his heart, but he was wise enough to know he could avoid even the hint of impropriety by some simple precautions. He protected his reputation and that of his ministry.

Do you remember the presidential election from a couple of years ago when a Christian leader was running for president? This man was accused of having an improper relationship with one of the people on his campaign staff. He had a door to his office that was a solid door and for some reason wouldn't put a window in the door. The whole plan of escape was as simple as putting a window in the door so that folks who had these concerns could look in the window and see what was truly happening. Pride must take a back seat to common sense and caution.

Sometimes we are so pigheaded that we create problems for ourselves that we could eliminate immediately. Beware of the slippery slope from temptation to sin. Sin can be pleasurable, but you must live with the consequences and the memories forever. When you pick up the coin of sin, just like any coin, it has two sides. There's the pleasure side, and there is also the consequence side.

Another truth about sin is that it is like putting a nail in a board. You can remove the nail, you can stop the sin, but you can't remove the indentation. The indentation is the consequence from the fact that the nail was in the board. Can you be forgiven? Sure. But forgiving doesn't mean forgetting. Recognize that if someone has sinned against you, then just because you have forgiven them doesn't mean that you have forgotten the issue. Be constantly on the alert, testing your thoughts and motives. Honor Jesus; make Him proud!

My understanding of forgiveness is that it is basically choosing to never bring up the sin and using it against the person. That doesn't mean it has been forgotten. I have had people tell me before that God forgets. Well, God can't forget. He is omniscient (all knowing). He knows everything. He is God. However, God chooses to put your sin as far as the east is from the west (Psalm 103:12). Corrie Ten Boom used to say, "God throws your sin in the deepest ocean and then places a sign that says, 'no fishing.'" That is a choice God makes. Aren't you glad? And, by the way, if you've got a problem with your wife or with your children, you know as well as I do that forgetting is a tremendously difficult thing. It's a whole lot easier not to sin than it is to have someone forgive us.

Why avoid temptation if it isn't sin? To remain pure. It's easier and better to keep evil out of your soul than it is to try and remove it after it gets in. I'm not sure we understand how tempting and insidious sin truly is. If you start with a clear glass of water and you take a dropper filled with dirty water, then you squirt one tiny drop of dirty water in the clear glass, what do you have? You have dirty water. Even a little sin can contaminate our purity. Sometimes people tell me that they are going to bars or strip clubs to minister to folks. You better take people with you to hold you accountable. You better have your act together because when you get around sin and temptation, it's awfully easy to give in to it. It is much simpler to stay away from sin and temptation. You must know yourself. You must know your areas of personal weakness. You can't stand next to a mud puddle while people are running and biking through it without getting splashed. And Paul says very clearly, "Flee immorality" (1 Corinthians 6:18). He doesn't say "get up and walk away." He says, "get up and run, flee immorality." That's one of the best ways to keep yourself pure.

How insidious is sin? St. Augustine was known as a brilliant theologian. Augustine wrote a report about stealing pears, which Charles Colson talked about in one of his books. Certainly, stealing pears is not what many people would conceive of as a devastatingly sinful event. Yet to Augustine, the incident illustrated the depth of his sinful heart.

> Augustine recorded that late one night a group of youngsters went out to 'shake down and rob this tree. We took great loads of fruit from it, not for our own eating but rather to throw it to the pigs.' He went on to berate himself for the depth of sin this incident revealed. 'The fruit I gathered I threw away, devouring it only out of iniquity (wickedness). There was no other reason, but *foul was the evil and I loved it.*'

> Contemporary critics, though generous in their praise of Augustine's literary genius and profound philosophical insights, mock him for his seeming obsession with the pear tree episode. Why would one harmless prank loom so large in the saint's mind? By his own admission he had taken a mistress, fathered a child out of wedlock, and indulged in every fleshly passion. Surely any of these were more serious than stealing pears.
>
> But Augustine saw in the pear incident his "true nature" and the nature of all mankind: *in each of us there is sin—not just susceptibility to sin but sin itself.* Augustine's love for sensual pleasure could be explained as the natural arousing of his human desires; proving inner weakness or susceptibility to sinning. *But he had stolen those pears for the pure enjoyment of stealing* (he had an abundance of better pears on his own trees). Augustine knew his act was more than weakness; *it was sin itself—sin for the sake of sinning* (emphasis mine).
>
> And why do we love it when other people fall? What else accounts for our morbid fascination with violence on television? Why do we love the bloody carnage of horror films or the fall of television pastors? What causes this behavior? It's just human nature. Who has not found himself at some point smiling, boasting of a sin? Not only do we sin, but at some level we start to boast of our sins. We start to brag about them. So pervasive is the sin in us that we are subject to lonely shame if we cannot share in the sins of others.[3]

Let's look at two Bible stories about temptation with two very different endings. The first story is about King David, who is described in the Bible

---

3 Charles Colson, *Loving God: The Cost of Being a Christian* (Grand Rapids: Zondervan, 2018).

as "a man after His [God's] own heart" (Acts 13:22). How would you like to have God say that about you? What an honor. What a statement, and yet, what a flawed man David was. David fell to the evils of sin when he seduced Bathsheba. 2 Samuel 11 describes the affair, which starts off this way: "In the spring when armies went out to fight…" Let me ask you a question. Where is the leader of the army supposed to be when the army goes out to fight? He's supposed to be with the army. As king, David was the leader of the army, so where was David? He was at home when he should have been out with his men. Verses 2–3 tell us he got up from his bed, looked out his window, and saw a woman bathing—Bathsheba. He was tempted for sure. But just because he saw her, it wasn't sin yet. Unfortunately, he didn't stop there. David not only saw Bathsheba, he sent for her, knowing full well she was another man's wife. As king, he could do that, but he shouldn't have. He took what didn't belong to him, a temptation, and began to act on it. He sent for her. She came. He was the king, so she had to.

If there is any question, this was David's sin. He made plans even knowing she was married. He exposed himself to ever greater temptation by being in her presence. The Bible says, he "took her and lay with her" (2 Samuel 11:4). Sin, which had only been temptation before, was now completed. It followed with the murder of Bathsheba's unsuspecting husband. The consequences of his sins followed him the rest of his life. He had a horrible life, hunted down by his own son. David's life ended as a mess for a man who was described as "a man after God's own heart." You should read the rest of the story.

We see David's sin as a horrible mistake. Yet God is a big God, and Jesus Christ was born through the line of David and Bathsheba. As terrible as David's sin was, God was able to overcome the consequences and use them for good. Truly remarkable!

The second example I want to review is Joseph—Joseph of multicolored-tunic fame. This man responded to a very difficult situation like a champion, which you can read in Genesis 39. He responded like a man of action.

Potiphar's wife asked Joseph to lie with her. He said, "No." Given that she was used to getting her way, she was unhappy. Joseph explained to her that Potiphar had been good to him, so "How then could I do this great evil and sin against God?" (Genesis 39:9).

It's important to recognize all sin is against God. David said that in 2 Samuel 12:13. Joseph said that too. It is clear. All sin is against God. Often, we sin directly against another person, but that sin is against God, first and foremost.

Potiphar's wife continued to try to seduce Joseph and falsely accused him of rape. He was thrown in jail for an action he didn't commit. Forgotten by his friends, hated by his jealous brothers, and sold into slavery, Joseph was abandoned. In fact, the only thing that kept his brothers from killing him was they just didn't quite have the guts. They really wanted to kill him. Yet, Joseph never lost faith in God. "As for you," speaking to his brothers, "you meant evil against me, but God meant it for good in order to bring about this present result to preserve many people" (Genesis 50:20).

God is so powerful that He took pure evil and made it work for His good. Sometimes we miss that. Before we become too harsh on the people in these events, I want to remind you of something. Remember that without the Holy Spirit, each of us could do any sin. Many of you are thinking, "I could never do that. I could never molest a child. I could never rob a bank." Yes, you could. Were it not for the power of the Holy Spirit restraining us, we could commit any sin or atrocity.

I know a man whose father ripped out a man's eye because the man shorted his father a nickel. Ripped his eye out! Now, that's evil. But I would contend that all of us are capable of this or any sin if not for the fact that we are restrained by the Holy Spirit. For that I am eternally grateful and thankful.

Let us consider some specific ways that we can help keep our minds and actions pure. I have listed ten of them for you with the hope that they give you something to think about and evaluate in your own life.

TEN WAYS TO PRESERVE PURITY

1. ***MEMORIZE TEMPTATION-ORIENTED SCRIPTURES:*** Psalm 119:9 says that we need to read God's Word. "How can a young man keep his way pure? By keeping it according to Thy word." The reason that you memorize Scripture is so when you have difficult times or you're tempted, you can bring the Scripture to mind. By focusing on God's Word, we can ward off sin. Gil Stieglitz, author of *Mission Possible: Winning the Battle over Temptation*, recommends writing out Romans 6:1–23 and personalizing it, using your name and particular areas of temptation where appropriate.[4] This is powerful stuff.

   Not doing something or just thinking something is not enough. Saying to yourself, "I will not fantasize about that woman," will only cause you to think about her. You have to replace your tempting thoughts with pure thoughts. For example, if I tell you *not* to think about elephants right now, what are you thinking about? Elephants! You see, it's not enough to say, "Don't think about elephants." You must have good things to replace the bad thoughts. That's where God's Word comes in. That's why you memorize Scripture. I also appreciate 1 Corinthians 10:13 and James 1:2.

2. ***FEAR THE LORD:*** Proverbs 1:7 says, "The fear of the Lord is the beginning of knowledge." Fools despise wisdom and instruction, but people who fear the Lord look for wisdom and pursue righteousness. Fearing the Lord means to see God with such reverence and awe that we recognize not being obedient to Him is a big mistake. It bothers me that some want to take out the power

---

4 Gil Stieglitz, *Mission Possible: Winning the Battle over Temptation* (Roseville: Principles to Live By Publishing, 2017), 106–7.

of this statement. They wish to make this Scripture a soft warning from the God of Love. God *is* the God of Love, but He is not to be trifled with. People say don't mess with Texas. The heck with Texas! Don't mess with God!

3. **FLEE IMMORALITY AND SET BOUNDARIES FOR YOURSELF:** Temptations abound everywhere, so you need to decide in advance to flee anything that is outside of God's moral boundaries. This includes premarital sex and sex outside of marriage. No matter what certain men may say, God defines sex to include oral sex. We must teach our children honorable behavior. We will either model God's standard or Satan's lie.

   One boundary you can set is for when you travel and stay in a hotel room. What's on TV today puts you at risk. Pornography is just a click away. I have a friend of mine who had immense problems when he would travel for business. Pornography was a huge problem for him on TV. He needed to flee immorality by having those channels blocked. If you don't and you are a channel flipper, you will cause your own temptation.

   Another boundary you can set is to not have long talks with female co-workers. She could begin to listen to you in a way no one at home will. You could begin to believe she would be a better wife, a more kindred spirit. The whole relationship is built on a lie. She doesn't have to live with you, so it is easy to put up with your deficiencies. She can be your confidant, your supporter because she doesn't have to live with your faults. She can tell you how wonderful you are given that she does not have to deal with your peculiarities day after day. You better run, not walk, away from her. I also don't believe, for example, that it is appropriate for men to counsel women, period. I know men whose lives have been made far more difficult because they counseled divorced women, single women, and stepped over the line. Families and lives have been destroyed or at least harmed. You may have the best intentions in the world; your heart may be pure. Do not counsel women other than your wife and daughters. It makes you too vulnerable.

4. ***DO WHAT YOU'RE SUPPOSED TO DO WHEN YOU'RE SUPPOSED TO BE DOING IT:*** King David was in the wrong place at the wrong time, doing something he wasn't supposed to be doing. We can avoid some of this by adhering to what I call the "Eleven-o'clock rule." Very few good things happen outside of our homes after eleven o'clock at night. Most college coaches preach long and hard about this rule, but their players often violate the rule and get into serious trouble. Being where you shouldn't be always spells trouble. At some time in your life, you will get into situations where you must make a courageous decision. Don't wait until the situation arises to decide how you will act. Decide in advance to avoid tempting and compromising situations. Satan wants us to fail and he will use any and all of his tricks to destroy us. We are in a battle for our souls and the souls of our families.

5. ***PROTECT YOUR EYES AND GUARD YOUR HEART:*** David made his mistake by fixing his eyes on Bathsheba. He didn't protect his eyes or guard his heart. There's a great book by Fred Stoecker and Stephen Arterburn that talks about every man's battle. That, of course, is the battle for sexual purity. They emphasize the concept of "bouncing your eyes," a technique in which you intentionally look away from sin.[5] Like most techniques for averting sin, this

---

5 Fred Stoecker and Stephen Arterburn, *Every Man's Battle: Winning the War on Sexual Temptation One Victory at a Time* (Colorado Springs: Waterbrook Press, 2000).

works but only if you employ the technique. I have had men who have taken my seminar report back to me that "bouncing your eyes" works. Protect yourself, for the eyes are the portals of the soul. In Job 31:1, Job said, "I have made a covenant with my eyes; how then could I gaze upon a virgin?" He made a pact for purity. Will you? Using the technique for "bouncing your eyes" requires commitment. Don't expect instant perfection but keep practicing. In time you will develop a wonderful iron clad habit. Don't excuse yourself, improve yourself! Commit to be a man of honor and protect your eyes, guard your heart.

6. ***SAFEGUARD YOUR HOME:*** 1 Thessalonians 5:22 says, "Abstain from every form of evil." The J.C. Penney's catalog used to come to our home. If you have young boys, they will be drawn to the underwear section. Are you? If so, explain to your wife that she needs to help you by not keeping the catalogs around.

   My wife is really perceptive. She came to me one day and said, "Where's the Penney's catalog?" In my typical fashion, I said, "I have no idea." She found it in a strange place. It never dawned on me that it could tempt my young sons. God bless her instincts. Dad, do you want to help your kids? Don't put that kind of temptation in your home. Playboy? Put protections on your computer and phones as well. Only if you want to tempt the very children God has entrusted you to protect will you ignore this safeguard.

   You might say, "It's okay for me. I am an adult. My children can't handle that stuff but I can." You can't handle it either, Dad. You shouldn't handle it even if you can handle it; it's wrong. You might say to me, "Well, I've got Christian liberty." I would say that's true, but you are a knucklehead. Why in the world would you subject yourself to things that have no positive value whatsoever? Some guys, trying to be funny, say, "I'm off the market, but I can look at the menu." Well, only if you want to play with fire and hope not to get burned. It isn't worth it. Remember, purity is a heart issue as well as a physical issue.

I'm trying to be funny, but I'm also trying to make sure you understand this is serious stuff. Guys fall every day; guys that you and I respect. Sin is insidious. Pastors fall when women come and throw themselves at them. They didn't set out to fall but they didn't protect themselves. Sin must be avoided, so flee. Sin can ruin homes, reputations, and lives. If you've got a pastor, you ought to be praying hard for him that he remains pure in all things.

7. ***BE DILIGENT IN YOUR THOUGHT LIFE:*** God clearly says in 2 Corinthians 10:5 that we must be diligent in our thought life. "We are destroying speculations and every lofty thing raised up against the knowledge of God, and we are taking every thought captive to the obedience of Christ." Our thought life, if not controlled, will lead to sin against the Lord Jesus who died for us.

   Masturbation for men is a difficult issue. A lot of men want to avoid talking about the problem. Is masturbation a sin? Personally, I think it is, and I know this is true: you can't masturbate if you don't have thoughts of lust in your head. Sorry, guys, you just can't do it. There's only one way to masturbate, and that is to have lustful thoughts. Now, is that a sin? Yes!

8. ***GUARD THE TEMPLE:*** 1 Corinthians 6:19-20 says, "Or do you not know that your body is a temple of the Holy Spirit who is in you and whom you have from God and is not your own. For you have been bought with a price, therefore glorify God in your body." I

understand that this refers to sexual sin. But it seems to me that if the Holy Spirit resides in you there is more to it than only God watching you. God is in you, if you're a Christian. God is more than watching you, He is in you.

If God came back today would he be pleased with what you are watching on TV? Would He approve of your relationships? Only you can decide that. But I'll say this: honor and purity need to remain top of mind all the time. When you go through your day, do you realize that God is with you? Since He is, then it's important to think and do things of which He would be proud. Watch TV as if Jesus were watching with you.

As Randy Alcorn says in his book *The Purity Principle*, "Purity is always smart; impurity is always stupid."[6]

9. ***PRAY HARD:*** Jesus says in Matthew 6:13 to pray that you are not led into temptation but that you are delivered from evil (paraphrase mine). I guess I've made enough mistakes in my life that if I'm around evil long enough, I will cave in. To avoid the fall, I just try to stay away from sin. It's a simpler and easier way to stay pure.

10. ***TEACH ABSTINENCE:*** As fathers, we must teach our children to abstain from sex before marriage. The emotional and physical consequences are very heavy. In our society today, we are told that waiting isn't possible. Garbage! My sons and their wives were pure at their weddings. Aside from the emotional consequences, the impact of disease is very real. Society is against us on this. Take a look at Robert Layton's story below about abstinence, which gives

---

6 Randy Alcorn, *The Purity Principle* (Colorado Springs: Multnomah Publishing, 2003).

us a vivid picture of the dangers of pre-marital sex and the carefree "everybody-does-it" attitude of our society:

> I was holding a notice from my 13-year-old son's school announcing a meeting to preview the new course in sexuality. Parents could examine the curriculum and take part in an actual lesson presented exactly as it would be given to the students. When I arrived at the school, I was surprised to discover only about a dozen parents there.
>
> As we waited for the presentation, I thumbed through page after page of instructions in the prevention of pregnancy or disease. I found abstinence mentioned only in passing.
>
> When the teacher arrived with the school nurse, she asked if there were any questions. I asked why abstinence did not play a noticeable part in the material. What happened next was shocking.
>
> There was a great deal of laughter, and someone suggested that if I thought abstinence had any merit, I should go back to burying my head in the sand. The teacher and the nurse said nothing as I drowned in a sea of embarrassment. My mind had gone blank, and I could think of nothing to say.
>
> The teacher explained to me that the job of the school was to teach "facts" and the home was responsible for moral training.
>
> I sat in silence for the next twenty minutes as the course was explained. The other parents seemed to give their unqualified support to the materials.

"Donuts at the back," announced the teacher during the break. "I'd like you to put on the nametags we have prepared. They're right by the donuts and [you can] mingle with the other parents."

Everyone moved to the back of the room. As I watched them affixing their nametags and shaking hands, I sat deep in thought. I was ashamed that I had not been able to persuade them to include a serious discussion of abstinence in the materials. I uttered a silent prayer for guidance.

My thoughts were interrupted by the teacher's hand on my shoulder.

"Won't you join the others, Mr. Layton?"

The nurse smiled sweetly at me. "The donuts are good."

"Thank you, no," I replied.

"Won't you please join them?" she coaxed.

Then I heard a still, small voice whisper, "Don't go." The instruction was unmistakable.

"Don't go!"

"I'll just wait here," I said.

When the class was called back to order, the teacher looked around the long table and thanked everyone for putting on nametags. She ignored me.

Then she said, "Now we're going to give you the same

lesson we'll be giving your children. Everyone please peel off your nametags.

"Now then, on the back of one of the tags I drew a tiny flower. Who has it please?"

The gentleman across from me held it up.

"Here it is!"

"All right," she said, "The flower represents disease. Do you recall with whom you shook hands?"

He pointed to a couple of people.

"Very good," she replied. "The handshake in this case represents intimacy. So, the two people you had contact with now have the disease."

There was laughter and joking among the parents. The teacher continued, "And with whom did the two of you shake hands?"

The point was well taken, and she explained how this lesson would show students how quickly disease is spread.

"Since we all shook hands, we all have the disease."

It was then that I heard the still, small voice again. "Speak now," it said, "but be humble."

I noted wryly the latter admonition, and then rose from my chair. I apologized for any upset I might have caused earlier, congratulated the teacher on an excellent lesson that would

> impress the youth, and concluded by saying I had only one small point I wished to make.
>
> "Not all of us were infected," I said. "One of us…abstained."[7]

Jerry Bridges, in his book *Pursuit of Holiness*, says this, "It's time for Christians to face up to our responsibility for holiness. Too often we say we are defeated by this or that sin. No, we are not defeated, we are disobedient." There's a distinction here. We are simply disobedient. "It might be well," he says, "if we stopped using the terms victory and defeat to describe our progress in holiness and rather we should use the terms obedience and disobedience."[8]

Sin doesn't defeat me in the sense that you and I talk about losing the game. My disobedience defeats me. I know what's right and wrong. Morality is a simple thing. It's the practice of morality that becomes difficult. However, pursuing purity takes more than discipline. Pastor Beau Stanley makes this point, "Discipline is necessary to succeed, but without passion, you will never be able to maintain the discipline."

You know what a sin is and what is not a sin. That is not the issue. The issue is, will you be a man who pursues purity? Will you be committed to having and holding on to honor?

---

7 Robert Layton, "Abstinence," Inspirational Christian Stories & Poems, last modified 2020, http://www.inspirationalarchive.com/texts/topics/learning/abstinance.shtml.

8 Jerry Bridges, *Pursuit of Holiness* (Colorado Springs: NavPress, 2006), 80–81.

TO PRESERVE PURITY...

- MEMORIZE TEMPTATION-ORIENTED SCRIPTURES.
- FEAR THE LORD.
- FLEE IMMORALITY AND SET BOUNDARIES FOR YOURSELF.
- DO WHAT YOU'RE SUPPOSED TO DO WHEN YOU'RE SUPPOSED TO BE DOING IT.
- PROTECT YOUR EYES AND GUARD YOUR HEART.
- SAFEGUARD YOUR HOME.
- BE DILIGENT IN YOUR THOUGHT LIFE.
- GUARD THE TEMPLE.
- PRAY HARD.
- TEACH ABSTINENCE.

When glancing at this list, are there two or three items that convict you? Purpose to change them intentionally today.

> *Lord, men are creatures driven by sight. You know that better than I do. I don't ask that You take away our manhood but that You help us flee immorality and Honor You. Amen.*

P. **A.** U. L.

A MAN OF HONOR IS:

ACCOUNTABLE TO CHRIST

The A in Paul stands for Accountable to Christ. We must allow the Lord God to be in control of our lives and that means we should be subject to, or submissive to, Jesus's will. Therefore, we need to start this section with what true submission is. Jesus said, "My food is to do the will of Him who sent me and to accomplish His work" (John 4:34). That was His mission. And in the garden of Gethsemane, He said, "Father, if You are willing, remove this cup from Me, yet, not My will, but Yours be done" (Luke 22:42). Because He was committed to doing what God had asked Him to do, Jesus "humbled Himself [submitted] by becoming obedient to the point of death, even death on a cross" (Philippians 2:8).

The key for accountability lies in two words: consistent and intentional. Jesus was *consistently* and *intentionally* submissive to God the Father. Understanding this, how then, should we behave as biblical men? The clearest test of our being accountable to Christ is shown in our everyday relationships. You can tell the heart of a man most easily by watching how he treats those closest to him. Most men treat perfect strangers far better than they treat their family. We are kind, we are nice to people outside our family. But with the people at home, we become aggravated and intolerant because they have flaws. Well, guess what? So do we!

We tend to forget our shortcomings, but we certainly remember theirs. We know that we are supposed to be kind and generous to strangers, but we don't even demonstrate that same kindness and generosity in our own homes.

Specifically, I would like to focus on marriage to give us a living guide as to how properly centered relationships work when the man has truly *submitted to Christ*. This is a crucial concept for biblical manhood. The Bible explains, "Christ is the head of the church" (Ephesians 5:23). "The church is subject or submissive to Christ" (Ephesians 5:23b). "Christ gave himself up [died for the church]" (Ephesians 5:25b). Paul says in 5:25a, "Husbands, love your wives as Christ loved the church." Submission only works properly when all the biblical requirements are in place.

Oftentimes, radical feminists try to misrepresent the Bible and assert that submission is akin to being a doormat for a man to wipe his feet on.

Nothing could be further from the truth. Biblical submission is like a ranking order in the armed services. Some are generals, some are captains, and some are privates. A private has no lesser value as a human being than a general does, but the private should submit himself to a general because his rank is higher. No organization, including the family, can operate efficiently unless everyone knows their role. Submission is freeing because we don't have to do everything on our own. James 4:7 says, "Submit therefore, to God." So we all should be submitting to God.

For example, if I had a daughter, and I could help it, I would never allow my daughter or my granddaughter to marry someone who wasn't "born again." In fact, if I had my way about it, she wouldn't even date someone who wasn't "born again." If you start doing what is commonly called "missionary dating," that is, dating someone to save them, more than likely you will end up with a big problem in your family. Missionary dating is a no-no. Has it ever worked? Yes, it has worked, but it has also failed tragically.

I love my wife, but it's hard work being married. It's worth it, but it's hard. When a man is submissive to Christ, then his wife can submit safely to him. That's the whole key. Many women will not submit to their husband's leadership because their husband's leadership is garbage. He doesn't submit himself to Christ.

"WHEN A MAN IS SUBMISSIVE TO CHRIST, THEN HIS WIFE CAN SUBMIT SAFELY TO HIM."

If you're married and God is not the head, then here's the problem: there is no head of the family. You can't break ties. If she's not a Christian and you're not a Christian, then as far as she is concerned, she's God and you think you're God. Everything is a 50-50 tie with no way to break the ties.

Submission, however, cannot be forced. You can force somebody to obey, but you can't force them to submit to you. Think about the American prisoners in Vietnam; many were beaten and forced to obey but they never submitted to the enemy; they never gave in. They obeyed what they were told to do because they didn't want to get beaten senseless, but their hearts never changed. You can make your children obey you, but you can't make them submit to you. As men, we need to earn our children's respect, honor, and love. Submission occurs only through somebody's free will.

1 Peter 3:7 says, "You husbands in the same way, live with your wives in an understanding way, as with someone weaker, since she is a woman; and show her honor as a fellow heir of the grace of life, so that your prayers will not be hindered." To live with her in an understanding way means to study her, becoming an expert in knowing her wants and needs. In fact, this verse has a very serious consequence if we fail to know her. We are told our prayers could be hindered if we don't show her honor. God is very serious about men knowing and honoring their wives.

In fifty years of marriage, there have been fewer than five big issues on which my wife and I have really disagreed. To choose judiciously whom you marry, spend some time dating them for a couple of years. If you get to know them, and you understand them, then you can see whether your values, ideals, and goals match. My wife and I were not Christians, yet we shared most values, such as how we wanted to raise our children and how we would treat money. For women to feel safe and secure about submitting to their husbands, the husband must give his wife *all* the information he has before he makes the final decision. Wives are incredibly discerning with a special perception that I at least often miss. I think you will avoid a lot of mistakes if you consider your wife's opinions before you make the final decision. However, there are times when you must make decisions with which your wife doesn't agree. Nevertheless, if you've really informed her about everything often your wife will say, "Do what you think is best because I know that you have my best interest at heart."

I don't want to hurt my wife. I want to honor my wife. She knows that. How does she know that? Because of the years of experiences we have had where I have protected her. It should be that way in all marriages. God calls the man to be the tie breaker; otherwise the wife rules the house by veto. Don't miss that concept. If you have to agree on every decision, your wife will rule your home by veto. But when you assume the proper role of a biblical man correctly, your wife will experience the following benefits:

She will feel safe.

She will feel secure.

A woman's number one need is security. When you make good decisions, systematically, year-after-year, involving her along the way, then she can be all that God wants her to be! Often men say they would die for their wives, but the greater question is, will you lovingly live for her?

Bill McCartney, the founder of Promise Keepers, started the ministry after his pastor gave a sermon asserting that you could tell how good a husband was by the countenance of his wife. If you've got a great thing going with your wife, her countenance will glow. She'll be effervescent and glowing. Bill McCartney left coaching when he looked at his wife one morning as the pastor was speaking and he saw that his wife was broken. He realized that he was responsible for her joy, as much as an earthly person he could be. But he also recognized that her countenance was down because of what was going on in their lives and he knew he had to change that. So, he left coaching to focus on her. That is true Manhood in Action!

One note of caution, men—never bully your wife with your voice. A male voice can be very scary. You've got to be sensitive about your tone. 1 Peter 2:16 gives us a sober warning: "Act as free men and don't use your freedom as a covering for evil." You shouldn't manage your household as if you were king. In fact, men are called to servant leadership. This type of leadership demands that we are more concerned for our family's needs than for our own.

I'm going to give you some guidelines I have given to young men for appropriate dating. If you are already married, give your sons these dating guidelines.

First, pray and ask for wisdom before you ask someone for a date. Dating doesn't have to happen immediately. Know what your drop-dead issues are. Pray that God will reveal the true character of the other person. You want to know what their character really is, and time is necessary to see the real person. You can fake who you are for a while, but you can't fake it for a long while. That's why I think it's important for people to date in excess of a year and probably closer to two years before marriage.

Second, be healthy spiritually yourself. I can't tell you how many guys I counsel who are a spiritual mess. It worries me when they talk about getting married. To date biblically, you must be able to say no and accept no. If you begin to date someone and you know they are not the person you intend to marry, stop dating them! Have that courage in reverse so that if she says to you that you're not the one for her, you won't pine away about it. Thank God that you didn't marry her and find out later that she only married you because she didn't want to break up and hurt your feelings. Praise God and then get on with life. Be thankful. Realize your mate is not going to meet all your needs anyway. God wouldn't allow it. God doesn't want any gods before Him, and that includes your wife.

Third, date only born-again Christians. Time spent in group events will help verify their claim to be a Christian. Many people claim to be Christians, sometimes with very evil motives. Spend time with them; find out whether the fruits of their life verify their claims. Don't be a notch on somebody else's belt. Some women are like gunfighters in the Old West. Instead of notches on their belts for killing someone in a gunfight, they notch their belts with virgin young men they cause to stumble. Flee immorality! We are accountable to Christ.

I heard a story once about a young man who was a virgin in college. His friends ridiculed him for not having sex. They told him they would set him up with a woman so he could have sex. His response was that of a man of honor. He said, "I can join your club any time I want but you can never be in my club again because you have given away your virginity, your purity." Praise God for such an unwavering young man.

Finally, date only to find a mate. When you know it's not the right person, call it off. Consider it a gift from God if it is called off because you can't make marriage work alone. One of the serious risks of dating too much is that we learn how to divorce or break relationships easily. When we have established a pattern of abandoning relationships casually, then divorce becomes easier to do. Failure in marriage just simply isn't an option.

It's your responsibility, Dad, to teach your children about sex. Here's the choice…either you're going to teach them, or they are going to learn on the playground. Your choice! Have the strength and courage to be the man you need to be and the model of which they can be proud. James Dobson's book *Preparing for Adolescence* is a great tool.

We're accountable to Christ to teach our children God's best and to be men of honor.

BIBLICAL DATING GUIDELINES

- PRAY AND ASK FOR WISDOM BEFORE YOU ASK SOMEONE FOR A DATE.
- BE HEALTHY SPIRITUALLY YOURSELF.
- DATE ONLY BORN-AGAIN CHRISTIANS.
- DATE ONLY TO FIND A MATE.

P. A. **U.** L.

A MAN OF HONOR IS:

UNPRETENTIOUS

So, a man of Honor is like the apostle Paul. He is Pure in mind and action; he is Accountable to Christ. He is also Unpretentious, which means humble. Who controls your life, you or God? Humility is not thinking less of yourself; it is not thinking of yourself at all. Most people think they are humble when they are just downcast, feeling worthless. They say, "I'm not worthy, I'm not worthy." No, that doesn't make you humble; that makes you proud of being so unworthy and so worthless.

Pride is the opposite of humility, and the Bible warns us, "Pride goes before destruction and a haughty spirit before a fall" (Proverbs 16:18). We use the sucker trap in football all the time to take advantage of a person's weakness. On a trap play, the defensive player encounters very little or no resistance. He charges ahead with his eyes on the target and then another player hits him from the blind side. So does Satan. He sets all kinds of traps.

As men and fathers, we will be criticized from time to time if we are following God's call. When we are criticized, we need to remember this quote from J. Oswald Sanders, "No leader is exempt from criticism and his humility will nowhere be seen more clearly than in the manner in which he accepts and reacts to criticism."[9] I know that for myself as a leader, the most difficult thing is not to become defensive when someone criticizes me. A quick temper and an urge to respond are often brought on when we think too highly of ourselves.

---

9 J. Oswald Sanders, *Spiritual Leadership: Principles of Excellence for Every Believer* (Chicago: Moody Bible Institute, 2007).

"NO LEADER IS EXEMPT FROM CRITICISM AND HIS HUMILITY WILL NOWHERE BE SEEN MORE CLEARLY THAN IN THE MANNER IN WHICH HE ACCEPTS AND REACTS TO CRITICISM."

The following is an excerpt from a *Sports Illustrated* article that shares the story of Mike Sweeney, an all-star first baseman baseball player for the Kansas City Royals. But Mike Sweeney hasn't always been a star. Let's take a look.

> [Tony] Muser, who had taken over for [Bob] Boone midway through '97 [was] disenchanted with Mike Sweeney's skills behind the plate – he says that while Sweeney had a strong arm and the overall athletic abilities to be a good catcher, he was "overloaded and confused" when it came to calling a game – he made it clear that Sweeney had no future as his starting catcher. In January '99, a Kansas City coach told Sweeney he had "zero percent" chance of sticking with the big-league club for the following season.
>
> On Ash Wednesday, 1999, two days before he was to leave for spring training in Davenport, FL, Sweeney exercised at a gym and then drove to the Church of the Nativity, a Roman Catholic Church where he was a parishioner. He was tired and drained, wearing baggy sweats and running shoes. A service was under way, so Sweeney quietly found a spot in the back and dropped to his knees. He began to weep. "I had this vivid picture in my head of a tandem bicycle," he recalls. "I'm thinking, the bike represents my life, and I'm on the front seat, and I'm trying to pedal and steer the bicycle. But I don't know where I'm going."
>
> As he prayed, the image changed. He saw Jesus on the front seat, holding the handlebars. Says Sweeney; "I was on the back, pedaling my heart out, realizing the Lord will steer me if I agree to follow."

> Sweeney recalls that he silently prayed; "Lord, there are six weeks until Opening Day. I don't know where I'm going, I don't know what city I'll end up in, but I know that you control my life. As long as I'm in the backseat pedaling, everything will work out. No matter where I am, I will get on my knees and praise you."
>
> The next day Sweeney received more phone calls about trade rumors. This time, however, he was at peace. He reported to camp with a clear mind, batted .361 and made the Royals as the third-string catcher, behind Chad Kreuter and Tim Spehr.
>
> During the year the Royals needed a first baseman. The coach asked if anyone had ever played first base before. Sweeney had played one game in Little League, so he volunteered. Mike Sweeney has gone on to become a perennial All-Star at first base.[10]

Mike Sweeney learned a valuable lesson about how to best live life. It is summed up really well by a quote from Doctor Samuel Brengle, once introduced as "the great Doctor Brengle." He said, "If I appear great in their eyes, the Lord is most graciously helping me to see how *absolutely nothing I am without Him* and *helping me to keep little in my own eyes.* He does use me. But I am so concerned that *He uses me,* and that it is not of me that the work is done. The axe cannot boast of the tree it has cut down. It could do nothing but for the woodsman. *He made it, He sharpened it and He used it.* The moment he throws it aside, it becomes only old iron. O that I may never lose sight of this [emphasis mine]."[11]

---

10 Jeff Pearlman, "A Run of Luck: Last Year Mike Sweeney Found His Batting Stroke, a New Position and Inner Peace. Now the Royals' First Baseman Is a Big Hit at the Plate and with Kansas City Fans," *Sports Illustrated,* July 24, 2000, 50–51.

11 J. Oswald Sanders, *Spiritual Leadership*: *Principles of Excellence for Every Believer* (Chicago: Moody Bible Institute, 2007), 62.

A man of Honor would conduct his life using the advice and admonition from Philippians 2:3–4, which says, "Do nothing from selfishness or empty conceit, but with humility of mind, consider others as more important than yourself. Do not merely look out for your own interests, but for the interests of others." I think these verses should be in every wedding ceremony. If men and women intentionally lived that way, we would have fewer divorces. Every teammate on every team should commit to these verses. Read them from the perspective of an athlete. There truly is no "I" in team. Being Unpretentious comes from knowing we are flawed, but God is in control, and we are better off for it.

P. A. U. **L.**

A MAN OF HONOR IS:

LAUDABLE

The L in Paul stands for Laudable. Laudable defines a man who is praiseworthy or worthy of honor. If we are living our lives keeping our minds and actions pure, and if we are Accountable to Christ and Unpretentious, we will be Laudable.

In Matthew 26:24–27, Jesus gives us our marching orders as to how we must live to be praiseworthy. He also asks us one of life's most critical questions. "Then Jesus said to his disciples, 'If anyone wishes to come after me, he must deny himself, and take up his cross and follow Me. For whoever wishes to save his life will lose it; but whoever loses his life for my sake will find it. *For what will it profit a man if he gains the whole world and forfeits his soul?* Or what will a man give in exchange for his soul. For the Son of Man is going to come in the glory of His Father with His angels and will then repay every man according to his deeds" (emphasis mine).

What will it profit you, what will it profit me, if we gain all the world has to offer yet lose our souls? Now that would be a tragedy!

I can think of no better source to explain the traits of an honorable man than Almighty God Himself. The Holy Spirit through the apostle Paul defined the traits of a laudable man in 1 Timothy 3:2 when he defined the qualities an elder or overseer would have. He would be a man above reproach. The Greek for "above reproach" gives the picture of a man with "no handles." There would be nothing to grab onto by those inside and outside the church. He is a husband of one wife. This is a man who is committed to, and sold out to, one woman. He is temperate, prudent, respectable, hospitable, able to teach, not addicted to wine, and is not pugnacious, which means he is not a brawler or fighter. He is gentle, free from the love of money. He is one who manages his household well, keeping his children under control with dignity. If a man does not know how to manage his own household, how will he take care of the church of God?

An elder should not be a new convert. Why? So the elder will not become conceited and fall into the trap of pride set by the devil and his forces. If you let people take on too much responsibility too soon, you often ruin them. A new convert to Christianity should not be out leading the charge, because he just doesn't have a strong enough foundation. He must have a good reputation with those outside the church so that he will not fall into reproach and the snare of the devil. Even if you can't see yourself as an elder, this is still God's guideline for a man of honor. Strive hard to "show yourself approved" (2 Timothy 2:15).

I'm not an elder, but I strive to be eligible. Not being an elder does not hinder me from following God's call for my life or serving Him fully. I want to be known as a man who has the qualities of an elder. God Himself wrote the job description. I never want to be disqualified because I lack the necessary traits.

Sometimes in life, we clearly see a person who is to be lauded and to be respected. The following story tells us about such a man.

World War II produced many heroes. One such man was a lieutenant Commander Butch O'Hare. He was a fighter pilot assigned to the aircraft carrier Lexington in the South Pacific.

One day his entire squadron was sent on a mission. After he was airborne, he looked at his fuel gauge and realized that someone had forgotten to top off his fuel tank. He would not have enough fuel to complete his mission and get back to his ship. His flight leader ordered him to return to the carrier.

Reluctantly he dropped out of formation and headed back to the fleet. As he was returning to the mother ship, he saw something that turned his blood cold. A squadron of Japanese bombers was speeding their way toward the American fleet. The American fighters were gone on a sortie and the fleet was all but defenseless. He couldn't reach his squadron and bring them back in time to save the fleet. Nor could he warn the fleet of the approaching danger.

There was only one thing to do. He must somehow divert them from the fleet. Laying aside all thoughts of personal safety, he dove directly into the formation of the Japanese planes. Wing-mounted 50 calibers blazed as he charged in, attacking one surprised enemy plane and then another. Butch wove in and out of the now broken formation and fired at as many planes as possible until finally all his ammunition was spent.

Undaunted, he continued the assault. He dove at the planes, trying to at least clip off a wing or tail, in hopes of damaging as many enemy planes as possible and rendering them unfit to fly. He was desperate to do anything he could to keep them from reaching the American ships. Finally, the exasperated Japanese squadron took off in another direction.

> Deeply relieved, Butch O'Hare and his tattered fighter limped back to the carrier. Upon arrival he reported in and related the event surrounding his return. The film from the camera mounted on his plane told the tale. It showed the extent of Butch's daring attempt to protect his fleet. He had destroyed five enemy bombers. That was on February 20, 1942, and for that action he became the Navy's first Ace of WWII and the first Naval Aviator to win the Congressional Medal of Honor.
>
> A year later he was killed in aerial combat at the age of 29. His hometown would not allow the memory of that heroic action die. And today, O'Hare Airport in Chicago is named in tribute to the courage of this great man. So, the next time you're in O'Hare, visit his memorial with its statue and Medal of Honor located between Terminals one and two.[12]

This story about O'Hare would be inspiring on its own merits but what makes it even more amazing is this next the story of another man.

> There was a man in Chicago called Easy Eddie. At that time Al Capone virtually owned the city. Capone wasn't famous for anything heroic. His exploits were anything but praiseworthy. He was, however, notorious for enmeshing the City of Chicago in everything from bootlegged booze and prostitution to murder.
>
> Easy Eddie was Capone's lawyer and for a good reason. He was very good. In fact, his skill at legal maneuvering kept Big Al out of jail for a long time.

---

12 Jack Cousins, "Butch O'Hare: Navy's First Ace of WWII," last modified 1998, http://www.cannon-lexington.com/Other%20Stories/Butch%20O%27Hare.html.

To show his appreciation, Capone paid him very well. Not only was the money big, but also Eddie got special dividends. For instance, he and his family occupied a fenced-in mansion with live-in help and all the conveniences of the day. The estate was so large that it filled an entire Chicago City Block. Yes, Eddie lived the high life of the Chicago mob and gave little consideration to the atrocities that went on around him.

Eddie did have one soft spot, however. He had a son that he loved dearly. Eddie saw to it that his young son had the best of everything: clothes, cars, and a good education. Nothing was withheld. Price was no object. And despite his involvement with organized crime, Eddie even tried to teach him right from wrong.

Yes, Eddie tried to teach his son to rise above his own sordid life. He wanted him to be a better man than he was. Yet, with all his wealth and influence, there were two things that Eddie couldn't give his son. Two things that Eddie sacrificed to the Capone mob that he could not pass on to his beloved son: *a good name and a good example.*

One day, Easy Eddie reached a difficult decision. Offering his son a good name was far more important than all the riches he could lavish on him. He had to rectify all the wrong that he had done. He would go to the authorities and tell the truth about Scar-Face, Al Capone. He would try to clean up his tarnished name and offer his son some semblance of integrity. To do this he must testify against the Mob, and he knew that the cost would be great. But more than anything, he wanted to be an example to his son. He wanted to do the best to make a restoration and hopefully have a good name to leave his son.

> So he testified, and within the year, Easy Eddie's life ended in a blaze of gunfire on a lonely Chicago street. He had given his son the greatest gift he had to offer at the greatest price he would ever pay.
>
> This story would be inspiring on its own merits. However, what makes it so special is that Easy Eddie's son was Butch O' Hare, the World War II hero.[13]

I use this story because it points out that even if our lives haven't been all that we want them to be, there's hope. It's never too late to do the right thing. You get a chance every day to earn your reputation; every decision you make, every action you take. Honor is earned one thought, one decision, one action at a time. Are you happy with your reputation? If you are not, then today is the day to begin to change your behavior intentionally.

---

13 Cousins, "Butch O'Hare."

A MAN OF CHRIST

COMMITMENT = A PROMISE COMPLETED

HONOR = CHARACTER ABOVE REPROACH;
LIVING BY A BIBLICAL STANDARD

RESPONSIBILITY = TRUSTWORTHINESS DEMONSTRATED OVER TIME

INITIATIVE = BOLDNESS WITH INTEGRITY

SERVICE = INTENTIONALLY PUTTING THE NEEDS OF OTHERS FIRST,
EXPECTING NOTHING IN RETURN

TRUTH = A STATEMENT OR PRINCIPLE THAT APPLIES TO ALL PEOPLE,
IN ALL PLACES, AT ALL TIMES

C. H. **R.** I. S. T.

A MAN OF RESPONSIBILITY

T. I. M. O. T. H. Y.

TRUTH IS ABSOLUTE

ILLUSTRATES FORGIVENESS

MATURE DISCERNMENT

OVERCOMER, NOT A VICTIM

TEAMMATE

HATES EVIL

YES IS YES

CHAPTER FIVE

A MAN OF RESPONSIBILITY

T.I.M.O.T.H.Y.

WE HAVE DISCUSSED THE FACT that a godly man starts with a goal; he starts with the end in mind. Some men never do. My goal is very simple—to stand before Jesus Christ and have him say, "Well done, good and faithful servant" (Matthew 25:25, KJV). Everything I do in life centers around that goal. I try to filter my thoughts, actions, and motives through this question: what would really honor Jesus?

A man of responsibility will have the following traits like Timothy, a man who knows that truth is absolute. We live in a world where truth is situational, but as Christians, we should be able to know the truth of God's Word and stand on it as the incontrovertible, authoritative message from God, himself.

A man like Timothy illustrates forgiveness. On the one hand, a godly man is a man who has strength and courage and is unwavering. And yet he is also a man who can demonstrate or illustrate forgiveness. God asks us to forgive those who sin against us. Jesus talks about forgiveness a great deal. It is a very difficult concept, but if you are going to be a godly role model and accurately reflect God for your children, one of the things you need to teach them is how to forgive. Some of us who are mountaineers at heart have a hard time forgiving. But children don't just learn how to forgive. They need to see it modeled.

We know that a man like Timothy is a man of mature discernment. He is an overcomer, not a victim. He is a teammate, recognizing that going through life properly requires having teammates. A man like Timothy also hates evil, recognizing the areas he needs to flee that are evil. He needs to recognize that God's Word is very clear and he, like God, needs to hate evil.

And finally, and maybe most importantly, a man of responsibility is a man whose yes is yes, and no is no. He is a man of unquestioned integrity. He is a man you can *trust*.

Let's begin with the first trait of a man of responsibility.

T. I. M. O. T. H. Y.

A MAN OF RESPONSIBILITY BELIEVES: TRUTH IS ABSOLUTE

"Truth is absolute" is the foundation for a man of responsibility. God's Word, the Bible, is the revealed, unchanging, and definitive source for truth, yesterday, today, and forever.

Our lives can be built on a solid rock, not sinking sand, because absolute truth *never* changes. Many people in society today have bought into the lie that everyone has their own truth. But in truth, there is a right and there is a wrong, and they can be known. The Bible teaches truth for living each day. Most of us know how we should behave but often we choose not to. We are disobedient to God's instructions for living. It's not that we don't know the instructions, we just don't follow them.

So, what is absolute truth? It is "a statement or principle that applies to all people, in all places, at all times." In other words, for something to be absolutely true, it must be true for everybody, everywhere, every time!

When I first heard about absolute truth, it stopped me in my tracks. Could it be that stealing was wrong two thousand years ago in Europe, as well as one thousand years ago in Africa? How about today in America? This is exactly what it means. If something is true, it is true for all people, in all places, at all times. For example, since adultery is a sin (Matthew 5:27), that means it was a sin then, it is a sin now, and it will be a sin in the future.

Truth is by definition absolute because if it isn't always true, then it isn't the truth. It is critical to understand that when something is true, it's true all the time. Situational truth is an oxymoron and a lie. As Christians, the foundation of how we live depends on biblical truth, which started at creation.

Society has tried to destroy the foundation of the Christian community over the years by attacking God. They ridicule His account of the beginning of the world, creation. Ken Hamm, the founder of "Answers in Genesis," says that we Evangelical Christians are in a war with evolutionists. It's a war. The problem is that many of us don't realize it is a war. We think it is simply a debate.[1]

There is an illustration that Ken Hamm uses to make his point. Picture two circular medieval castles. You have a castle on each side of a moat. The evolutionists are in the tower of one castle and the creationists are in the tower of the other castle. In the top of each castle is a cannon. From their tower, the creationists are shooting at issues, like homosexuality, adultery, abortion. I'm not demeaning the importance of these issues; I'm simply saying that we shoot at the issues. However, the evolutionists have trained their cannon right at the base of the creationist tower. They shoot at the foundation of the creationist's belief, which is the account of creation. The evolutionists tell us that we are not created by God, that we evolved out of a slime pit. They recognize that if they can convince you and me that we evolved out of a slime pit, then there is no God. If there is no God, there is no one who will hold us accountable, and we can essentially do anything that we want to do. There are no moral imperatives, because without God each of us makes up our own rules and morals.

---

1 Greg Hall, "Chapter Two: Welcome to the War," Answers in Genesis, published September 10, 2016, https://answersingenesis.org/the-word-of-god/welcome-to-the-war/.

The people who are deeply driven by evolution are either misguided or they are doing sinful things and need a reason or an excuse not to be judged. If they know and understand that God exists and that He will judge their behavior, suddenly it changes the way they need to live their lives.

In our society, we are enamored by the scientific community. If the scientific community says evolution is a fact, even though there are no transitional forms, even though there's never been another human who has evolved, even though there is no logical explanation for where the material for the "big bang" came from without God, we are intimidated by their intellect and assume God's explanation must be flawed.

Think of it like this: If you take all of the pieces of a human being in cut up form, and you stick them all back together, why don't you have life? You've got all the parts; you've got all the necessary ingredients, so why don't you have life? The answer is because God alone gives life. "Professing to be wise," the Bible says, "they become fools" (Romans 1:22). When I was a youngster in high school, I totally believed in evolution because my teachers told me it was true. When I was in biology, we studied the concept "ontogeny recapitulates phylogeny." The only reason I remember this phrase is because the words flow so easily. The essence of the phrase means this: while a baby is in the womb, it goes through all the natural progression stages of the human being. In other words, the baby has a tail because man had a tail as he evolved. The baby has gills because man came from the ocean and was a fish at one time. That's what I was taught.

Eventually, the scientific community knew this theory was wrong, but they didn't or couldn't un-teach us. What's the tail? The tail is simply a piece of cartilage that sometimes doesn't disappear in the development of a human youngster and he's born with a tail. So what do they do? They cut it off. Well, it's not a tail at all; it's a piece of cartilage. What are the gills? The gills are folds of skin. If you take a picture of an unborn baby, you'll see that there are folds in the neck. They're not gills; they're just folds in the skin. But for years people thought they were gills, and they taught their false belief. We, as a society, are so in love with science that we believe anything scientists tell us is true. Generally, we don't bother to challenge their assertions even when they defy common sense. For a moment, reflect on these three critical points about the truth of Genesis chapter one:

1. In Genesis 1:1, what does the text declare that is impossible for God to do?
2. God didn't need seven days; in fact, the text claims that creation was accomplished with the spoken word in six days.
3. If God can do all the text says, why would He lie to me about how He did it?

One of science's early claims of a transition form was called "Lucy." They found a tooth and hypothesized that if the tooth looked as it did, then surely the jaw would look this way, and if the jaw looked like that, then the head must have looked like this. So, if the head looked like that, then you needed to have this particular kind of body to support it. Now suddenly they had this whole creature developed to defend the concept of evolution. Then, lo and behold, they discovered the tooth was the tooth of a pig. Unfortunately, many students had been taught incorrectly and there was no way to go back and correct the error. It seems that much of evolutionary science isn't science at all. It is simply a thinly veiled effort to prove evolution because creationism is so unpalatable to the intellectual elite.

I want to share a story with you that illustrates the arrogance of many in society and their condescending attitude about the Bible and its truths.

> There was a boy sitting on a park bench with one hand resting on an open Bible. He was loudly exclaiming his praise to God. "Hallelujah! Hallelujah! God is great!" He yelled without worrying whether anyone heard him or not.

Along came a man who had recently completed some studies at a local university. Feeling himself very enlightened in the ways of truth and very eager to show this enlightenment, he asked the boy about the source of his joy. "Hey," asked the boy in return with a bright laugh, "Do you have any idea what God is able to do? I just read that God opened up the Red Sea and led the whole nation of Israel right through the middle."

The enlightened man laughed lightly, sat down next to the boy, and began to try to open his eyes to the "realities" of the miracles of the Bible.

"That can all be very easily explained. Modern scholarship has shown that the Red Sea in that area was only 10 inches deep at that time. It was no problem for the Israelites to wade across."

The boy was stunned. His eyes wandered from the man back to the Bible lying open in his lap. The man, content that he had enlightened a poor, naïve young person to the finer points of scientific insight, turned to go. Scarcely had he taken two steps when the boy began to rejoice and praise louder than before. The man turned to ask the reason for these resumed jubilations.

"Wow!" exclaimed the boy happily, "God is greater than I thought! Not only did He lead the whole nation of Israel through the Red Sea, He topped it off by drowning the whole Egyptian army in 10 inches of water."[2]

---

2 Gwen Smith, "See the Red Sea: Nothing Is Impossible With God," Crosswalk.com, published January 27, 2010, https://www.crosswalk.com/church/worship/see-the-red-sea-nothing-is-impossible-with-god-11625480.html.

As an aside to that story, I want you to know that the Bible says the Israelites crossed on dry land. We must know the Bible. It's the remedy to not being misled. I've heard intellectuals make this assertion for years and never recognized that a thorough reading of the Bible would clear up the issue. Sometimes the brightest among us let their pride and ego rule over common sense. Believe God. He's never been wrong. Since the Bible's account of creation is God's account, creation must be true, or God lied. God cannot be God if He were to lie. That's clear, isn't it? God has held Himself to a standard that says, *I will not lie* (Titus 1:2). Therefore, if the creation account is not truthful, He is not God. Don't miss how important the creation account is because the evolutionists certainly haven't. There is much at stake. If there is no God, there are no moral absolutes. If there are no moral absolutes, we can do anything we want and answer to no one. We become the God of our own lives, the very opposite of fearing the Lord.

The human heart knows instinctively all sin is against God. Remove God, and you don't have to answer to anyone other than yourself. This allows people to follow their own desires and not fear any repercussions. David, after his sin with Bathsheba, said, "I have sinned against the Lord" (2 Samuel 12:13). Joseph reinforces this concept, when in Genesis 39:9, he says, referring to Potiphar and then to God, "There is no one in this house greater than I, and he (Potiphar) has withheld nothing from me except you, because you are his wife. How then could I do this great evil and sin against God?" The average person would believe David's sin was against Uriah or Bathsheba, and Joseph's sin would have been against Potiphar. However, both men knew the truth: all sin is against God.

When a Christian knowingly walks in deliberate sin, a common result is that he begins to lose confidence in his salvation. He knows he's doing wrong and he begins to really wonder if he could really be saved. Sin separates us from God, and we sense that. Live your life knowing that your foundation is solid, unshakable, because it is based in the absolute truth of God's Word.

A man of responsibility is a man who recognizes that truth is absolute as it is revealed in God's Word.

Is your world built on absolute Truth from God's Word? I pray that you build your house on the rock of God's Word. Life is easier when we don't have to guess what *the* Truth is.

T. **I.** M. O. T. H. Y.

A MAN OF RESPONSIBILITY: **I**LLUSTRATES FORGIVENESS

The I in Timothy stands for Illustrates Forgiveness. The big issue for most of us is that the other guy doesn't deserve to be forgiven. That's true; however, we didn't either. So, the first thing we need to do is understand why we should forgive. It's just not natural. It's something to be learned. In Ephesians 4:32, the Bible says, "Be kind to one another, tenderhearted, forgiving each other *just as God in Christ also has forgiven you*" (emphasis mine). We're told to forgive because God, through Christ, has forgiven us, not because the other person deserves it.

The danger in having an unforgiving heart is what happens to us personally. Pastor Bill Snell once said, "Unforgiveness is the poison we drink, hoping it will kill our offender." God's instructions to forgive were given to us because He loves us so much. He knows we will die a slow, bitter death from the inside if we refuse to forgive.

We are to model God. That's what he really asks us to do. Paul encouraged us to be imitators of Him. Hebrews 10:17 says, "Their sins and misdeeds I will remember no more." In Psalm 103:12, God tells us He removes our sin as far as the east is from the west. Words are critically important here. If God's Word said, "as far as the north is from the south," it would mean He only chose not to remember for a short time. If we start going north, after we go over the polar ice cap we begin to move south, and after going past the South Pole we head north again. However, when we start going east, we will never be going west. God will never remember our sins!

Forgiving doesn't mean forgetting. It means deciding in your heart and mind not to bring up the offense to zing the offender. If you really want to know if someone has forgiven you, all you have to do is see how many times they throw that sin back in your face. If they're throwing it back in your face, they really haven't forgiven you.

Many people, Christians and non-Christians alike, do not know how to properly ask for forgiveness. Most people simply say "I'm sorry" for the slight and move on. If you are the offender, the proper way to ask for forgiveness is to say, "I was wrong when I ______________ (name your sin). Please forgive me." It is so important to name the sin or slight and to acknowledge that you are agreeing that what you did was wrong. Then you specifically ask for forgiveness. If the person forgives you, you can work on restoring the relationship. If they don't, you cannot do any more humanly. But pray because God can.

Realize that when we sin against others, just because they forgive us and choose not to bring it up against us, doesn't mean they forget it. It doesn't mean that God forgot it. God intentionally chooses not to remember it. And therefore He asks us to model Him.

A note of caution: Trying not to think about something makes us think about it even more. Remember the story of thinking about elephants I told earlier? True forgiveness means that we need to replace our negative thoughts with pure, lovely thoughts. Like Mr. Miyagi taught Daniel-san in *Karate Kid:* "Wax on, wax off; wax on, wax off."[3] Focus on the new and don't dwell on the old.

---

3 *The Karate Kid,* directed by John G. Avildsen (Los Angeles: Columbia Pictures, 1984).

If you were the offended one, pray for the offender. Teach your children when somebody sins against them that they need to forgive, and they need to pray for the offender. Forgiveness is not an overnight thing. It is not a normal human response. It is a choice, not a feeling. At some level, your ability to forgive is directly proportional to your ability to understand what God has done for you. If you are so arrogant as to believe that you deserve God's mercy and favor, you'll never forgive anybody. You can't understand why they don't match your standard, meaning you don't truly understand God's standard.

Forgiving doesn't mean restoring all of someone's previous rights. Teach your children this critical lesson. I once had a manager who stole from me. I forgave the man, but I didn't give him his job back. I was not going to put him back in charge of the cash because he had lost that right based on his behavior. If the man worked in some other capacity for an extended period of time and regained my trust, then perhaps his rights could be restored. However, it would take a long time for him to regain trust.

That's what happens in relationships where spouses cheat on one another; it is so difficult to rebuild the trust. It impedes the ability for someone to trust you again. But make no mistake; trust can be rebuilt if both parties are committed to making it work. In fact, Tryon Edwards tells us that "right actions for the future are the best apologies for wrong ones in the past."[4] The Bible says the only real reason for divorce is adultery, but nowhere does Christ demand divorce even for adultery.

Forgiveness was important to Christ. In the Lord's Prayer in Matthew 6:9–13, Jesus says, "Forgive us our debts as we have forgiven our debtors." In Matthew 6:14–16, Christ says, "For if you forgive others for their transgressions, your heavenly Father will also forgive you. But if you do not forgive others, then your Father will not forgive your transgressions." In some

---

4 Tryon Edwards, C.N. Catrevas, Jonathan Edwards, editors, *The New Dictionary of Thoughts* (Whitefish, MT: Literary Licensing, LLC, 2012).

ways this is a confusing concept. If we are saved, nothing can separate us from the love of Christ. But what is hindered is our relationship, our fellowship with God Almighty.

T. I. **M.** O. T. H. Y.

A MAN OF RESPONSIBILITY EXERCISES: **M**ATURE DISCERNMENT

Mature Discernment comes from knowing the Holy Spirit and obeying His wisdom. That takes time, but as Paul told Timothy in 1 Timothy 4:12, age isn't the issue; it has to do with wisdom. It is so critical to recognize that you can be forty or fifty years old and be incredibly immature.

Most parents would tell you they want the best for their children. I want to challenge you a little bit. I think sometimes we miss the mark because we're striving for earthly success instead of maturity and wisdom. Ask yourself: do I want my son to be a great athlete, a great musician, a great painter, or do I pray that my son will have maturity and wisdom; that my daughters will have discernment. When they go on dates with their fellows, do they have their spiritual antenna up? Are they are looking for the kind of behavior a godly man would portray?

If we are honest with ourselves, I think we pray and push for earthly success more than developing wisdom, but Solomon asked for wisdom realizing it was God's greatest gift. In 1 Kings 3:5, God said to Solomon: "Ask what you wish Me to give to you." And Solomon replied, "So give Your servant an understanding heart to judge Your people to discern between good and evil. For who is able to judge this great people of Yours?" (1 Kings 3:9). Because Solomon asked for wisdom instead of earthly possessions, God gave him wisdom and health and wealth as well. Why is it that we get so fixated as parents on earthly success for our children instead of what their character is like?

I'm preaching to myself as well as you. I've struggled with this. I want my children to be successful. Part of the reason I want them to be successful on an earthly basis is because they want to be. I don't like to see my children hurt. But I think that God's Word points us to the fact that wisdom is much more important than being the greatest tennis player there ever was. Being a great tennis player is terrific, but only if you use your position to honor Jesus. All of life's successes mean very little in the eternal scheme of things. "Whatever you do in word or deed, do all in the name of the Lord Jesus, giving thanks through Him to God the Father" (Colossians 3:17). Try to see things from His perspective; pray for His discernment and maturity.

I commented to a man once that his son was a really terrific shortstop. He said, "You know what? I would far prefer that my son would give his life on the mission field for Christ than be a great shortstop." I thought the man was wacko. However, this man had mature discernment. Still, it is really hard to see that truth. It takes a deep level of maturity to understand that your child is not yours. God simply gave them to you for a season to help them grow up, to help them find *God's plan* for their lives.

I don't know about you, but if one of my children wants to go overseas to the mission field, it would concern me. Something might happen to him. My goodness, one of them left and went to Chicago. Think about that. One of them lived in New York City. Talk about the mission field! We tend to think missions are only overseas. At some level, we are just being selfish because we recognize we don't want them to go, and that partly because we like seeing them. We've got a long time in heaven to talk about the experiences they had on the mission field and the things they accomplished if we allow them to do the things that God really puts in their heart.

Contentment comes from wisdom. It is critical for having a peaceful life. If you could give your children anything, pray for their contentment in whatever situation they are in. When they learn how to be content as Paul was, in all circumstances, life will be a whole lot better for them.

Someone once asked the professional golfer Scott Simpson how he felt coming down the 18th fairway with the match on the line. He responded, "I know who I am in Jesus Christ. So, I play well being content in Him." The reporter said, "Doesn't that keep you from being really competitive?" To which Simpson replied wisely, "There's a big difference between contentment and complacency." You see, the world believes that if you are content, you're complacent. There are professional sports teams who don't want Christians on them because they feel Christians are complacent. Actually, Christians are challenged by the Bible to do our best at all we do and with passion as for the Lord Jesus Christ. "Whatever you do, do your work heartily as for the Lord, rather than for men" (Colossians 3:23).

I heard a story once about Tommy Hume, who pitched for the Cincinnati Reds. The story goes that he got shelled one evening. After being pulled from the game, he was in the locker room. A teammate came in the room and found Hume sitting there smiling and humming. The fellow walked over to him and said, "Hummie, they just lit you up. They killed you. How can you be in here smiling?" And he said, "Let me tell you what I do. Every time I go out to pitch, I imagine that Jesus Christ is sitting in the third base box seats. I go out every night and pitch as hard as I can for Christ. If I do well, I give Him the glory. If I don't do well, I know He still loves me. So, I just do the best I can every night for Jesus Christ. I play a lot better that way and I am content with what I do." He didn't have to mope around and make everyone around him miserable. When I was a young man and we lost a ball game it took me a week to get over it. I felt that to show I cared, I had to be nasty to live with for a week. That's misguided, but it was where I was. I was terribly lacking in discernment and wisdom.

The apostle Paul said it best in Philippians 4:11–13, when he said, "Not that I speak from want, for I have learned to be content in whatever circumstances I am. I know how to get along with humble means, and I also know how to live in prosperity; in any and every circumstance I have learned the secret of being filled and going hungry, both of having abundance and suffering need. I can do all things through Him who strengthens me."

The more mature you become, the more you will begin to understand that you really do reap what you sow. If you sow good, you will reap good. If you sow bad, you will reap bad. One of our friends, Nancy Hartsook, says that occasionally in praying for our children we need to pray for a crop failure.

People who are bullies and fly off the handle all the time are really people who lack confidence and self-esteem. It takes a real man to be able to be criticized and not overreact. It takes a real man not to become defensive when questioned. That depth of confidence can only come from an inner understanding of the fact that the God of the Universe loves you so much that he came to earth and died for you. You are valuable and priceless in Christ's eyes. When you know how much he cares for you, you can recognize your worth as a human being. When you internalize this truth, it is easier to be confident.

When my mother was dying in 1996, she and my father had a truly perceptive conversation. My father asked her, "Jo, outside of me, who was the most memorable man you have ever known." Instantly, she replied, "Grandfather Stephens." Dad then asked why she felt that way, and she said, "Because he was the most *gentle* man I have ever known." "Why do you believe that was so?" Dad questioned. Mom said, "Because he was so confident."

Confidence comes only when you are at peace with who you are and Whose you are. Grandfather was an attorney and a lay preacher. As a child of God, he was able to be gentle and not defensive. He knew he had immeasurable worth according to the King of kings and Lord of lords.

Often, I think Christian men are not encouraged to dedicate work heartily to the Lord. In fact, many in Christian circles believe that work is an evil and only family life is important to God. That is simply poor theology and a poorer understanding of God's character.

When I was a McDonald's operator, some of my poorest performers were Christians. I believe that we need to balance our work and our families.

Now listen to me carefully; I'm probably the only guy in the world that makes this assertion. I believe that men need to work. I believe that's what the Bible says. I believe that men don't need to overwork. I believe that men need to care for their families. I believe we need balance. There are people in our society today who want to say that men don't need to work, or that if they work intensely, somehow or another that's bad. I don't know one single person in the world, unless they inherited wealth, who is financially successful today if they only work forty hours per week. I don't know one. It takes more effort than that, but balance is the key.

I personally enjoy work because it gives me the satisfaction of a job well done. I think there are many people today who don't get that satisfaction because they don't think that working is important or mandated by God, while others have their whole self-esteem tied up in their work. Balance is the key! Don't forget God's message to men in Genesis 3:17: "Cursed is the ground because of you; in toil you will eat of it all the days of your life." God expects us to work and work well, but not overwork. This next story shows you where balance comes in.

> An American businessman was at the pier of a small coastal Mexican village when a small boat with just one fisherman docked. Inside the small boat were several large yellowfin tuna. The American complimented the Mexican on the quality of his fish and asked how long it took to catch them.
>
> "Only a little while," the Mexican replied.
>
> The American then asked why he didn't stay out longer and catch more fish?
>
> The Mexican said he had enough to support his family's immediate needs.

The American then asked, "What do you do with the rest of your time?"

The Mexican fisherman said, "I sleep late, fish a little, play with my children, take siesta with my wife, stroll into the village each evening where I sip wine and play guitar with my amigos. I have a full and busy life, señor."

The American scoffed, "I am a Harvard MBA and could help you. You should spend more time fishing and with the proceeds, buy a bigger boat; with the proceeds from the bigger boat, you could buy several boats; eventually, you would have a fleet of fishing boats. Instead of selling your catch to a middleman, you would sell directly to the processor, eventually opening your own cannery. You would control the product, processing and distribution. You could leave this small coastal fishing village and move to Mexico City, then LA and eventually NYC where you will run your expanding enterprise."

The Mexican fisherman asked, "Señor, how long will this all take?"

"Only 15-20 years," replied the businessman.

"But what then, señor?"

The American laughed. "That's the best part. When the time is right you would announce an IPO and sell your company stock to the public and become very rich. You could easily make millions!"

"Millions, señor? Then what?"

"Then what?!" said the American. "Then you would retire. Move to a small coastal fishing village where you would sleep late, fish a

> little, play a little, play with your kids, take siesta with your wife, stroll to the village in the evenings where you could sip wine and play guitar with your amigos."[5]

Like the fisherman, we need to develop enough mature discernment to know the difference between what we really need in life and what we desire. I just love that story. I feel like I've been in that rat race before.

Maturity can be gained one of two ways; making lots of mistakes and hoping to do better next time or walking with the Holy Spirit. Gaining knowledge is a matter of studying books and keeping your ears open when others teach. Maturity, however, is taking the knowledge you have and making sound, virtuous decisions.

Some Christians teach men to do things with the family to the exclusion of doing well at work. That is not mature discernment because balance in life is the key. A man of Responsibility must provide for his family, but he must also lead and be there for his family. That requires balance, which requires Mature Discernment. Fortunately, the Bible teaches principles that help us learn how to discern the best for our lives and families.

T. I. M. **O.** T. H. Y.

A MAN OF RESPONSIBILITY IS AN:

OVERCOMER, NOT A VICTIM

The O in Timothy reflects the fact that godly men are Overcomers, not Victims. I get tired of the American-victim mentality. "Oh, woe is me; I'm a victim!" The truth is, no matter what your circumstances are or what

---

5 Heinrich Böll. "The Story of the Mexican Fisherman," KidzShortStories.com, last modified August 10, 2013, https://kidzshortstories.wordpress.com/2013/08/10/the-story-of-the-mexican-fisherman-by-heinrich-boll/.

condition your life is in, you can still serve God. We told our children over and over that they could not allow themselves to be victims. "Yeah, but Dad, you don't understand. The coach doesn't do this, or the coach doesn't do that." Yes, I do understand. Life is not fair. The only thing that would make life fair from your perspective would be if you were God. Then you would get to determine everything that happens. I only know two things in life. There is a God, and I'm not Him. Actually, I know a third thing—you're not God either. So, guess what? Some things are going to be unfair. In fact, a man we know got T-shirts for his family that said, "Life is unfair, deal with it." That may be a bit harsh, but it's right on the money.

Charles Swindoll beautifully points out how much we really impact our own lives. Many people have seen the quote about attitude by him. Please read this carefully:

> The longer I live, the more I realize the impact of attitude on life. Attitude, to me, is more important than facts. It is more important than the past, than education, than money, than circumstances, than failures, than successes, than what other people think or say or do. It is more important than appearance, giftedness, or skill. *It will make or break a company...a church...a home.* The remarkable thing is we have a choice every day regarding the attitude we will embrace for that day. We cannot change our past. We cannot change the fact that people will act in a certain way. We cannot change the inevitable. The only thing we can do is play on the one string we have, and that is our attitude. I am convinced that life is 10% what happens to me and 90% how I react to it. And...so it is with you. We are in charge of our attitudes.[6]

---

6 Bill Hybels, Charles R. Swindoll, Larry Burkett, *The Life@Work Book* (Nashville: W Publishing Group, 2000), 125.

So it goes with you and I. We are in charge of our attitudes. You can't control your circumstances, but you can control your reaction to them. The key ingredient to being an overcomer is deciding you are not a victim. Start with the decision to see yourself as a victor, not a victim.

Athletics really helped me prepare for adversity. I came to learn that a bad call, a bad bounce, or a great play by an opponent shouldn't change my perspective. I learned that sulking about my circumstances or even asking "Why me?" did nothing to help me reach my goal. A bad call or a bad bounce should be viewed simply as reality. It is what it is.

I remember playing Mount Vernon High School my senior year. Both teams were highly ranked in the state. They had a young punter named Greg Kundrat. With about three minutes left in the game, our defense stopped them on their forty-five-yard line. Kundrat punted the ball from his forty-five-yard line to our six-yard line. We ran three plays and punted to them. They ran a few plays and called on their punter once again. This time, he punted the ball out of bounds on the four-yard line. This is in high school football! We ran a couple more plays and punted the ball back to them. They ran a few more plays, our defense forcing another punt. This time he punted dead on the four-yard line. Three punts in a row dead on target.

At this point, we had a choice. We could just quit and say, "It's not in the cards for us tonight." However, we ended up going ninety-six yards in a minute and thirty-four seconds and winning the ball game. There was one second on the clock when we scored to win the game. Now, that's a happy ending for me to that story. But the fact is that nobody in our huddle was complaining about our lack of luck or our own misfortune. We knew we had a job to do and we set about doing it. One reason I believe so strongly in athletics is that it teaches life lessons in a real laboratory setting. The more energy I wasted on being frustrated with poor circumstances, the less energy and focus I had to solve the problem. So it is in life!

A pastor named Rick Nuzum once shared with me why God allows such trials in our lives. He said, "God is not as interested in your comfort as He is interested in your character." He did not promise us an easy path to follow. Daily, we are challenged to take up our cross and follow Him. We're urged to take His yoke upon us. He assured us that the way would be narrow and there are few who find it. It's a tough road. We must expect to be tried and weighed on the scales of adversity. Through this, we will be stronger, more focused disciples in the service of our Savior.

You might ask how this applies to everyday living. God understands us. He made us. He gives us perspective in the Bible for the various trials we encounter. I think the Bible has a clear message in 1 Peter 2:19–20: "For this finds favor, if for the sake of conscience toward God a person bears up under sorrows when suffering unjustly. For what credit is there if, when you sin and are harshly treated, you endure it with patience? But if when you do what is right and suffer for it you patiently endure it, this finds favor with God."

What I find interesting about people is this: Some persecution we experience in life is because we are being God's men and suffering righteously for Him. However, some of what we suffer we bring on ourselves. Often people whine about being persecuted. They complain about how they've been treated harshly. For example, when you're late to work and you're disciplined for it, you should be! I am amazed when people complain about being disciplined when they deserve it. You're not supposed to be late. If your work is poor, you ought to be disciplined. Some people try to pass off their employer's criticism by saying, "That's righteous persecution." No, it isn't! You are being scolded because you're doing a crummy job. You should be disciplined.

When God talks about righteous persecution, He is talking about times you take a stand for Him in a way He would approve of. That can happen to us in school, in the workplace, in any number of places, but He's not referring to the things we bring on ourselves. Righteousness occurs when we stand for God through the difficult times. Roger Crawford, the first and only person in American history to be a United States Professional Tennis Association athlete and play a Division I college sport with a severe disability, has said, "Being challenged in life is inevitable, being defeated is optional."[7]

Remember, God says those He loves He disciplines (Hebrews 12:6). That's tough. As a coach, it's tough for young people to understand that if you really care about them, you're going to correct them when they do things poorly. Failure does not define you; it is how you respond to failure that defines you.

This is one of my favorite topics. One of the things that drives me nuts today is misunderstood positive parenting. Some people assume that the child can do no wrong. Little Joey is in the field and a ground ball is hit to him. He goes down to make the play and the ball rolls right between his legs and he misses it. Then someone in the stands and yells, "Oh, Joey, great play!" No, Joey, it was a lousy play. You are a wonderful child, but it was a lousy play. You must be honest with children. You must tell them the truth. If you are not honest with people, here's what happens: They begin to believe a bad play was a good play and they expect to be rewarded for poor performance.

Be especially aware not to use sarcasm. It is ineffective and demeaning. It confuses children and adults.

We need to teach our children the ability to have people discipline them without automatically assuming that those people hate them or want bad for them. People who want to help them get better are going to correct them. They are the ones who really care about them. Our society seems to have the basic feeling that if you say anything cross or sharp to a person, it means you don't like them. Hogwash! How can you ever help somebody get better? How

---

7 Roger Crawford > Quotes > Quotable Quotes. "Being Challenged In Life…" Goodreads, last modified 2020, https://www.goodreads.com/quotes/496796-being-challenged-in-life-is-inevitable-being-defeated-is-optional.

can you ever help them improve if you don't point out the mistakes? John Neal makes a terrific point when he says, "A certain amount of opposition is of great help to a man. Kites rise against, not with the wind."[8]

"A CERTAIN AMOUNT OF OPPOSITION IS OF GREAT HELP TO A MAN. KITES RISE AGAINST, NOT WITH THE WIND."
—JOHN NEAL

It's true that you have to point out the good things they do as emphatically as you do the mistakes. I know that as a football coach I have a jaundiced perspective. If there are eleven guys on the field and one guy messes up, I see the one guy. It goes with coaching but if I never correct or discipline you, I really don't care about you. Only when I care about you will I make the effort to help you improve. As a note of caution: Parents who don't want their children corrected must be assuming the child is perfect and can't get any better. That's silly. Those who really want to improve must be taught to expect and desire correction and discipline.

God says, "All *discipline* for the moment seems not to be joyful, but sorrowful; yet to those who have been trained by it, afterwards it yields the peaceful fruit of righteousness" (Hebrews 12:11). That is the fruit of peace, patience, kindness, love, goodness, faithfulness, and self-control.

Almost every successful person I have ever met doesn't make excuses. Whether they are at fault or not, their focus is on correcting the problem instead of being exonerated. Joseph was thrown in jail unfairly, but he became the highest helper because he didn't take a victim's mentality. Job was similar, frankly, as was Daniel. They knew that their ultimate judge was God; but just as importantly, if they were mistreated, they knew God allowed it for their

---

8 John Neal > Quotes > Quotable Quotes. Goodreads, last modified 2020, https://www.goodreads.com/quotes/310680-a-certain-amount-of-opposition-is-of-great-help-to.

growth. When we take our eyes off Jesus, it's easy to become a victim as opposed to being an overcomer. Overcomers rise, victims fail; overcoming is better.

T. I. M. O. T. H. Y.

A MAN OF RESPONSIBILITY IS A:

TEAMMATE

The second T in Timothy stands for Teammate. Men truly need support groups, and "no man is an island," as the Joan Baez song goes.[9] Each of us has various kinds of teammates to help us along in life.

Your wife, if God so wills you to have one, should be your first and best teammate. The Bible's picture of marriage is so beautiful and accurate. Ecclesiastes 4:9 says, "Two are better than one because they have a good return for their labor." Married couples can multiply the work they get done. Ecclesiastes goes on to say, "If either of them falls, the one will lift up his companion, but woe to the one who falls when there is not another to lift him up" (4:10). In other words, don't go through life independently. Ecclesiastes 4:12 paints the picture of marriage of a man and woman with Christ at the head as a cord of three strands, which is not easily broken. You, your wife, and Jesus Christ form an unbeatable team. If Satan attacks you or your wife, the other two can resist and defeat him.

If you have no wife, I strongly urge you to get an accountability partner. In fact, even if you are married, find one to help with those male areas that you don't wish to burden your wife with. I don't believe in keeping secrets from my wife. Yet, I believe in protecting my wife from some of the dumb things I might say to her that would hurt her. How many of you go home and say, "Boy, I was at lunch today and a babe walked in; she was hot." That

---

9 Joan Baez. "No Man Is An Island." Recorded 1968. Track 11 on *Baptism: A Journey Through Our Time*. Vanguard.

does not help your wife. She does not need to be burdened with that. A male friend can help hold you accountable by asking the right questions. Did you bounce your eyes? Did you flee immorality? You can even call a male friend and report successes. Discussing these things with your wife only burdens her and eats away at her security. Have an accountability partner but make them male. As an aside, I need to add: Do not lie to your accountability partner. As my friend Dr. Duke Heller says, "You cannot counsel a lie." So true.

One way to get an accountability partner is to join a small group. You will spend time hearing the hearts of other men and seeing their commitment to the Lord. From this small group, you can approach someone with whom you sense a kindred spirit to have as a teammate. I would never try to get somebody to form an accountability team with me if I hadn't spent a lot of time with him first. I want to know what they're about. An accountability relationship needs to be open and transparent. You need to know that you can trust your teammate. You need to know whether they're going to run their mouth about your issues. You need to know whether or not they're really going to care and pray for you.

The test of time is critical for a deep relationship to occur because you go deeper as your trust level grows. It is not appropriate to dump your whole life on someone until you know they're committed to the relationship. One of the problems with accountability in small groups is that many people are more than willing to tell you all their troubles, but they are not particularly interested in yours. That is not an accountability team; that is a monologue. That relationship will not serve the needs of both men, which is critical in a healthy accountability team. The opposite of this example will also kill any chance you have of a special teammate. If he tells you his concerns and you don't share yours, the team will fail. Give and take is a must. By the way, just because somebody asks you a question doesn't mean you have to answer it.

When President Clinton was running for office, he appeared on MTV and someone asked him whether he wore boxers or briefs, and he answered! My general response to that would be, "It's none of your business." Sometimes, because we are in an accountability team, we think we have to answer a question just because it was asked. No, there are things that you may choose not to discuss at this time. Just because you get in a small group doesn't mean you must answer every question asked. I find it funny that I have to tell people that, but I find people are doing that more and more often today. We just automatically assume if someone chooses not to answer a question it means they are rude. No, it's not rude; it's sensible. There are lots of things that people don't need to know about you.

Another team is a community of men. It's from this group that we have support in raising our children and growing personally. I want my sons to be exposed to the finest men I can find. Many people have their sons in the Crusader program not because of the football or even the Bible teaching, but because they want their sons around godly role models. I am so fortunate to work with such a fine group of men who help me grow in my walk with Christ. Often, I have had parents say to me, "I can't tell you what a blessing it is that my son is around Coach so and so." That's a community of men.

At the Christian school run by our church, it is customary for staff members to present diplomas to their own children at graduation. I asked one of the pastors whose son was graduating if he was planning on doing the presentation. When he responded no, I asked him why. He said, "I want as many men of godly character in my son's life as I can find. Sometimes I may not be able to be there. I want him to know there are other men who can step in for me." All parents know there comes a time when opinions carry more weight when someone else gives them. I'm not sure why, but people often listen more closely when instruction or advice comes from someone outside the family. Jesus said in Matthew 13:57, "A prophet is not without honor except in his hometown and in his own household."

Don't just hope your children are around godly men; be intentional about it. Pursue godly men to be in your son's life. You can do it all kinds of different ways. Find somebody who your son or daughter looks up to, maybe their piano teacher or sports coach. It doesn't have to be a fifty-five-year-old pastor. You need to get somebody in their lives who is living out their faith. In my opinion, if a child is in fourth or fifth grades, it is better to encourage them to be around younger adults. There tends to be a mindset among the younger generation that older folks can't understand or relate to teenagers. Teenagers watch the lives of those older than them and believe that what they see now reflects consistently good choices all throughout their elders' lives; they assume older folks just don't know what it means to mess up and have problems. But of course, "All have sinned and fallen short of the glory of God" (Romans 3:23). It may be beneficial to hook young people up with younger adults who are living God-honoring lives as an example to them, as well as encouragement that it is possible to honor God with their life-choices even at a young age.

In the book *Raising a Modern Day Knight*, Robert Lewis talks about special ceremonies as an opportunity for fathers to validate their sons. This group of community teammates is the group you would call upon to help with special ceremonies in your son's life. The Crusaders bless our seniors at the last practice of their senior year to let them know that from that time forward we will treat them as men. I can't give a Crusader player a father's blessing; I am not his father. But I can give him my blessing. I can tell him I think he is special. Ceremonies help drive a stake in time when a special event or commitment occurs. Lewis talks about the fact that ceremonies can be costly, yet it is better to do a simple one planned carefully to reduce the expense than to forego the ceremony completely because of money. However, cost does have an impact because it demonstrates value and worth. It employs symbols. It empowers a life with a vision.

One time we had some parents give their son a team jacket on his birthday. It was a very special time because it was right there among the people who the young man admired most and those who thought highly of him. The parents came out and said publicly, "We value you. We think you are really important, so we give you this jacket in front of your peers, mentors, and teammates." The young man will never forget that. I'll never forget it! It was a great, great time.

One of the scariest things to do in the world is to be transparent with another human being. Despite that fear, a wise man will surround himself with men who are striving to be like Christ. Together they can help one another with life's issues. In some circles, it may be unpopular, but men should not tell their wives everything. It only hurts your wife and creates insecurity if you deal with your issue of pornography by discussing it with her. Sometimes I want to bounce ideas about finances off other men before I consult my wife. Transparency develops over time as you live life with your men's group. Teammates are critical to a maximized life.

T. I. M. O. T. **H.** Y.

A MAN OF RESPONSIBILITY:

HATES EVIL

A man of responsibility Hates Evil. Evil is anything which doesn't conform to God's standard, like when we murder the innocent, when we abuse our wives, when we don't raise up our children as we should. That is evil because it doesn't conform to God's plan for mankind.

Because society is convinced there is no absolute truth today, our society worships at the altar of tolerance. Why? Because lack of tolerance forces people to believe that they are somehow unfair if they don't accept any and all viewpoints about morality. Their mantra is, "I don't criticize you, so don't tell me what I can and cannot do." Therefore, if there is no absolute truth, they can do whatever they wish with no criticism or judgment.

Our country has decided that marriage is between Adam and Eve as well as Adam and Steve, though God makes his position very clear, "A man shall leave his mother and father and be joined to his wife; and they shall become one flesh" (Genesis 2:24). Society is looking for all kinds of reasons why Billy has two moms and why that's okay. But God said that's not okay. He said there is something missing in that relationship. There is something that the child will never have growing up in that kind of environment. We need to care for children, but not by perverting God's very clear will.

Our society has chosen to allow abortion virtually on demand. Life begins at conception. It's a baby, not a fetus. Why won't we protect the weakest among us?

We are legalizing drugs, assisted suicide, and all forms of things that must be an abomination to God. If Christians would band together and be all out for God, these issues could be righted.

Martin Niemoller wrote about the evil under Adolf Hitler and the unwillingness of people to speak up. He said, "First they came for the socialists and I did not speak out…because I was not a socialist. Then they came for the trade unionists, and I did not speak out…because I was not a trade unionist. Then they came for the Jews, and I did not speak out…because I was not a Jew. Then they came for me…and there was no one left to speak for me."[10]

A man of responsibility does not worship at the altar of tolerance. If you want to become very unpopular, tell people what God says. Stand up for living that way because it is God's way. People don't like that very much these days. People believe it's wrong to judge right and wrong actions. Everyone I know living a lifestyle of sin knows Matthew 7:1, which says, "Judge not lest you be judged." However, they do not know the next verse which says, "For in the way you judge, you will be judged and by your standard of measure, it will be measured to you" (Matthew 7:2). So if I say, "You're a thief and that's sinful," and I am also a thief, I am going to be judged by the same standard. What God says matters; it doesn't matter what I think. If I judge others by

---

10 Franklin H. Littell, "First They Came for the Jews," *Christian Ethics Today,* February 1997, 29.

God's standards, then yes, He will judge me by the same standards. However, I must keep this in mind: I can judge the actions, but I am not God and so I cannot judge the person. I must have a level of tenderness and mercy when I deal with sin, because I, too, am a sinner.

A popular bumper sticker says, "Hate is not a family value." That bumper sticker is a terrible distortion of truth. The slogan is driven by parts of our society who claim that anything but tolerance and love couldn't possibly be a family value. The subtle implication is that a loving God wouldn't hate anything. But the truth is God calls us to love one another and yet hate evil, as He does. The assertion is that if you hate abortion or homosexuality or drunkenness, you are a narrow-minded bigot. The folks who feel this way must not wish to accept that God Almighty Himself hates many things. Yes, God hates! His Word teaches us that He hates many things, and as men of responsibility, we should as well. We should imitate God; if He hates certain behaviors and actions, we should as well.

What does He hate? He hates divorce (Malachi 2:16). He hates evil (Proverbs 8:13). He doesn't sort of dislike evil; He hates it. God recognizes that in human morality and in our human economy there are some things that are so destructive and terrible that we shouldn't even dabble with them. Proverbs 6:16–19 lists seven things God hates and are an "abomination" to him: haughty eyes, a lying tongue, hands that shed innocent blood, a heart that devises wicked plans, feet that run rapidly to evil, a false witness who utters lies, one who spreads strife among his brothers. There are lots of things God hates. Surely, we should as well.

If there were no absolutes, everyone could do what's right in their own eyes, just like it says in the book of Judges. Doing anything we want with no restraints causes anarchy. Worst of all, it leads to situational ethics, which is just another term for lies based on the perceived need of the moment. Situational leadership makes some sense. I may need to coach Josh differently than Jared because of their personalities and temperaments. But situational ethics are garbage. If I tell Josh that I'm going to bench him for the first half if he comes late to the game, but I tell Jared I won't bench him, then that's wrong.

It is important to note that if we confront improper behavior, we ought to do so in "truth and love." Ephesians 4:15 says, "But speaking the truth in love, we are to grow up in all aspects into Him who is the head, even Christ." Don't be cowed into a position that says you can't tell someone a particular behavior is wrong; if God says it's wrong, that settles it. The old cliché "hate the sin, but love the sinner" is difficult to enact, but it is proper. Men of responsibility live to please Christ, not society. As my friend Gene Graves says, "Decisions often give you two choices; easy or right. As men of Christ, we need to do the right thing."

T. I. M. O. T. H. **Y.**

A MAN OF RESPONSIBILITY LETS HIS **Y**ES BE YES AND HIS NO BE NO

All good relationships are built on trust; not just you and your wife, but also you and your children, you and your friends, and you and your co-workers. Trust takes time to build. A man who does what he says he is going to do can be counted on to honor his word; therefore he becomes a man you can trust. His yes means yes, and his no means no, so we can have confidence in him to do the things he says he's going to do or not do.

When our actions match our words, this builds trust and respect. One of my favorite Bible stories is in 2 Kings 12:11–15. In this story, the king asked the priest, "Why did you not repair the damages of the house (temple)?" (v. 7). The priest had no good answer:

> When they saw that there was much money in the chest, the king's
> scribe and the high priest came up and tied it in bags and counted
> the money which was found in the house of the LORD. [11]They gave
> the money which was weighed out into the hands of those who
> did the work, who had the oversight of the house of the LORD; and
> they paid it out to the carpenters and the builders who worked on
> the house of the LORD; [12]and to the masons and the stonecutters,
> and for buying timber and hewn stone to repair the damages to the
> house of the LORD, and for all that was laid out for the house to
> repair it. [13]But there were not made for the house of the LORD silver
> cups, snuffers, bowls, trumpets, any vessels of gold, or vessels of
> silver from the money which was brought into the house of
> the LORD; [14]for they gave that to those who did the work, and with
> it they repaired the house of the LORD. [15]Moreover, they did not
> require an accounting from the men into whose hand they gave the
> money to pay to those who did the work, for they dealt faithfully.

These men were so trustworthy because their yes was yes and they had integrity. They remind me of Mike Cheeseman, the founder of the Crusaders, who is also a builder. He can be trusted; he has integrity. Speaker and professor Brené Brown said, "Integrity is choosing courage over comfort; choosing what is right over what is fun, fast, or easy; and choosing to practice our values rather than simply professing them."[11]

A man once said to me, "I've got a problem with my sons because I tell them no and they just badger me until I change my position to yes." Sadly, his sons have come to realize their father is not a man of his word—his yes is not yes and his no is not no. My uncle, Roger Stephens, sent me a clip that talked about times when your children come to you and say, "You don't

---

11 Brené Brown, "Integrity Is…" PassItOn.com, last modified 2020, https://www.passiton.com/inspirational-quotes/7655-integrity-is-choosing-courage-over-comfort.

understand. You should really let me go down to my friend's and watch that video." If you stand by your "no," they may whine and complain that you don't understand—kids want to be understood. But at that point, you can say, "I *do* understand, and the answer is *NO*." It's not a question of whether you understand; the answer you gave is *no*. If we don't confront their whining, if we don't say, "Hey, I do understand," they may assume we can't understand, and the answer isn't legitimate to them in their mind. But we can build trust when we convey that we truly made our decision based on what we believe to be the best decision for them or the family and then stick with that decision. They'll respect you more for it in the long run.

Being a man who stands by his word develops character like nothing else. A wonderful Christian man, and perhaps America's best college basketball coach ever, gave this advice: "Be more concerned with your character than your reputation. Your character is what you really are, while your reputation is merely what others think you are." Coach John Wooden understood the biblical truth, "Like a sparrow in flittering, like a swallow in flying, so a curse without cause does not alight" (Proverbs 26:2). You see, if you keep your character pure, even when you are attacked, the criticism will not stick.

Trust is earned every day by fulfilling your commitments, being a man of honor, and completing your responsibilities. But keep in mind that trust is harder to restore than it is to earn. I tell members of the team that I will always believe them until I know they lie to me. Once they lie to me, then I have a problem. I don't know when to believe them. The only way that you know when to trust somebody is if they tell you the truth all the time. Pastor Jim Custer says, "There's a big difference between being forgiven and being trusted." Heed this statement. You may have somebody forgive you, but it is quite another thing for them to trust you if you have broken their faith. We must demonstrate trustworthiness over time.

Let me emphasize what I mean by trust established "over time." It is done over years, not days. While trust takes a long time to build, it can be destroyed in one short breach of said trust. In marriage, men and women who take "yes is yes" seriously and their vow before God can take hope from the following study:

> In the late 1980s, the National Survey of Family and Households studied 5,232 married adults. Of those couples, 645 reported being unhappily married. Five years later these same adults, some of whom had divorced or separated, and some of whom had stayed married, were interviewed again. The results of these interviews were astonishing. They revealed that a full two-thirds of the unhappily married spouses who stayed married were actually happier five years later! Among those who initially rated their marriages as "very unhappy" but remained together, nearly 80 percent considered themselves as "happily married" and "much happier" five years later.
>
> Surprisingly, the opposite is found to be true for those who divorced. The Institute for American Values study confirmed that divorce frequently fails to make people happy because, while it might provide a respite from the pain associated with a bad marriage, it also introduces a host of complex new emotional and psychological difficulties over which the parties involved have little control. They include child-custody battles, emotionally scarred children, economic hardships, loneliness, future romantic disappointments, and so on. This helps explain why of all the unhappy spouses in the initial survey, only 19 percent of those who got divorced or separated were happy five years later.[12]

---

12 Linda J. Waite, Don Browning, William J. Doherty, Maggie Gallagher, "Does Divorce Make People Happy? Findings from a Study of Unhappy Marriages," Institute For American Values, 2002, https://healthymarriageandfamilies.org/library-resource/does-divorce-make-people-happy-findings-study-unhappy-marriages.

A man of Responsibility models "trustworthiness demonstrated over time." He is a man who provides for his family; you can take his word to the bank, always. He is willing to do the right thing, not the easy thing. A young man who used to work for me told me at one point he knew he added to the truth a lot. He doesn't anymore! The fact is that you can change your old behaviors. Get started now!

A MAN OF CHRIST

COMMITMENT = A PROMISE COMPLETED

HONOR = CHARACTER ABOVE REPROACH;
LIVING BY A BIBLICAL STANDARD

RESPONSIBILITY = TRUSTWORTHINESS DEMONSTRATED OVER TIME

INITIATIVE = BOLDNESS WITH INTEGRITY

SERVICE = INTENTIONALLY PUTTING THE NEEDS OF OTHERS FIRST,
EXPECTING NOTHING IN RETURN

TRUTH = A STATEMENT OR PRINCIPLE THAT APPLIES TO ALL PEOPLE,
IN ALL PLACES, AT ALL TIMES

C. H. R. **I.** S. T.

A MAN OF INITIATIVE

P. E. T. E. R.

PROACTIVE

ELITE FORCE

TEACHER

ENCOURAGER

REJECTS PASSIVITY

CHAPTER SIX

A MAN OF INITIATIVE

P.E.T.E.R.

INITIATIVE IS DEFINED AS "boldness with integrity." A biblical man avoids being passive, letting life just happen to him. We need to realize that nothing happens unless God wills it, but when it happens, God uses us to accomplish His will. When speaking about Men of Initiative, we stress that men need to be proactive in their lives. They need to reject the assertion in society that a man of initiative is aggressive, pushy, and overbearing. In my experience, lack of initiative is the average man's weakest trait of all the C.H.R.I.S.T. traits.

Some men won't act because they're lazy. Some men won't act because they fear the consequences. Some men won't act because they have believed the feminist lie that leading offends and demeans women. The truth is that wives can be most alive when their husbands lead and behave as God has called them to. Initiative and abuse are nothing alike for a man of Christ. In every case, a man who lacks initiative misses out on God's best.

The Council on Biblical Manhood and Womanhood contends that the single greatest issue facing men today is their inability to reject passivity. That sounds so strange in our society where many people think of men as being overbearing and abusive. Such men do exist, but the more common problem lies with men who will not be proactive or bold with integrity.

The sub-acrostic we will use for a man of Initiative is P. E. T. E. R. A man of Initiative is Proactive, the head of the Elite Force, a Teacher, an Encourager, and one who Rejects Passivity.

Peter was a man of deep passions and he acted on them, sometimes to his benefit and sometimes his detriment. Remember, he is the disciple that got out of the boat to walk on the water and met Christ. How amazing must that have been! Then there was the time when he cut off the slave's ear when the soldiers came to arrest Christ—not his finest moment. Yet with all of his passion and conviction, he denied Jesus three times. Isn't that strange? Peter was a man of action yet passive at other times. So are we! Many of us are critical of Peter because he took his eyes off Christ when he got out of the boat and sank in the water. But keep in mind that he is the only one who had the courage to get out of the boat. Everyone else stayed in!

While it is true that Peter denied Christ three times, wonderfully the story doesn't end there. Peter became the early leader of the church and became the spokesman for Christ.

To be a man of Initiative, we must constantly look to our goal of standing before Christ to have him say, "Well done." From a leadership perspective, we should never take our eyes off the prize. If you focus on the obstacles, you will lose sight of the end-goal much like missing the forest as you see the trees. As you might expect, the Bible explains how to apply this principle in life. Hebrews 12:2 says to fix our eyes on Jesus, the author and perfecter of our faith (paraphrase mine).

My old high school coach, Marv Moorehead, used to stress that we should "see it clearly," that is, our objective had to be perfectly clear before we can reach it. The concept applies to men living their lives as well. Without a clear goal, a guide, and an effective game plan, you will flounder in life. When you are confused, life is extremely difficult. As a coach, you are constantly trying to mediate between giving your team enough plays and schemes to defeat the opponent without overwhelming and confusing them. The K.I.S.S. strategy works well in football and life: Keep It Simple, Stupid. In life, as in this book, we need to be constantly reminded that during each day, all our choices and decisions must be filtered through our personal goals to honor Jesus.

With that in mind, seeing the goal clearly, let's explore the part of our game plan represented by Peter.

P. E. T. E. R.

A MAN OF INITIATIVE IS:

PROACTIVE

A godly man is Proactive. He is someone who looks for ways to achieve his goal, and he is (key word) *intentional.* So many people I know in life simply get up in the morning and let things happen to them. All of us have seen the bumper sticker that says "Life Happens," or similar ones that are far cruder but preach the same message. The implication is that you and I are like leaves blowing in the wind, out of control. I believe if you have a clear goal and an intentional lifestyle you will be able to affect how life happens to you. The Bible is clear that "whatever a man sows, this will he also reap" (Galatians 6:7). It certainly sounds as if we affect our own lives.

John Eldredge's book *Wild at Heart* is a wonderful book; most people think it is a great book for men. I think it is a pretty good book for men... but I think it is a tremendous book for women. It defines and explains what drives and motivates many men. Eldridge asserts that society and especially the church are much more comfortable with passive, pleasant, well-mannered men. Being pleasant and well-mannered are true traits of a biblical man but being passive is not. Eldredge said, "God made men the way they are because we desperately need them to be the way they are. Yes, a man is a dangerous thing. So is a scalpel." Amen and amen.

"GOD MADE MEN THE WAY THEY ARE BECAUSE WE DESPERATELY NEED THEM TO BE THE WAY THEY ARE. YES, A MAN IS A DANGEROUS THING. SO IS A SCALPEL."

The real issue should be that since men have the capacity to be dangerous, how can we best channel and direct our passions and actions? You wouldn't tell a doctor not to use a scalpel because it is dangerous. Most of us wouldn't say we should stop driving cars because they are dangerous. Men have a God-given role. Part of their role is protector and defender. How will men ever learn to protect their wives, daughters, and mothers if they must remain passive?

Men need to learn how to become men. We need to know that we have what it takes to measure up. Most of us are asking ourselves constantly, "Do I have what it takes to be a man?" "Can I measure up?" "Can I compete?" Mothers need to understand that good intentions to make her son just like a nice young lady will kill his spirit. There are times you need to fight. Many in society think a man or boy should never fight. They are wrong! There are times you need to fight. But you need to know when those times are. You can't just be the playground bully. You must be taught when violence is appropriate.

When my youngest son was playing basketball, he played with incredible intensity. A pastor once told me that he should tone it down and remember that he played for Jesus Christ. I was stunned by that. I guess the pastor felt that being intense and playing "all out" was too aggressive and, therefore, wrong for a Christian. I think Jesus would play hard. In fact, I think He would play as hard as He could within the rules to win. My son's college baseball coach described his play this way: "He plays as if he were going a hundred miles an hour with his hair on fire." That's a pretty good picture. That's the way I want the young men on our team to play.

Often, the church wants our boys to be docile. They want them to be girls. Jesus was not docile. In John 2:15, the Scripture says, "And He made a scourge of cords, and drove them all out of the temple, with the sheep and the oxen; and He poured out the coins of the money changers and overturned their tables." He knew what He was going to do, and He intentionally prepared for it. Some are misteaching weakness for godliness. We must not emasculate our sons. That would be horrible. Meekness isn't weakness at any age. Meekness is "controlled power." We teach men to be passive; we teach them to be weak. Then when we need them to stand up and fight in an honorable way, they're not ready. They don't know how.

Some women want men to be more like women; yet when that happens, they don't like us. Real women need real men, ones who can and will fulfill God's role for men. Men are called to lead their families, protect their families and provide for their families. This requires strength and courage and drive, traits which are often looked down upon in our world.

So how do we teach men to be proactive? Life often requires men to lead, and leadership requires dealing with the ups and downs of life. As a leader, you will face adversity and difficulty. If you are a husband, you are intended to be the leader of your home. It will not always be smooth sailing. We must teach men how to confront and deal with tough issues, whether in the home or at work. One of these issues is how to honestly evaluate how we are doing raising our children. Often, I ask my children and my wife if I have offended them in some way. I must be proactive to keep our relationship strong. It is hard for our dear ones to be open and honest with us as the following story shows. Tom wrote this to encourage other parents not to miss how their actions may affect their children.

> Dear Parents,
>
> Almost all parents exist in an irrational state of mind when it comes to their child's performance in various after-school

activities. I know, because I was as guilty as anyone! This letter is in the form of a plea…

My son, Clay, who is now 23 years old, participates in a Bible Study with me and two other men every Thursday night. A few meetings ago he told the group that as a twelve-year-old, he was afraid to get into the car for the ride home after many of his basketball games, because he feared I would not be happy with his performance. My displeasure always stemmed from whether or not I thought he played hard enough. This was obviously one of the salient memories of his childhood participation. If he would have taken a knife and stabbed me through the heart it would not have hurt more. I've apologized to him no less than twenty times. He has forgiven me, God has forgiven me, but it is almost impossible for me to forgive myself.

For the longest time I thought I was the only overbearing parent who meddled in his son's career. However, as the years have gone by, I've learned that many, many, parents "meddle" with their child's participation. I thought Clay didn't play enough, or didn't get enough shots, or the other boys didn't pass the ball to him enough, or whatever. My worst personality traits exhibited themselves through his basketball career. I was selfish, self-centered, and always irrational. It was "me, me, me." Oh, how I wish I could go back and do it over—but it's too late.

For the parents who have children participating now, it's not too late. "Get a grip." Believe me, I know your arguments seem sound (I always thought mine were well thought out and rational). But I promise you'll look back someday and wonder how in the world

> your child's participation could have been as important as you made it. Take it from me, you'll be embarrassed.
>
> So, if you are thinking about talking to the coach concerning your child's playing time or points or whatever...emulate the Beatles' song "Let It Be." A coach's number one problem (by a long shot) is parents—people like me, who thought they posed a good argument, but were in fact self-centered and irrational.
>
> Do a better job than I did, and your child won't bring up your poor behavior in a Bible Study five years after his performance is totally forgotten. Butt out and let the chips fall where they may.
>
> —Tom Smith

I admire Tom for his courage to write this, but most of all, I admire his relationship with Clay. They truly love one another.

Life is a paradox at times. Sometimes we are called upon not to rush in, but to wait, to be patient. On the one hand I'm telling you not to be passive, and on the other hand I'm telling you there are times to wait. That's correct. Sometimes the Holy Spirit is doing a work and needs us not to interfere. Here is a critical, critical point: an untrained man cannot tell the difference between waiting on the Lord and avoiding conflict. How do you respond? Do you back off or do you go full speed ahead?

Sometimes the problems are just too overwhelming, and we sort of shut down. When this happens, let us remember the words of Edward Everett Hale, when he said, "I am only one, but still I am one. I cannot do everything; but still I can do something; and because I cannot do everything, I will not refuse to do the something that I can do." Put aside all excuses and ask yourself, "What should I be doing?" You alone can make a difference. The question is, will you?

If we haven't trained our sons, and if we weren't trained along the way, often we will interpret our waiting as cowardice. And when you perceive that you are a coward, you may overreact to prove you aren't one. This may lead to unwise, even macho behavior. It takes a man with supreme confidence derived from the knowledge of who he is in Jesus Christ not to blow up, verbally or physically, when he is backed into a corner. This is the real essence of a biblical man, one who models and honors Jesus.

When a man knows he could and would address an issue instead of waiting, then he can have the courage to wait without doubting his manliness. If you confront me and I know that I am fully prepared and willing to deal with you, then I can wait for God to work, not doubting my manhood. Knowing I would act if necessary, allows me to be patient. Bullies are often the biggest cowards. They try to control the situation by fear. When they can't control people by fear, the level of violence escalates because they know deep in their hearts that they are trying to hide their fear by their actions. Biblical men *never* try to control those they love through fear and intimidation.

ABOUT BIBLICAL CONFRONTATION...

It is critical for fathers to teach their sons and daughters about biblical confrontation. Let me say at the outset that you may have taught someone the biblical method for confrontation, but this concept really needs to be modeled as well as taught.

James 4:17 says, "Therefore, to one who knows the right thing to do and does not do it, to him it is sin." If you know that you need to deal with an issue and you don't, you're in sin. I know this—if there is a conflict and I'm not willing to deal with it, then I am in sin. I must accept that fact, and I need to deal with it swiftly and biblically.

Matthew 18:15–17 gives us a four-step process about biblical confrontation:

1. "If your brother sins, go and reprove him in private. If he listens to you, you've won a brother." Isn't that terrific? If a brother sins against you or you perceive that he has sinned

against you, the first thing you need to do is go to the brother, not gossip behind his back. One of the big problems in our society is that we don't go to the brother; we go to every single person in the neighborhood except the person involved. We gossip and we talk behind his back and we create all kinds of problems. It is totally unbiblical. God is very serious about people who gossip and use their tongues in the wrong way.

This step may be simple, but it is not easy. Going to someone who has wronged you in some way one-on-one takes guts. It takes a true man. If you can begin to teach biblical confrontation when they are young, you will raise wise children. One of my sons, Beau, had a second-grade teacher that used to pick on him. We made him go and deal with the issue instead of us dealing with the issue for him. It was hard for him, really hard for him. The man was one of those mean sarcastic teachers. I was so proud of my son! I think that incident has really helped him learn how to confront problems.

One of the peculiarities about confrontation is that it is a lot worse in your mind than it is in reality most of the time. Not always, but most of the time. Often you stew with dread, thinking "what if" this and "what if" that, when in fact most people will listen if approached in a civil manner. They won't necessarily agree with you, but they will at least listen.

2. The next step is this: If he does not listen to you, "Take one or two with you so that by the mouth of two or three witnesses every fact may be confirmed." The person or people I take should be someone we both respect and trust. When one or two go with you, they might even show you how you were

wrong. Part of confrontation is helping everyone see the facts the same way. So if you feel like someone has offended you, go to him first to discuss the matter. If he will not listen to you, take two or three others with you and try to address it again. As the problem is discussed, the third-party listeners may find that you are the one in the wrong. If they are truly wise friends, they will honestly assess the situation and tell you the truth. Then the onus is on you to make the situation right. The goal is reconciliation, not proving you were right in the first place.

3. The third step is taken if he still refuses to listen: tell the church. Telling the church means it is appropriate to talk to the pastor or elders. It does not mean publicly announcing something during Sunday morning worship. Often, we forget that the purpose of confrontation is reconciliation. The word confrontation in our society means fight. That's not what it should mean. It should mean dealing with an issue in such a way that the situation can be made better, not worse. Therein lies the purpose of biblical confrontation. I can't say that all confrontation is well-meaning because some people may just want to embarrass or hurt you. Biblical confrontation was never intended for that reason.

4. And, finally, "If he refuses to listen even to the church, let him be to you as a Gentile and a tax gatherer." If you have gone through the biblical confrontation process and the person refuses to accept responsibility and ask for forgiveness, yet in the process, nothing has been pointed out to you that would lead you to believe that your position is wrong, you have the right, biblically, to treat the other person as a pariah.

> Paul turned people over to Satan at times. However, I think it is awfully presumptive to assume that we can turn people over to Satan. I'll let God deal with that. All I can do is go through the biblical confrontation process. Our world would be a lot better off if we didn't hold on to so many offenses, perceived or otherwise. Family feuds might be averted if biblical confrontation had occurred.

Men also need to be taught to confront issues directly and avoid "garbage bagging." Garbage bagging is when you collect frustrations and put them in an imaginary garbage bag. Then at some future point, the person you have been collecting frustrations about bothers you again and you hit them with all their past perceived indiscretions. The person you attack is startled by your ferocity over the current, seemingly small issue. Your reaction seems disproportional to the offense. Feelings get hurt and relationships can even be destroyed all because you didn't deal with the frustrations as they occurred. A man who is proactive will deal with the issues right away.

Jesus said that the world would know Christians if we have "love for one another" (John 13:35). Sometimes love requires making hard, tough choices. But it is all based around the desire to improve relationships, not make them worse. Remember when you confront someone, it should only be using God's standards. Confront only in love with the hope of reconciliation. Never confront to hurt or for revenge. Hebrews 10:30 says, "Vengeance is Mine, I will repay, says the Lord." This means that vengeance is not yours and vengeance is not mine. No matter how much we know that to be a true statement, human beings tend to believe that what is best for them is truth. Fortunately, you are not God, and neither am I. God is a lot smarter than all of us and He will take care of justice in His timing.

Most of us want justice for others but mercy for ourselves. We are truly blessed if we have friends who are proactive and will tell us the "truth in love" (Ephesians 4:15). Proverbs 27:5–6 says, "Better is open rebuke than love that is concealed. Faithful are the wounds of a friend, but deceitful are the kisses of an enemy." We all need people in our lives who will tell us the hard truth.

On Father's Day, our pastor gave a sermon that included an incredible story. He explained that two older couples went to lunch after church one Sunday. A family of three generations, grandmother, mother and father, and three early-teen daughters came into the restaurant. The young teenage girls were dressed in midriff halter tops, short skirts, and sandals. In other words, they were dressed in a very revealing, provocative manner. After seeing the family walk in, one of the older gentlemen commented on the way the girls were dressed and expressed his disapproval. The other wiser gentleman replied, "I don't blame the mother or the grandmother. I blame the *father,* because the father knows what every man in this restaurant is thinking right now. The ladies don't."

Where was this father's leadership? Where was his proactive protection of his daughters? That father should never have allowed those girls out of the house looking the way they did. That is wrong. We need to recognize it as wrong. It takes great courage to say to your daughter, "No, you can't wear that." You see, women don't think about sex like men do, which is to say—constantly, all the time. When women dress up, it is to look beautiful, not sexy. Most often women dress for other women and don't recognize or understand the impact or effect it has on men. You do, Dad, so one way you can be proactive is to protect your daughters and your wife.

FOUR STEPS FOR BIBLICAL CONFRONTATION

- IF YOU THINK SOMEONE HAS SINNED AGAINST YOU, GO TO HIM ONE-ON-ONE.
- IF HE DOES NOT LISTEN TO YOU, "TAKE ONE OR TWO WITH YOU SO THAT BY THE MOUTH OF TWO OR THREE WITNESSES EVERY FACT MAY BE CONFIRMED."
- IF HE STILL REFUSES TO LISTEN, TELL THE CHURCH—THE PASTOR OR AN ELDER.
- "IF HE REFUSES TO LISTEN EVEN TO THE CHURCH, LET HIM BE TO YOU AS A GENTILE AND A TAX GATHERER."

REMEMBER THAT THE GOAL IS RECONCILIATION. DEAL WITH AN ISSUE IN SUCH A WAY THAT THE SITUATION CAN BE MADE BETTER, NOT WORSE.

P. **E.** T. E. R.

A MAN OF INITIATIVE LEARNS TO LEAD AN:

ELITE FORCE

The first E in Peter stands for Elite Force. In God's plan, the family is the frontline fighting unit—they are an Elite Force. The reason that Satan attacks the family so fiercely is because destroying the family diverts attention away from fighting him. It creates lasting wounds that cause us to spend time healing instead of reaching out. If Satan can destroy the family, he believes he can slow or stop God. As Christians, we should have marriages that the world would envy and desire for themselves. There can be no question that God intended for men to lead and were directed to lead the family. You are the leader of this force whether you like it or not.

Often, men are portrayed on TV and in films as bumbling idiots. Before I was a Christian, I led my family based on the principle of "delegation by abdication." In other words, I let them do whatever they wanted. Some people thought I was an enlightened male when actually I was uncaring. When I was not a Christian, my wife would ask to do something, and I would say, "Sure, go ahead." Sometimes it was because I really didn't care, but sometimes it was because I did not have the courage to assume my leadership role. It is much easier to be passive.

When women try to find husbands, they look for men they respect. They want to marry James Bond and then turn him into Mr. Rogers. Instinctively, they realize they need a man with courage and character. How can you respect a man with no backbone? Our society has confused the idea of backbone with the concept of being a bully. Men with real backbones have the courage not to be bullies. It takes more courage to walk away from a fight than to react impulsively.

Children have an innate love for Dad and Mom placed in them by God. One of my most vivid memories as a teenager was of my father coming to a baseball game when I was playing in a city an hour away. The significant thing about this game was that it was played in the spring, during budget season for state government. My father was a budget analyst for the state and worked long, long hours during the dreaded budget season. But somehow, he managed to carve out time to come and watch me play baseball. I vividly remember him walking down the left field line while we were playing. It was remarkable! I felt so honored and loved that my father cared enough about me to put his work aside for a time and come to that ball game. I knew how difficult it was for him. I know I am not alone in feeling that time with my dad was very special. Dads, make memories with your children.

In his book *Man in the Mirror*, Patrick Morley recounts a story about James Boswell, the biographer of eighteenth-century English writer Samuel Johnson, as told by Gordon McDonald. Boswell frequently mentioned a special childhood memory of a day spent fishing with his father.

> Apparently, Boswell's life had been deeply etched for the better on this single day, for *he constantly referred to the many matters his father had tutored him about on that one occasion.* Many years later someone stumbled across the following entry in his father's journal. These are the words penned by Boswell's dad, "Gone fishing today with my son; a day wasted."
>
> I believe this is a positive story about Boswell's father. Whatever personal feelings he had; he must have effectively suppressed them since his son profited so much from the day. It would be more common for us to express our selfish displeasure and ruin the day for everyone.
>
> Instead, his son had been deeply encouraged by the mundane affair, and the memory became a cornerstone of his entire life. We don't have to be the sweetest guy in the world to have an impact on our kids. What seems like a bore and a waste of time can be a great inspiration to them. They just need our time and attention. If we can learn to control our selfish desires, not lose our tempers so often, and encourage our kids, they will inherit a great legacy from us.[1]

---

1 Patrick Morley, *Man in the Mirror* (Grand Rapids: Zondervan, 1997), 122.

This father made a great impact on his son just by being present. Whoever developed the term "quality time" was misguided. Quality time is intended to prevent guilt for lack of a quantity of time spent with our children. Quantity of time produces opportunities to have quality time. You don't just go to your child and say, "Listen, I've got fifteen minutes, can we have a quality discussion?" Quality time occurs when you spend time with your children and then suddenly something profound occurs because you are spending a quantity of time with them.

What a blessing it is to be chosen by God to be the hero in our child's life. We've been given a great opportunity. Let's not waste it!

I realize that many men grew up without a father at home. Or maybe he was home but was a poor dad or an often-absent dad. I'm sorry about that for you, but please remember that "God is the father to the fatherless" (Psalms 68:5). He loves you and will never fail you. This book is intended to help you know how to be a godly man even if you have no one at home to teach you. Perhaps you could even find a male mentor to go through it with you.

I know there have been young men who have assumed that because their father was gone, through death or divorce, they were automatically worse off than guys who had fathers at home. Not so! We often assume that when a father lives at home, he is automatically a good father. That is not necessarily true. The critical issue is that no matter what your situation, you control how you will live the rest of your life. Whether your dad was good, bad, or indifferent, you will ultimately be held responsible for how you live, what kind of man and father you become. Commit to acting responsibly, and to be a man of honor and a man of truth.

If you take the opportunity to spend time with young people who have come from single-parent homes, teach them that they are not victims. They have the right to make of their life what they want to make of it. "With God all things are possible" (Mark 10:27). Some fathers are merely sperm donors even if they are in an intact home. A good mentor and role model can make all the difference.

In the next story, think about how a man of Christ should strive to be thought of as the wife thinks of her husband.

> Many years ago, when the Grecian armies were in search of world conquest, their army was invading the barbaric areas of what is now northern Europe. They captured all these villages easily because of their superiority of numbers and weapons. They finally attacked a small village; but, due to the superior ability of one great warrior, the Greeks were unable to overcome this small village. This warrior was a man of great height, strength, and led his men with such cunning and in such a fearless manner they stymied the Greeks; however, as time wore on the superior power of the Greeks overcame the village. People were taken slaves, as was the custom of the time. The great warrior, his wife and son, were also taken prisoners and transported back to Greece. The King heard of this warrior. He had been impressed with the cunning, courage and bravery he exhibited against the Greeks, and asked that this soldier and his wife and son be brought before his throne. He was very impressed with his size, his stature and his noble features. His wife was beautiful, and his son was a lad of tender years but who displayed in his countenance, greatness like that of his father.
>
> The King asked this fine soldier what he would do if he would spare his life. The soldier explained he would be his slave and serve him always. The King then asked what he would do if he would spare his son. "I would fight for you," he answered. "I would use all my cunning, strength, my wisdom of warfare, my leadership and all my weapons to help Greece conquer the world." This

> pleased the King very much. He then asked the great warrior what he would do if he spared the life of his wife. The soldier answered, "I would die for you." The King then told the soldier he was far too brave and wise a man to be a slave and set him free.
>
> As the warrior and his wife and son left the palace, the soldier remembered how his wife had been impressed with the jewels and finery she had seen in Greece. She had never seen these things in her barbaric country. He asked his wife had she not seen the ring the King wore. She said she had not noticed it. He then said, "Surely you noticed his crown. There were so many brilliant jewels there I could scarcely see his face." "No," she replied, "I never noticed his crown at all." In dismay, the soldier asked her what she was looking at then. She replied, "I just couldn't take my eyes off the one who loved me so much he was willing to die for me."

A friend gave me a plaque that speaks to how the Elite Force can be kept strong. It says: *"The greatest thing a father can do for his children is to love their mother."* I have found that to be helpful and accurate. Remember, men, that while you may lose a battle or two, the objective is to win the war. Grow closer as a couple, raise godly children, and stand firm against the devil in God's frontline defense.

Biblically, one of the most fearful proclamations in God's Word is given to fathers: "You shall not make for yourself an idol, or any likeness of what is in heaven above or on the earth beneath or in the water under the earth. You shall not worship them or serve them; for I, the LORD your God, am a jealous God, visiting the iniquity of the fathers on the children, on the third and the fourth generations of those who hate Me, but showing lovingkindness to thousands, to those who love Me and keep My commandments" (Exodus 20:5–6).

The first time I heard that verse it scared the dickens out of me. To believe that what I do could negatively impact my children and grandchildren for three or four generations astonished me. This was startlingly clear to me one day when I was arguing with one of my sons and caught myself, actually caught myself, as I was arguing and realized I was arguing just like my dad. I hated the way my dad argued. He acted as though he thought the person whose voice was loudest wins. The arguments in our house went back and forth, escalating in volume. Dad was bigger, older, stronger, and he could speak louder. So he always won. Yet, here I was, sitting at the table on a Sunday afternoon with my son realizing I was arguing just like my dad.

Dave Simmons, founder of *Dad the Family Shepherd*, told a poignant story about his father. His dad was an ex-military man, hardnosed and demanding. After every game Dave played, football or basketball, his father would go over the game play-by-play telling him and sometimes literally showing him what he should have done instead. Dave promised himself he was never going to be like his "old man" in this area. As the story continued, Dave told of his own son's basketball game. After filming the first half he became more and more furious with his son's poor play. By the time the second half began he had put the camera away and sat fuming throughout about his son's performance the rest of the game. Instead of going out for their traditional post-game ice cream, they went directly home. All the way home Dave berated his son for his play, commenting on everything from lack of defense to poor offensive technique. Dave parked the car, walked up to the house, opened the door, and stepped aside for his family to pass. As his wife walked through the door, she turned and said one word, "Amos," Dave's father's name. With that one word he saw so clearly how he had become his dad and violated his promise to himself. That experience changed his life.

If you didn't like the way your own father behaved, you must change the cycle. When men hate God, the Bible says the consequences of their sin affects the third and fourth generations. That is a very sobering idea, but the good news is that God goes on to say that He will shower blessing and mercy to thousands of generations that love and keep His commandments. Will you and I learn the hard way, or will we let the Holy Spirit mold us? Most of us love and want the best for our children. When God allows us to recognize the cycle of generational sin in our families, He also gives us the power to break that cycle.

God repeats the warning of generational sin in Exodus 34:7 and Deuteronomy 5. It can be a fearful thing. As dads, we have a powerful challenge to help our children love God and keep His commandments. We can break the cycle of generational sin with God's help by loving Him and honoring Him. Just because it is true that the consequences of past sins may be visited upon you by no fault of your own, it doesn't mean they have to continue through another generation. If your parents or grandparents were divorced, it does not mean it is inevitable for you. You can break the cycle.

My great-grandfather was known in the vernacular as a "traveling man." He had a couple of children in Kentucky and then moved to Oklahoma alone without notice. When my grandfather was thirty-five years old and running his wholesale business, a man walked in unannounced one day and introduced himself as my grandfather's father. He stayed in town a few days and then left again. Even though he did not have a good role model of committed marriage from his mother and father, my grandfather remained married to my grandmother and broke the cycle of divorce in their generation. My parents were married for fifty-two years before my mother died, and my wife and I have been married now for fifty years. Generational cycles can be broken.

You may have to deal with some of the consequences of generational sin, but you don't have to pass it down to your children. If one generation has a problem with alcoholism, it increases the likelihood of alcoholism in the next generation should they choose to drink. But it doesn't force the next generation to be alcoholics. God holds each of us personally responsible for our own choices regardless of the example given them by the previous generation. Ezekiel 18:4 says, "Behold all souls are mine. The souls of the father as well as the soul of the son. *The soul who sins will die.*" You are responsible for your own actions no matter what kind of dad you had. Your father's sin does not doom you to follow in his footsteps. God says in Ezekiel 33:11, "As I live, I take no pleasure in the death of the wicked, but rather that the wicked turn from his way and live." God wants us to make good choices.

Be encouraged by Exodus 20:6: "But showing love and kindness to thousands of those who love me and keep my commandments." The thousands in this verse refers to thousands of generations. God says the iniquity of the fathers and their sons are passed down to the third and fourth generations, but for those who love and honor Him, kindness and love will follow them for thousands of generations. What a wonderful promise of hope we have.

What kind of father did you have? Do you see yourself in him? Do you use him as an excuse for your misbehavior? Be intentional; change the cycle.

P. E. **T.** E. R.

A MAN OF INITIATIVE IS A:

TEACHER

The T in Peter stands for Teacher. The best example of how to teach is written in Ezra 7:10, "For Ezra had set his heart to *study* the law of the Lord and to *practice* it and *teach* his statutes and ordinances in Israel." This verse helps us understand how we should teach and lead our families (our Elite Force).

When I was a very new Christian, I remember being very concerned about how I would ever know what the Bible said. I was afraid my children would ask me questions and I would not know how to answer. As time passed, I learned more, read the Scriptures more, and continued to ask questions. My children did come to me with questions. If I did not know the answer, I searched out the answer. It is remarkable to me how many times the answer was given to me while I was reading God's Word; just the right Scripture at just the right time. It still amazes me. To study, to practice, to teach; a very practical guide for training ourselves as well as our children. Study, practice, and teach!

Ezra followed his own advice. He put a lot of emphasis on modeling what he knew to be right. Many behaviors are caught rather than taught. When our children were young, we tried to do devotions at night. I might as well have been doing root canals with no anesthetic. Even I was bored. It was horrible. Deuteronomy 6 tells us the way you teach life is by doing the things of life. Spend time with your children, and opportunities to teach them will come naturally. In our football program, the best teaching times come when someone is late or if something gets stolen. At those times, the lessons are no longer theoretical, they become real. In order to take advantage of such teachable moments, you must be looking for opportunities. When they occur, take advantage and act on it. Those are the best teaching times.

Many years ago, I learned from my wife that sarcasm is a terrible teaching technique. Occasionally I revert to my old ways, but I really try not to be sarcastic. There are two reasons for it. The person who is not perceptive enough to understand that you are being sarcastic thinks you're giving him a compliment. Let's say a young football player misses a block. If I say, "Nice block," and he is not perceptive, then all he hears is a compliment and thinks he made a great block. "Thanks, coach. I appreciate that." The person who is perceptive enough to understand that you are being sarcastic is saying to himself, "Why can't the guy just say what he really means?" Sarcasm is a lousy tool. Are you sarcastic to your children? Are you sarcastic to your wife? She won't respect you if you demean her. Sarcasm verbally rewards poor performance, but it belittles the person by not dealing with the issue in a straightforward way. Sarcasm has no place in leadership or love.

Sometimes we have to be creative in the way we teach our children. Some people who have been teaching or coaching twenty years have twenty years of experience, but some only have one year of experience twenty times. This story reflects twenty years of experience.

> According to a news report, a certain school in Garden City, MI was recently faced with a unique problem. A number of twelve-year-old girls were beginning to use lipstick and would put it on in the washroom. That was fine, but after they put on their lipstick, they would press their lips to the mirror leaving dozens of little lip prints. Every night, the maintenance man would remove them and the next day, the girls would put them back. Finally, the principal decided that something had to be done. He called all the girls to the washroom and met them there with the maintenance man. He explained that all these lip prints were causing a major problem for the custodian who had to clean the mirrors every night. To demonstrate how difficult it had been to clean the mirrors, he asked the maintenance man to show the girls how much effort was required. He took out a long-handled squeegee, dipped it in the toilet, and cleaned the mirror with it. Since then, there have been no lip prints on the mirror. The moral of this story…there are teachers and then there are educators.

God's method of teaching is different than society's. Society says, "Show me and I'll do it." God says, "Do it and I'll show you." That can be very hard. God often asks us to follow Him when the whole picture isn't clear. How will I know if it's absolutely God's way? I take a three-step approach to understanding God's way:

1. ***FILTER IT THROUGH SCRIPTURE.*** Is the direction you think you are getting from God consistent with His revealed Word?

2. ***GET GODLY COUNSEL.*** Many people make decisions and never consult with anyone, especially anyone with a Christian

background. If you have a real problem and you go to a counselor who doesn't have a Christian background, what will you get? You're going to get worldly counsel. You need to get with people who know God's Word and will speak the truth to you.

3. ***PRAY ABOUT IT.*** When deciding a tough matter, a pastor I know prays first. After he has prayed and has an idea of the right thing to do, he tells God his plan and then commits to pray for another period of time. During that additional time, he prays that if this is not God's will on this particular matter that God would prevent him from executing his original idea.

Emotions run high with us. It might be true that I need to be more emotional about some things and less about others, but as it relates to seeking God's wisdom, I am serious about being sober, logical, and thoughtful. I want to filter the decision through God's Word, seek godly counsel about it, and pray about it.

Men, we must teach, we must lead. Teach your children what God has done for you. Share your praises with them. We must know what to teach by knowing the Bible and then modeling it, living it. Keep in mind that what you say is of no value if you don't live it. Walk your talk!

3 STEPS TO UNDERSTAND GOD'S WAY

- FILTER IT THROUGH SCRIPTURE. IS THE DIRECTION YOU THINK YOU ARE GETTING FROM GOD CONSISTENT WITH HIS REVEALED WORD?
- GET GODLY COUNSEL FROM SOMEONE WHO KNOWS GOD'S WORD AND WILL SPEAK THE TRUTH TO YOU.
- PRAY ABOUT IT.

P. E. T. **E.** R.

A MAN OF INITIATIVE IS AN:

ENCOURAGER

Now, the second E in Peter is Encourager. To be a true encourager, we must be enthusiastic. In fact, did you know enthusiasm means "God in you?" However, sometimes God needs to get our attention so that we're enthusiastic about what we need to be enthusiastic about. For example, we may be enthusiastic about bowling or football, but we're not enthusiastic about church. We may not be enthusiastic about reading the Bible or praying, but sometimes God needs to redirect our lives and passions. One thing we need to understand as parents is that we are to be our children's best cheerleader. Yes, we are to be their teacher and mentor, but we are also to encourage them mightily in the things they want to do.

Pastor Jim Custer believes that Barnabas may have been the most important man in the New Testament because he is the man who got the Jerusalem Council to accept the apostle Paul as a true apostle. Barnabas means "son of encouragement." That was a pretty scary task because Paul had been involved in killing Christians. But Barnabas paved the way for Paul to be accepted by Peter and the other apostles. He was an encourager.

We all need encouragement. All of us wish we would get more encouragement from our wives, children, bosses, and friends, right? Consider this young fellow. A boy went to his father and said, "Let's play darts. I'll throw and you say wonderful." This is a cute story that reflects a deep truth; we all need encouragement occasionally. We need someone to give us a pat on the back, letting us know that we are okay. So today, go out and encourage someone; be Jesus with skin on in their life.

The noted speaker and writer Zig Ziglar said, "Anything worth doing is worth doing poorly." This seems like a silly statement until you realize that we must encourage people when they fail to keep trying and improving. No one starts as an expert, so do it poorly until you can do it well.

I remember coaching a wrestler who became a state champion as a junior. Because he was a state champion, he wouldn't wrestle in summer tournaments because he "might lose." While he won another state championship as a senior, he never improved very much because he was afraid to fail.

On the other hand, Dan Gable was one of the best wrestlers America has ever had. Dan would wrestle most anyone in practice and always had a strategy for each practice. In the summer before Dan won his Gold medal at the Olympics, he and I were working at a wrestling camp. One day as we walked to the mats, I asked him if I could wrestle him. (I wanted to test my manhood.) Dan's strategy that day was to work on the defense to a single leg takedown on his right leg. I scored a point on him by taking him down one time, but he didn't care because he was improving. The funny part of the story to me is that I scored one point while he took me down sixteen times, and on thirteen of those, he pinned me directly from my feet. But I survived with a great story to tell my children.

We must be encouraging, not negative, to our children. There are enough negatives just living every day. I'm reminded by a true story about how our negative words can wound. A three-year-old girl was mad at her father. She yelled at him, she screamed, "I hate you!" The father's response was, "That's okay, I hate you, too!" Perhaps he thought it was funny, but his wife didn't. He didn't really mean that. He was just being sarcastic. This young lady is nearly forty years old and married but still remembers it. It was a significant event in her life.

Many years ago, I thought it was funny to call one of my children "Stinkpot." To me, it was a term of endearment. I intended to be cute and funny, until one day, he came to me and said, "Dad, I don't like that." I was stunned. So I did the only reasonable thing that I could do: I started calling him "Champ." He likes that, and frankly, it really matches my perspective of him.

I believe this next story sums up the need young people have for positive people in their lives.

> He was in the first third grade class I taught as Saint Mary's School in Morris, Minnesota. All 34 of my students were dear to me, but Mark Eklund was one in a million. Very neat in appearance but had that happy-to-be-alive attitude that made even his occasional mischievousness delightful. Mark talked incessantly. I had to remind him again and again that talking without permission was not acceptable. What impressed me so much, though, was his sincere response very time I had to correct him for misbehaving: "Thank you for correcting me, Sister!" I didn't know what to make of it at first, but before long I became accustomed to hearing it many times a day.
>
> At the end of the year, I was asked to teach junior-high math. The years flew by, and before I knew it Mark was in my classroom again. He was more handsome than ever. Since he had to listen carefully to my instructions in the "new math," he did not talk as much in ninth grade as he had in third. One Friday, things just didn't feel right. We had worked hard on a new concept all week, and I sensed that the students were frowning, frustrated with themselves and edgy with one another. I had to stop this crankiness before it got out of hand. So, I asked them to list the names of the other students in the room on two sheets of paper, leaving a space between each name. Then I told them to think of the nicest thing they could say about each of their classmates and write it down. That Saturday, I wrote down the names of each

student on a separate sheet of paper, and I listed what everyone else had said about that individual. On Monday I gave each student his or her list.

Before long, the entire class was smiling. "Really?" I heard whispered. "I never knew that meant anything to anyone!" "I didn't know others liked me so much." No one ever mentioned those papers in class again. I never knew if they discussed them after class or with their parents, but it didn't matter. The exercise had accomplished its purpose. The students were happy with themselves and one another again. Several years later, after I returned from vacation, my parents met me at the airport. As we were driving home, Mother asked me the usual questions about the trip—the weather, my experiences in general. There was a lull in the conversation. Mother gave Dad a sideways glance and simply said, "Dad?" My father cleared his throat as he usually did before something important.

"The Eklunds called last night," he began. "Really?" I said. "I haven't heard from them in years. I wonder how Mark is." Dad responded quietly. "Mark was killed in Vietnam," he said. "The funeral is tomorrow, and his parents would like it if you could attend." The church was packed with Mark's friends.

The pastor said the usual prayers, and the bugler played taps. One by one those who loved Mark took a last walk by the coffin and sprinkled it with holy water. I was the last one to bless the coffin. As I stood there, one of the soldiers who acted as pallbearer came up to me. "Were you Mark's math teacher?" he asked. I nodded as I continued to stare at the coffin. "Mark talked about you a lot," he said.

After the funeral, most of Mark's former classmates headed to Chuck's farmhouse for lunch. Mark's mother and father were there, obviously waiting for me. "We want to show you something," his father said, taking a wallet out of his pocket. "They found this on Mark when he was killed. We though you might recognize it." Opening the billfold, he carefully removed two worn pieces of notebook paper that had obviously been taped, folded and refolded many times. I knew without looking that the papers were the ones on which I had listed all the good things each of Mark's classmates had said about him. "Thank you so much for doing that," Mark's mother said. "As you can see, Mark treasured it."

Mark's classmates started to gather around us. Charlie smiled rather sheepishly and said, "I still have my list. It's in the top drawer of my desk at home." Chuck's wife said, "Chuck asked me to put his in our wedding album." "I have mine too," Marilyn said. "It's in my diary." Then Vicki, another classmate, reached into her pocketbook, took out her wallet and showed her worn and frazzled list to the group. "I carry this with me at all times," Vicki said without batting an eyelash. "I think we all saved our lists." That's when I finally sat down and cried.

The purpose of this letter is to encourage everyone to compliment the people you love and care about. We often tend to forget the importance of showing our affection and love. Sometimes the smallest of things, could mean the most to another.[2]

---

2 Jack Canfield, "Appreciation, by Helen P. Morals," *The Original Chicken Soup for the Soul 20th Anniversary Edition,* (Cos Cob: Chicken Soup of the Soul Publishing, 2013).

This story was the catalyst for how we developed the recognition award for our middle school football team. We had the team members write down the traits they appreciated in their teammates. We then presented the top five or so to each eighth grader as he graduated to the high school level to serve as a lasting reminder. Middle school is such a needy age for affirmation. It is such a tough, tough time. I love this story because it shows the power of encouragement.

Unfortunately, the opposite of this story is often the case when we as fathers push our kids instead of loving, caring for, and encouraging them. Can you see yourself in this story? I hope not, but if you do, use it as a prompting from the Holy Spirit to change!

> In truth, I played better when my mother attended my matches than when my father did. I suppose that's no surprise. Whereas my mom—profoundly unathletic, with only casual interest in tennis—didn't care about wins and losses, my dad was decidedly results-oriented. He taught me the American twist serve and the two-handed backhand, and I admired him very much, but living up to his expectations was difficult. He wanted me to be a hardscrabble winner in the mold of Jimmy Connors, his once and forever favorite player. Dad kept statistics—first serve percentages, unforced errors—and jotted them down on pads of legal paper that he left on top of my dresser the following morning. At the bottom of the page was his list of conclusions, which were always a bit too obvious to be helpful: "(1) cut down on your double faults and you'll win more service games; (2) an average rally ends on the fourth shot; visualize hitting five—keep the ball in play!"
>
> He took losing as badly as I did, especially when I lost to someone who had less talent. When this happened, it had the effect of rigor mortis on him. He would stand stock-still in the spot where he

> had been watching the match, dumbstruck, brooding, his necktie loosened and askew. He came to be known at these statuesque moments as the perfunctory pillar of salt, a monument to any father ever vexed by a son's inadequacy.[3]
>
> *(Kevin Heath teaches writing at Cedarville College in Cedarville, Ohio and is a PhD candidate in creative writing at the University of Cincinnati.)*

We may say something to our kids, trying to be funny and never mean for it to hurt, but it could hurt them terribly. When I was young, this phrase was the rage, "You don't sweat much for a fat kid." That is intended to be funny, but it isn't. My wife will never forget making her first strawberry pie and asking her father what he thought. He said, "Pretty good strawberry pie, if you like strawberry pie." He wasn't being mean, he was just matter of fact, but it bothered her.

Your favor is so critical to your children, Dad. Sometimes parents have to support their children in areas we don't care for. Proverbs 22:6 says, "Train up a child in the way he should go / even when he is old he will not depart from it." "The way he should go" refers to the child's God-given desires and talents. Not everybody is bent the same way we are. Some of your children may have an academic bent, or a vocal or instrumental music bent. To be a good parent is to enthusiastically encourage your children in the direction God has gifted them, not to force them to be like us or succeed where we fell short.

Robert Lewis, the pastor who wrote *Raising a Modern-Day Knight,* made a comment that struck me forcefully. He said, "Psychologically, men are more fragile than women." I was astonished when I read that. "Men struggle with their identity much more than women do, though feminists would have us believe that poor self-esteem is largely a female problem caused by primary

---

3 Kevin Heath. Personal communication.

social inequities, the evidence tells a different story."[4] When I reflect on that statement, I know it to be true. Most men, when pressed man-to-man, deep-to-deep, are some of the most insecure human beings I know. Not because they are bad people, but because they never feel quite sure they measure up to others or even their own expectations. Therefore, a huge percentage of men feel inadequate. In some cases, it is because their dad kept telling them they were no good. After a while you begin to believe it, even if it is hogwash. The most critical encouragement that a man needs to give his son is his blessing. Fathers, heed this well!

Bill Glass of Bill Glass Prison Ministries visited all the men on death row in a state prison and asked them the same questions. He said 100 percent of the men had one trait in common. Do you know what that was? *Every single man on death row hated his father.* They hated their father and acted out that hatred in such a way that they ended up on death row.

Bill Glass used to play football for the Cleveland Browns and has two boys of his own; one of them is 6 feet 8 inches tall, 260 pounds, and the other is 6 feet 6 inches tall. Bill Glass is a pretty big fellow himself. He explains how to deliver a blessing so your boys will never again wonder if they are a man in your eyes. If you've given them the C. H. R. I. S. T. acrostic as a definition of Manhood; if you have spelled out the Goal, Guide, and Game plan, then they have a clear direction for life. All they need now is your blessing. A biblical blessing is modeled after what God the Father said after Jesus was baptized, "This is my beloved son in whom I am well pleased." This blessing conveys belonging, value, and love—the three necessities of a clear and powerful blessing.

Bill Glass says, "You are mine and I am glad" (belonging). Imagine how many children there are in the world today whose parents have never said "you're mine and I'm glad." In fact, some parents have said, "You're mine and I'm disgusted. You're a mistake!" What a way to grow up. Let's give our

---

4 Robert Lewis, *Raising a Modern-Day Knight* (Colorado Springs: Focus on the Family, 2007), 46.

children encouragement. I look my boys in the eye, and I tell them, "You're mine and I'm glad."

Then Bill Glass says, "You're special and I'm proud of you" (value). I am sure your children are special or unique in some good way.

And lastly, Glass says, "I love you and I always will" (love). Some parents have never told their children they love them. Even if you love your children, have you formally, face-to-face blessed them? Men say to me all the time, "I know my dad loved me, but he never said so." Stop the cycle now. Be a man. Bless your children unconditionally and do it out loud.

Each year we bless our graduating senior class of Crusaders. I can't give a young man his father's blessing; only his father can do that, but I can let him know that he is a Crusader forever, that he has value and is loved by us. We all need encouragement.

If your father is dead or missing, form a relationship with a mentor and get his blessing. Teach him what a blessing is and ask him to give it to you. I insisted my father bless me. I played a taped message from Bill Glass for him while we were on a trip to Evansville, Indiana. After checking in to the hotel, I wouldn't let my dad leave until he blessed me. Oh, he didn't use Bill Glass's words or mine, but he blessed me out loud and hugged me. A loving touch is so important when blessing someone. I will never forget that moment.

I'm not a preacher, but I preached at my uncle's funeral because I knew him better than any pastor that lived near him. He was a believer and my favorite uncle. Perhaps one of the most significant things my father ever said to me was after the funeral. We got into the car with my brothers; my dad looked over at me and said, "That was great. It couldn't have been done better." That's all I needed to know. I didn't care what anybody else thought. My dad thought I did well. It was a powerful, powerful life moment for me.

Men need confirmation and encouragement from other men. They need appreciation. "Femininity can never bestow masculinity," says John Eldredge. You can't be told you are a man from a woman. You can be told you're respected, you're loved, and you're cared for, but you will never know you are a man until another man tells you that you measure up. The men of the church need to step up and fill a void left by absentee fathers.

Lord Jesus, I pray for the men who read this book that they would find a coach, a real-life mentor, and that he would bless them. I pray, Lord, that we can all feel Your closeness and love for us. You have made us men; may we make You proud by intentionally living life as You desired.

3 NECESSITIES OF A CLEAR AND POWERFUL BLESSING

- "YOU ARE MINE AND I AM GLAD": BELONGING.
- "YOU'RE SPECIAL AND I'M PROUD OF YOU": VALUE.
- "I LOVE YOU AND I ALWAYS WILL": LOVE.

P. E. T. E. **R.**

A MAN OF INITIATIVE: **R**EJECTS PASSIVITY

Lastly, a man of Initiative must be a man like Peter and Reject Passivity. As I said earlier, the group who studies manhood says if there is any one area where men fail on a consistent basis, it is that they are too passive. They will not stand up and be counted.

Lewis Yablonsky said, "Boys tend to be heavily involved emotionally with their fathers as role models even though they may spend more time with their mother, sisters, and peers. Boys look to their fathers for clues as to how to act out their male roles, and specifically, later on, their roles as fathers."[5] Dads, you are important! You are critically important! Homosexuality often occurs in homes where Dad is passive and does not fulfill his God-mandated role as a leader. It is staggering how many homosexual men come from homes with a domineering mother and a passive father. Be the leader, provider, and protector of your family.

One of the difficult things about Initiative is that being bold isn't a one-time thing. Day after day we are presented with opportunities to take initiative or become passive. This next story is my own, and it illustrates the diligence one must have to avoid falling prey to our natural tendency to passivity.

"PROMISE KEEPERS VS. DANBURY"

> In 1994, God gave me a true blessing in that I was able to attend the Promise Keepers rally in Detroit with my youngest son, Stephen. Because it was a three-hour-plus trip, we watched a movie on the bus's video system. The group was all men and the movie of choice was *Rudy*. As the film progressed, the men got more and more involved in the movie, but I was bothered by the language. You can imagine that with a group of forty-five men intensely interested in the film, I didn't quite know what to do. But following the prompting of the Holy Spirit, I stood up and said, "Men, we need to turn this movie off, because the language is obscene and of all things we are on our way to a spiritual conference. I can't imagine God would be pleased with the language." I was roundly booed, but we did in fact turn the movie off. My son was proud of me, and I was happy that I had not been passive even though the situation was very difficult.
>
> Now fast forward to 2003. I was the head coach of the Columbus Crusaders and we were making a trip to Danbury High School which is about two-and-a-half hours away. On the way up we watched

5 Lewis Yablonsky, *Fathers and Sons* (Bloomington: iUniverse, 2000), 13.

> "Remember the Titans," a solid and inspiring film with a few, but very few, objectionable parts. When we began the trip home, one of the young men suggested we put in a movie called "Major Paine." We asked the young man if it was an appropriate movie for our team and he assured us that it was. As the movie began to play, I began to feel more and more uncomfortable with the language of the movie. Yet, I did nothing because I was waiting for someone else to register their concerns. We must have been at least halfway through the movie before one of our coaches, Carlos Bing, spoke up and said, "This movie is just not acceptable. We need to turn it off." We did so immediately, but I was really frustrated with myself because it took me so long to act. In fact, I apologized to the players the next morning for having been so slow in stopping the film.[6]

Being a man of initiative takes *constant vigilance* and a willingness to act on each incident you experience, not just one incident. Sometimes our failures teach us more than our successes. Both of these incidents have taught me that doing the right thing is often unpleasant but well worth it. Saint Augustine once said, "Right is right even if no one is doing it; wrong is wrong even if everyone is doing it."[7]

How important is the father? While walking one day, one of the great generals of the Civil War, Robert E. Lee, turned to find his young son, Custis, walking in his tracks in the snow. "When I saw this," he said to a friend, "it behooves me to walk very straight when this fellow is already following in my tracks." Dads, you and I need to walk very straight as well. We need to do the right thing because our kids are following everything we do.

Don't be passive. Most men watch the movie *Braveheart* and get inspired as William Wallace leads his men into the charge against the English. At some

---

6 Mike Stanley, Columbus Crusaders, personal communication.

7 Augustine of Hippo > Quotes > Quotable Quote, Goodreads, last modified 2020, https://www.goodreads.com/quotes/126110-right-is-right-even-if-no-one-is-doing-it.

level we feel we are ready to follow Wallace into battle as well as he challenges us that: "Every man dies. Not every man really lives."[8] Martin Luther King Jr. said it very well when he said, "The ultimate measure of a man is not where he stands in moments of comfort and convenience, but where he stands at times of challenge and controversy."[9] Give me a sword and let's go! But then we find ourselves in a conversation with our wives who may ask us something that we ought to say no to, and we cower, we falter, we're passive. When Eve was being tempted by the serpent, Adam was right there next to her in the garden, not somewhere off in another section (Genesis 3:6). He should have challenged Satan's lies, yet he didn't, and it set a pattern for manhood ever since. It is a pattern we must break.

Rejecting passivity doesn't always require a fight. In fact, men of initiative are always looking for a better solution than fighting. When Beau was in the third grade, he went to the school playground. One of the neighborhood bullies threatened to bust his chops. Beau came home very upset and asked me what to do. My advice was very worldly. I told Beau the next time the guy threatened him he should hit him in the face as hard as he could. Get the first one in and make it a good one. So the next day, Beau went back to the playground. He was anxious but knew he couldn't back down from this bully. When the guy pushed Beau and told him he was going to bust him, instead of punching him, Beau simply asked him *why* he wanted to do that. The fellow was so taken by Beau's question, he left him alone and never bothered him again. Beau's response was so much better than mine. Thank you, Jesus!

I should point out that not fighting back often takes more courage than fighting; sometimes, but not always. A man of C. H. R. I. S. T. never wants to retaliate, but sometimes it is necessary. Knowing when those times are requires mature discernment and strength.

I learned a very important concept from Pastor Darryl DelHousaye: "The stronger always goes to the weaker." When disagreements arise, when

---

8 *Braveheart,* directed by Mel Gibson (Los Angeles: Icon Entertainment, 1995).

9 Martin Luther King, Jr., *Strength To Love* (Boston: Beacon Press, 2019).

feelings are hurt, the stronger person always approaches the weaker first. The stronger person rejects passivity and does what is right. Be the stronger person.

I shared with our coaching staff the story Pastor Jim Custer told about the family in the restaurant, the one with the little girls who were dressed inappropriately. One of our coaches, Paul Dwyer, has two young daughters, beautiful girls. At the time of this story, they were of high school age and were preparing to go on a mission trip. They came to their dad, saying they needed to find new swimming suits to take along. So they searched all over for appropriate swimsuits. When they came back, they said, "We want to show you this suit and want to know what you think. But we want you to know we have been all over town looking for these things. I think we've been to every store in Columbus." So, one of them modeled the bathing suit. His response was, "You are not going out in that suit." Of course, they protested, but to their credit they accepted his response. He said, "*No*, it's not appropriate." He rejected passivity. Can you imagine the pressure on him? It takes a real loving, caring man to say that's not good enough. A real man, a godly man, rejects passivity and makes the right decision, unlike the dad in the restaurant. Why? Because he knew what men would think as they looked at his daughters. He also knew who was responsible for protecting the daughters God had entrusted to him. That's true even if they don't know they need protecting.

Let me close with the final part of Peter's story. Yes, he denied Christ three times, which was a passive thing to do. But, like us, God gave Peter a second chance. Later, when the priests threw Peter in jail, the angel of the Lord opened the jail gate and let him out. He told Peter, "Go your way. Stand and speak to the people in the Temple the whole message of this life." That's the gospel. The angel freed Peter so he could go tell people the truth about Jesus Christ. Peter was a champion and did just that. He spoke at the Temple and the Temple guards and the priests had him brought before the council. In Acts 5:28, the High Priest said to him, "We gave you strict orders not to continue teaching in this name and behold you have filled Jerusalem with your teaching and intend to bring this man's blood upon us." And Peter's response was classic: "We must obey God rather than men." Sometimes we are far more worried about what our peers think of us than what God thinks about us. But Peter put it right; we must obey God rather than men. We must reject passivity and obey Christ.

If you have been passive before, and all of us have been, take heed of this lesson. This concept has changed my life more than anything I have learned in the last fifteen years. I consistently ask myself if I am being passive when I should act. If you have not been a man of initiative, commit to become one. Make a promise to obey God rather than men, and be the man God designed you to be—today, intentionally!

A MAN OF CHRIST

COMMITMENT = A PROMISE COMPLETED

HONOR = CHARACTER ABOVE REPROACH; LIVING BY A BIBLICAL STANDARD

RESPONSIBILITY = TRUSTWORTHINESS DEMONSTRATED OVER TIME

INITIATIVE = BOLDNESS WITH INTEGRITY

SERVICE = INTENTIONALLY PUTTING THE NEEDS OF OTHERS FIRST, EXPECTING NOTHING IN RETURN

TRUTH = A STATEMENT OR PRINCIPLE THAT APPLIES TO ALL PEOPLE, IN ALL PLACES, AT ALL TIMES

C. H. R. I. **S.** T.

A MAN OF SERVICE

J. O. S. E. P. H.

JOYFUL HEART

OTHERS FIRST

SPIRIT-CONTROLLED = SELF-CONTROL

EFFECTIVE LISTENER

PRAYER

HOPE

CHAPTER SEVEN

A MAN OF SERVICE

J.O.S.E.P.H.

IN COACHING, I ALWAYS FIND that it is good to review what I've already gone over to solidify what I am trying to get across. So, let's review what we have covered up to this point.

We have a *Goal* to have Jesus say, "Well done," a *Guide* who is Christ, and a *Game Plan* to become godly men by using the Manhood Language. Let me remind you that the reason for Manhood Language is so that men can use it to communicate man-to-man with our children, our fathers, and our friends. Every day of my life the manhood language is my preferred way of talking to other men. For example, if a man says he "bounced his eyes" from temptation, I can reinforce that he was pure in mind and action. If a man missed an appointment, it can be pointed out that he failed as a man of responsibility, yet he may demonstrate responsibility by calling to explain and ask forgiveness.

As men of *Commitment*, we want to exhibit the traits of Joshua. We want to be men who Judiciously choose, then finish the course; are Obedient to Christ, Strong and Courageous, have Habits of a Champion, are Unwavering, and men of Action. As a man of *Honor*, we would emulate Paul, who is Pure in mind and action, Accountable to Christ, Unpretentious, and Laudable. A man of *Responsibility* would model after Timothy, who recognized that the Truth is absolute; he will have Mature discernment, be an Overcomer, not a victim, a Teammate, Hate Evil, and would stay true to his word—his Yes would be Yes and his No, No.

A man of *Initiative* is like Peter. He is a man who is Proactive, a leader of the Elite force (his family), a Teacher, an enthusiastic Encourager, and one who Rejects Passivity. To be a man of initiative is to be someone who is bold with integrity.

For *Service*, I have chosen Joseph, the earthly father of Jesus, as our model. Imagine how Joseph must have felt when he found out that his fiancée was pregnant with God's son. Joseph isn't given much credit for the man of faith he must have been, not to mention the man of service that he had to be. Joseph is a forgotten fellow, especially in the Evangelical Church. There is always the fear that Mary and Joseph would be worshipped in place of the Lord Jesus. Jesus alone is worthy of our worship! Nevertheless, Joseph must have been quite a man if God entrusted His Son to him. He entrusted the woman that He chose to bring His Son into the world to Joseph. We don't know that much about him because the Bible does not say much regarding this man. But we do know that God chose him for this important position. He was called upon to encourage, train, and challenge Jesus as a child. God needed a special man for that task; that is exactly what he got.

The leader of the Christian singing group Salvador really made me think when he told the story of his parents sending him off to a life of singing for the Lord. They told him, "Don't serve Jesus alone; serve Jesus only." Our goal is to serve Jesus only.

For example, the right question for a man to ask while considering a wife should be, "Do I love her?" and, "Is this the woman I am willing to serve for the rest of my life?" Service is one of the most difficult things for me, both as a husband and as a father. I've long felt that Philippians 2:3–4 should be read as a commitment at all weddings. It says, "Do nothing from selfishness or empty conceit, but with humility of mind regard one another as more important than yourselves; do not merely look out for your own personal interests, but also for the interests of others." What a challenge! What a tremendous verse from the perspective of a wife and husband team. It is also a tremendous verse for athletic teams. If more of our teams really took the position that each player does nothing from selfishness or empty conceit, but with humility of mind, and would regard one another as more important than themselves, what a team that would be! That team would be one where there truly was no I in team. Marriage is best when we regard our mate as more important than we are. Regarding others' needs as more important than ours is the true essence of service.

REGARDING OTHERS' NEEDS AS MORE IMPORTANT THAN OURS IS THE TRUE ESSENCE OF SERVICE.

The longer we are with our families, the more difficult it is to serve them because "familiarity breeds contempt." Clichés become clichés because there is most often truth in them. And familiarity does breed contempt unless you are constantly vigilant. Lou Holtz once gave a speech in which he said, "We are generally far nicer to perfect strangers than we are to our own family." To be a true servant, we should treat everyone as we wish to be treated (Matthew 7:12). The key question we need to ask ourselves is "Are we improving?"

The sub-acrostic for a man of Service is J. O. S. E. P. H. This man has a Joyful Heart, puts Others First, understands that being Spirit-Controlled means having self-control, is an Effective Listener, engages in Prayer, and instills Hope. Let's learn more about becoming men like Joseph.

J. O. S. E. P. H.

A MAN OF SERVICE HAS A:

JOYFUL HEART

The J in Joseph stands for Joyful Heart. To be a man of Service you need to start with a joyful heart because a joyful heart provides the buoyancy for everyday living. At times, it is hard to live in this world. If you are fundamentally a pessimist, someone who always sees the negative viewpoint or perspective, it will be very hard to have joy in your heart. Therefore, it will be exceedingly difficult to serve others because of this bitter perspective of life. Knowing Jesus will prevail in the end, and knowing we are on the winning side allows us to be joy-filled even in the most trying circumstances. Society says, "God will love me if I'm good." Grace says, "God will love me because He is good." Let His love shine through.

One of the first verses I memorized when I first became a Christian was Philippians 4:4: "Rejoice in the Lord always. Again, I say rejoice." Sometimes I just don't feel like rejoicing! But the key is that we are supposed to rejoice in who we are in Christ and in who He is, not because of our circumstances. When I was a very new Christian, I really didn't understand the concept that joy is a byproduct of being in Christ and my relationship with Him.

After returning from a Bible conference all excited and on a spiritual "high," I caught pneumonia and ended up in the hospital. During the course of treatment, I was given a powerful antibiotic administered intravenously, and twenty minutes later, I vomited. Every time it was administered, I vomited without fail. It was terrible! Here I was a new Christian, and it was hard to rejoice with your head in the garbage can. I was thinking to myself, "Rejoice in the Lord? Are you kidding me?" It took a while for me to understand that it is not the circumstances that we are rejoicing in, but our relationship to the king of Kings and Lord of lords.

It is hard to understand that you *can* have joy in your heart if you stop relying on your emotions and stand on the fact that you are chosen of God to be born again, redeemed, a child of God, and a friend of Jesus. No matter what your circumstances, a joyful heart comes from being constantly tied to the Source of power, Jesus Christ.

We need to reflect daily on who we are in Christ. As an encouragement and reminder for you, let me remind you that as Christians, we are children of God. John 1:12 says, "For everyone who receives Him, to them He gave the right to become children of God." Also, our eternal Father owns and controls everything. As men, there is a tendency on our part to believe we control most things and we are in charge. But, in fact, we are not in control, not really; God is. Another amazing thing is pictured in John 15:15, "Jesus calls me friend." We are friends of Jesus Christ! What a remarkable thing to be a friend of God Himself—to know and be a friend of the Savior of the world.

One day during a discussion I had with our coaches, I stated that I think there are two kinds of competitors in life. The one who loves to win, and the other who hates to lose. I hope you are the first kind, that you are just overjoyed and excited about winning. I happen to be the latter category. I hate to lose. This type of thinking affects my spiritual attitude. Let me demonstrate. In my mind, Scriptures such as, "Work out your salvation with fear and trembling" (Philippians 2:12), and "To obey is better than sacrifice" (1 Samuel 15:22), far overshadow verses like, "So if the Son makes you free, you will be free indeed" (John 8:36), and "It was for freedom that Christ has set us free" (Galatians 5:1). My wife, on the other hand, has no trouble thinking of Jesus as her friend. She loves to win, and she knows she is already on the winning side! It is necessary for us to see Jesus not just as judge, but as savior, friend, and as someone who cares so deeply about us that He would give His life for us. Could I have joy in my heart recognizing that the God of the Universe would come and die for me even if I was the only person on earth? Absolutely! What an incredible thought.

Scripture says, "I am a new creation in Christ" (2 Corinthians 5:17). For most new believers, this verse is wonderfully freeing. The difficulty for many of us is that when you become a new creation in Christ, you don't immediately stop living as you did in every area of your life. It takes some time for the Lord to come and clean up all the facets of your life that need to be purified. An excellent illustration of how that cleansing occurs uses the concept of a normal home.

Imagine if Jesus comes to visit you in your ten-room house. He first walks into the living room and His very presence is so bright that all the clutter and dust are completely exposed. This is exactly how the sins and misdeeds of your life become so apparent to you. Because you are serious about your obedience to Christ, you clean up your act with the help of the Holy Spirit. The living room starts to look good, but then Jesus says, "Let's go into the kitchen." You protest because you know that room is a mess. He is about to see another area of your life just when you were feeling pretty good about how nice the living room looks. In the kitchen, there is a whole new set of dirty issues now visible that must be dealt with. Because it is Jesus asking and you want to please Him, you allow Him to clean up the house. *But that is the beauty of it.* Jesus does not tell us "clean this up" before we can be His friend, before He will be our Savior. Jesus wants you to come to Him just as you are. As you grow with Him, then you will begin to change.[1]

Another way I can experience a joyful heart is by embracing the idea that God loves me. John 3:16 tells us, "God so loved the world that He gave His only begotten son that whosoever believes in Him should not perish but have eternal life." Most of us know the words, but do we really feel the impact of the meaning? Ephesians 1:4 says that God chose us. Yes, the Bible says God chooses people. I don't pretend to understand the theology of how God chooses people and yet people have a free will. I heard Dr. Jerry Bridges once describe it this way: "You are walking down a street and you see an open door. Above the door the sign says, 'Whosoever will, may enter in.' You choose to go through that door and then look back at the doorframe. There you find another sign that reads, 'Chosen before the beginning of time.'"

Here's what I do know. I know it is beyond comprehension to think that God chose me to be in His kingdom. Yet, that is clearly what the Bible

---

1 Robert Boyd Munger, *My Heart, Christ's Home* (Chicago: InterVarsity Press, 2001).

teaches. God chose to pluck us out of our rebellion and save us. God chooses to save some humans, yet others die in eternal separation from God. The others should have no complaint, however, because they decided not to accept Christ's sacrifice for them. Peter makes it clear that God "is patient toward you, not wishing for any to perish but for all to come to repentance" (2 Peter 3:9b).

You see, the gates of hell are locked from the inside. Jesus says, "Behold, I stand at the door and knock; if anyone hears My voice and opens the door, I will come into him and will dine with him, and he with Me" (Revelation 3:20). The people that are in hell have chosen to be in hell because they've chosen not to open the door. The fascinating thing to me about Jesus is that although He loves us and chooses us, although He wants us to be saved, He will not force Himself upon us. It boggles my mind. If God were to force us to love Him, we would essentially be like programmed robots. If there is no free will, there can be no love and no true relationship. You can't have a true relationship unless each person has free will to accept or reject the other.

To know we are chosen by God reinforces how special He thinks we are. What can we do but thank Him with the quality of our lives? It reminds me of the hymn, "To God Be the Glory; Great Things He Has Done."

A joyful heart is summed up extremely well by the following testimony.

> As a third-century man was anticipating death, he penned these last words to a friend: "It is a bad world, Donatus, an incredibly bad world. But I have discovered in the midst of it a quiet and good people who have learned the great secret of life. They have found a joy and wisdom which is a thousand times better than any of the pleasures of our sinful life. They are despised and persecuted, but they care not. They are masters of their souls. They

have overcome the world. These people, Donatus, are Christians... and I am one of them."[2]

J. **O.** S. E. P. H.

A MAN OF SERVICE PUTS:

OTHERS FIRST

The O in Joseph reminds us that a godly man puts Others First. Let's keep in mind that we are talking about Service. Therefore, we are talking about a man with a joyful heart, which allows him to care about others and put their needs before his own. It is out of this joy that he is able to do this.

The man who founded the Crusaders, Mike Cheeseman, is probably the greatest servant I have ever known personally. He has an unbelievable caring heart for helping other people. I really admire him. Occasionally, I find myself coveting his gift because it does not seem to be mine. Nevertheless, I can improve. No matter how good or bad a servant one perceives oneself to be, one can get better. I am totally convinced that service and thinking of others first can be taught and improved upon. Jesus said, "It is more blessed to give than to receive" (Acts 20:35). What a challenging verse. For human beings, this is a counterintuitive statement because we naturally want to put ourselves first.

What is sin? The word *sin* in Greek means "missing the mark." It comes from a term used in archery when the archer misses the bullseye or mark. Another way to think about sin is "I want to do what I want to do when I want to do it." Putting others first means giving up our own selfish interests.

---

2 Ajai Prakash. "As a Third-Century Man Was Approaching Death He..." Sermon Central, published March 27, 2008, https://www.sermoncentral.com/sermon-illustrations/65584/on-stories-by-ajai-prakash?ref=TextIllustrationSerps.

We put our desires in the background and focus on the other person instead of ourselves. Satan delights in attacking you when you give up your position to someone else, doesn't he? When you have a legitimate claim to something and you put another first, Satan immediately attacks you. He whispers in your ear, "What a sucker you are! I can't believe you are going to give that up and let the other person go first! You let people step all over you!"

For men, to hear someone is stepping on us makes us want to fight, doesn't it? At the very minimum, I want to criticize them and gossip about them to everyone around me. Our nature is counterintuitive to service. We feel as if God isn't fair to put us in that position. Sometimes you make up an elaborate scenario and say to yourself, *If I go ahead and take my rightful spot, I can do something nice for the other person later.* Have you ever done that? We often sell God short assuming that if the company gives the promotion to the other person before us, then God can't, doesn't, or won't care for our needs. I have seen it happen where the favored person got the job and failed miserably.

A friend of mine, Dr. Ray Pongonis, played fullback in high school and was asked to change positions to quarterback. He was being heavily recruited as a fullback, yet he changed positions for the good of the team. Most all the recruiters forgot about him, yet he would tell you that he made the right decision because the team should supersede the individual. If it's all about you, you should play an individual sport. The team experience parallels life in that sometimes we must serve others and not just ourselves. No one likes selfish people, nor do they respect them.

Often in our life God asks us to take a less important role, or to make some sacrifice to help the team be more successful. Many people are kept in the background; many people never get their names in the press, in lights, or in the news. They are people who live a dedicated life for Christ doing a job less than being the quarterback, but an important role for the good of the team. I always like to think those "hawgs" up on the trenches are a good example of doing a job for the good of the team, often being bypassed with the ink.

Should God ask you to perform some insignificant job for Him, don't hesitate to give your best. Not everyone can be the quarterback, but everyone can play his very best game day after day in whatever role God has called him to serve. Be assured that Heavenly Father knows of your contribution and will bless you much for the sacrifice and dedication.

There's no question as a coach that if you don't have an offensive line, it doesn't matter how good your backs are; it will be a long game. We are all willing to give our best for God when He calls us to the front line for something that looks very important. But when He asks us to do something insignificant, that's when it is so difficult to follow His plan. Nobody is watching. Nobody will know. Yet God is! We must begin to act as if pleasing God is more important than pleasing men. Is God our God, or is some idol, like fame, money, toys, or relationships more important? God says we will have no gods before Him (Exodus 20:3), so I think we know the answer.

I have called young men into my office to ask them to consider a position change. Some of them have said *yes* and some of them have said *no.* I can't help but feel that those who say no are selfish and that they are not putting the team first. It's selfish! I won't force you to change positions because I believe that you will be bitter and frustrated and not help the team. God will not make you change positions either. He will give you opportunities to serve Him outside your comfort zone, but He won't make you do them. Oftentimes our attitude would be best described by the age-old radio station WIIFM, "What's In It For Me?" I'm glad Jesus didn't take that attitude on His way to the cross. He put us first so we could have a life with Him. We must resist the temptation to ask "what's in it for me?" as opposed to putting others first.

As you reflect on your life, can you see areas where your selfishness is impeding your job at work, in the church, or at home? To change requires reflection and examination and then *intentional* change.

J. O. **S.** E. P. H.

A MAN OF SERVICE IS: **S**PIRIT-CONTROLLED

The S in Joseph represents being Spirit-Controlled, or having self-control. In Galatians 5, Paul describes the lifestyle of a biblical man. He is a man of "love, joy, peace, patience, kindness, goodness, faithfulness, gentleness, and self-control" (5:22–23). This picture is illustrated in the following story.

> A little boy who, on the way home from church turned to his Dad and said, "Dad, the preacher's sermon this morning confused me."
>
> The father said, "Oh! Why is that?"
>
> The boy replied, "Well, he said that God is bigger than we are. Is that true?"
>
> "Yes, that's true," the father replied.
>
> "He also said that God lives within us. Is that true too?"
>
> Again, the father replied, "Yes."
>
> "Well," said the boy, "If God is bigger than us and He lives in us, wouldn't He show through us?"[3]

This is something we should really think about. When I owned my McDonald's franchise, I often wondered if my actions, my joy (or lack of joy), and my general approach to life reflected the Savior who came "that they may have

---

3 "God Is Bigger Than You and I," Kid's Korner, Skywriting.net, n.d., http://www.skywriting.net/inspirational/humor/KIDS-KORNER_03_on-going.html.

life and have it abundantly" (John 10:10). Only with the Holy Spirit will you have self-control, and only by receiving Jesus Christ as your personal Savior will you have the Holy Spirit. Your own self-control will invariably fail at the most crucial times.

Pastor Ed Jackson described men of great self-control as being like deep waters. Below the surface, the water may be churning, but on the surface, you see still waters, complete control. Men with quick tempers and little control are like shallow waters. When an event occurs, they have no depth and the surface is agitated very quickly.

No Holy Spirit equals no self-control.

You can fake it for a while, but only for a while. Being Spirit-controlled is easy when God is calling us to a situation that we want to be called to. If He calls me to be the quarterback and I want to be the quarterback, that's great; that's easy. But, if He calls me to be an offensive guard instead of the quarterback, that's hard. The real test of whether you are Spirit-controlled or controlled by your own nature is how you react when God calls you to represent Him in a situation you perceive as unfair.

I'm going to share some personal stories that have to do with me that are unfortunately failures on my part, but they illustrate my mistakes, which you can learn from.

My friend Rick Parcher, who was the head baseball coach at Tree of Life Christian High School, is a terrific person and coach. He has a favorite saying: "More athletes are ruined at the dinner table than are ever ruined on the playing field." It is hard not to be critical of the coaches and offer your own coaching nuggets at the dinner table. Even if you have some coaching experience, you don't work with the players every day and you don't know what the coach knows or wants.

My oldest son, Beau, played football in high school. In his junior and senior years, he was led to believe he had a legitimate opportunity to be the starting quarterback. In the off-season, he worked incredibly hard to be the best that he could be. While the circumstances and the particulars were different, each year the results were the same. He was treated unfairly. As his parents, we could document that different standards applied to him as opposed to others on the team. Can you see the situation clearly? Some of you are already siding with me and some of you are siding with the coaches, but for now, withhold your judgment.

To say that period of time was terrible in our family is quite an understatement. If you don't take anything else away from this book, *don't miss this, please*: No matter how unfairly Beau was treated, it was *my* actions that almost destroyed our family. I failed miserably as the head of God's Elite Force in this situation because I would not submit my prideful indignation to the Holy Spirit.

So, what happened in those two years? I polluted Beau's experience. Dinnertime was awful because I was critical and bitter about the coaches. After a while I didn't even try to disguise my feelings. I unloaded on Beau at the dinner table about what I thought. Then he had to go and spend the next afternoon with those men at practice. Somewhere along the line, Beau, in spite of me, moved into the role of encourager, becoming a wonderful teammate. But my constant complaining at home distorted his experience. I ruined it. My wife was literally physically sick during that time and afraid I would do something rash or foolish. She told me later on that for two years she really was anxious, in part because she was afraid that I was going to hit someone.

I have learned some things from these events and want to share them with you. I can't tell you in words how much anguish this brought to our home. In my son's senior year in high school, I missed the last five games that he played. I couldn't go to the games because I was so bitter. But my bitterness didn't hurt the coaches; they didn't care what I thought. The only people I was hurting was my own family.

What did I learn from that experience? First, unless a coach is immoral or abusive, we need to remember that God put him in a position of authority as stated in Romans 13:1. God appoints authority. That coach is there under God's authority. If you and I lose sight of the fact that God is in control, we begin to try to play God and get in the way of His plan. Earlier in the book we talked about men submitting to God as their wives submitted to them. I disobeyed 1 Peter 2:13 very clearly, "Submit yourselves for the Lord's sake to every human institution."

Romans 13:1 and 1 Peter 2:13 both apply to how we treat officials as well. As Christians, we have no business yelling at or demeaning officials. God is in charge, and if He wants a different outcome, He will make sure something else happens to secure His goal. In 1994, Worthington Christian High School lost the state basketball championship game in a heart-breaking fashion. Yet, the coach, Ray Slagle, wrote the following article. It shows a man who is Spirit-Controlled with Mature Discernment.

> The opportunity for a Christian to display God's gifts and talents is always available. To be able to do this with the world looking on is enviable. Such was the opportunity given to the members of the 1993–94 WCHS boys' basketball team as they competed in the State Final. Although that season will live on in the minds of some and certainly in relationships built, this will be for all intents and purposes its final legacy. Here are a few final, philosophical thoughts to ponder:
>
> - It's not the winning of the game that's important. In reality, neither players nor coaches can control outcomes. The important part of the game is performing to the best of one's ability.
> - The Lord will choose to use the outcome of a game for His glory. Therefore, it may be in His best interest for a team to "lose" in order for the gospel to be presented.

- It is the responsibility of each player and fan to conduct themselves in a way that Christ is honored. The world is not doing that. We can make a difference.

When my younger son, Stephen, later encountered some of those problems with coaches, I had vowed not to interfere. God worked out most of the issues without my help. It was remarkable that when I didn't get in God's way and create more problems, things seemed to work themselves out.

Secondly, I learned that high school athletics only have value in so far as they teach young people how to deal with real life. I love football. I love the game. I love the Xs and Os about football. I feel somewhat about football as General Patton did about war, "God help me, I love it!" However, football has little value short of what it teaches you about life.

One of my biggest concerns in the Crusader ministry is that we'll forget that truth and the emphasis in our ministry will change from having a great high school learning experience to focusing on athletic scholarships for college. If a youngster gets a scholarship, that's wonderful, but it's not the end of the world if you don't play college football. It is the end of your world if your priorities get so messed up that you lose sight of what is really important in life—God, relationships around you, and the way you can improve as a man.

I learned that a parent's job is to love their child and show them what God would expect of him. Beau couldn't learn from me about what God would expect of him in that situation because I totally blew it. I behaved so badly that what he learned from me was all wrong. Dads beware. You may think you just want the best for your child when you challenge the coach over playing time or position, but is the problem truly your child, or is it your bruised ego and pride? Seek what is really important to teach your child about life. I'm not saying the coach is right; I'm asking you what truths you are really teaching him. You may be unwittingly teaching him that he is a victim, that he should quit trying, and that God doesn't know or care about his situation.

I learned once again that if God gives you a wife, listening to her would be very helpful. Had I listened to my wife, I would have avoided many mistakes and missteps. My actions hurt my child and my wife. But the most important thing I learned is that putting that much focus on a child gives them the mistaken impression that they are the *center of the universe*. This can cause them to become totally self-absorbed, which is far from God's best. You can treat your child like they are the only ones with hardships and that only their hardships are important because the universe revolves around them. If the universe revolves around them, where does that put God? God's plan calls for not being selfish but being humble and serving others instead. As much as we love our children, we can hurt them in ways we could never imagine by acting as if they are more important than anyone else.

Because God is great, Beau has done very well, though he still carries many of the scars and aftereffects from that time in his life. You can get a pretty good read on your growth as a believer based on how you treat your wife and children and people in authority.

Most coaches just do their best. Many, if not most, see things differently than parents do. But, remember parents, you're not at practice every day. You don't know if your child hustles; you don't know if he knows his assignments; you don't know if he interacts well with his teammates; you don't know if he participates enthusiastically. And, even if you are at practice, you really don't get the subtle nuances of his instruction from the coaches.

In a junior varsity game one year, one of our coaches began to yell something to a player on the field. Since that coach did not work with that youngster's position, I found it odd that he was instructing that player. I turned to the coach and said, "Don't tell him to do that, that's wrong." He replied back to me, "Well, that's what his father was telling me to tell him."

I know many fathers coach the fifth quarter at home. They ask, "Why were you out of position on that defense?" But they don't know the defense. They think they know both the offense and the defense, but that is rarely the case. Dads, don't coach; just love, hug, and encourage your children. I can tell you that from hard experience. Fathers who coach at the dinner table almost invariably give not only poor advice, but usually the wrong advice.

Here's another classic Dad Stanley (me) story. My younger son, Stephen, played point guard on the basketball team at Worthington Christian High School. His job was to defend the opposing point guard. During the game, I would be in the stands yelling instructions to him to force the player to go to the left. Since the player was right-handed, I assumed he wanted to force him to his weaker side. However, that was not the system being taught by the coaches. They were teaching a system where the floor was split in half. It didn't matter which way the point guard went; the job of the defender was to keep him from coming back over the top. I didn't know that, but that didn't stop me from screaming instructions from the stands. Finally, my son had to come home and say to me, "Dad, you don't understand. That's not the system we play here." I felt like a total dolt and deserved to feel that way.

Dads, let the coaches do the coaching. You have a far more critical job to do in the lives of your children—model self-control by being Spirit-controlled.

J. O. S. **E.** P. H.

A MAN OF SERVICE IS AN:

EFFECTIVE LISTENER

As I've grown older, I realize one of the best indications of a person's servanthood is their willingness to listen. Selfish people talk too much; I often fall into this category. Selfish people talk all the time because the only person they think is important to listen to is themselves. Through the years, the Holy Spirit has really shown me that to be a man of Service you have to be an Effective Listener.

When I was first married, I would come home after practice and Sharilyn would ask me how my day went. I would lament about this youngster being hurt or the team not understanding the game plan. This went on for our first two or three months of marriage. Then one day it hit me that I never asked Sharilyn how her day had gone. Sharilyn was also a teacher and, frankly, a terrific one. One day, *after* she asked me how my day went, I decided in a magnanimous fashion to ask her how her day had gone. Her response was a classic. She said, "Why should I tell you? You don't really care anyway." I was stunned. If I really cared, I would have asked before. If I cared, I would have served her by listening carefully to her cares and concerns. It took me a long time to stifle my selfishness and listen more carefully to others. Truthfully, it's a battle I must fight every day.

To serve others you have to know their needs. To know their needs, you have to hear their concerns and care about the person. How can you care for a person's concerns if you don't know what they are? To know that requires effective listening. Why would someone share their heart with you if they know you're not really interested?

Do you care enough to turn off the television set when your children want to talk to you? I know a man whose son literally walked over to him, grabbed his face between his hands, and said, "Dad, I want to talk to you!"

Abraham Lincoln said it well when he said, "People don't care how much you know until they know how much you care." It doesn't matter how much information you have; if people don't think you care about them, they're not going to listen.

Biblically speaking, James 1:19 says, "Be quick to hear, slow to speak, and slow to anger." We are told to listen—to be men who are "quick to hear."

Listen first and well! Proverbs 1:5 says, "A wise man will hear and increase in learning and a man of understanding will acquire wise counsel." And Proverbs 12:15 says, "The way of a fool is right in his own eyes, but a wise man is he who listens to counsel." *Listens* not hears. Not just the physical act of hearing sounds, but the act of using all the senses to understand the other person's deepest felt needs.

Communication is so important. One of the classic stories from Sharilyn's family deals with my mother-in-law and father-in-law. I was so fortunate to have great in-laws, and I tell you this story with Helen's permission.

Dale and Helen had a car battery die in the early 50s, so Dale asked Helen to help him jump start the car. He told her he needed to get the stalled car up to thirty-five miles per hour before he could start it. So, Dale got in one car and Helen got in the other one. Dale was expecting Helen to nudge up against his car and push off slowly. To his surprise, as he looked in the rear-view mirror, Helen was speeding towards him at thirty-five miles per hour. Neither of them was hurt, but it does make a great story, illustrating how we need to communicate with each other very clearly and leave nothing for granted.

I used to teach a seminar in communication. If you are going to have a face-to-face conversation with someone you may need to confront or challenge, the first ten words that you say are the most critical words of the entire conversation. You will make the person relax or become defensive with your first ten words. If you have a situation where you have to communicate with somebody over a very touchy issue, write out your first ten words before you begin. If you don't actually write them out, you need to at least think about them really hard, because at the end of those ten words, you will have lost them if you opened the conversation wrong.

True listening requires active participation from you; serving others requires knowing that person and their needs. 1 Peter 3:7 says, "Husbands, live with your wives in an understanding way." This means to know her, which requires actively listening to her and asking questions.

This is a very touching story that demonstrates the fact that sometimes we assume too much:

> A man came home from work late, tired and irritated, to find his five-year-old son waiting for him at the door.
>
> "Daddy, may I ask you a question?"
>
> "Yeah sure, what is it?" replied the man.
>
> "Daddy, how much do you make an hour?"
>
> "That's none of your business. Why do you ask such a thing?" the man said angrily.
>
> "I just want to know. Please tell me, how much do you make an hour?" pleaded the little boy.
>
> "If you must know, I make $20 an hour."
>
> "Oh," the little boy replied, with his head down. Looking up he said, "Daddy, may I please borrow $10?"
>
> The father was furious, "If the only reason you asked that is so you can borrow some money to buy a silly toy or some other nonsense, then you march yourself straight to your room and go to bed. Think about why you are being so selfish. I work hard every day to provide for you and you greet me with such childish behavior."
>
> The little boy quietly went to his room and shut the door. The man sat down and started to get even angrier about the little boy's questions.
>
> "How dare he ask such questions only to get some money?"

After about an hour or so, the man had calmed down, and started to think: *Maybe there was something he really needed to buy with that $10. He really didn't ask for money very often.* The man went to the door of the little boy's room and opened the door.

"Are you asleep, son?" he asked.

"No daddy, I'm awake," replied the boy.

"I've been thinking; maybe I was too hard on you earlier," said the man. "It's been a long day and I took out my aggravation on you. Here's the $10 you asked for."

The little boy sat straight up, smiling. "Oh, thank you daddy!" He yelled.

Then, reaching under his pillow he pulled out some crumpled-up bills. The man, seeing that the boy already had money, started to get angry again. The little boy slowly counted out his money, and then looked up at his father.

"Why do you want more money if you already have some?" the father grumbled.

"Because I didn't have enough, but now I do," the little boy replied.

"Daddy, I have $20 now. Can I buy an hour of your time? Please come home early tomorrow. I would like to have dinner with you."[4]

---

4 "The Dad Gets Mad When His Son Asks About Money, But When He Sees Why, Everyone Should Read This," Newsner, published May 12, 2015, https://en.newsner.com/family/the-dad-gets-mad-when-his-son-asks-about-money-but-when-he-see-why-everyone-should-read-this/.

As a father, that's an arrow right through the heart. We often assume people, even our families, have some ulterior motive. Life is tough and sometimes we keep people at arm's length to protect ourselves from others' deepest needs. All this little boy wanted to do was spend time with his dad. I'm glad that story wasn't about me. I hope it's not about you either.

If we are Effective Listeners, we will avoid many of these mistakes. People who talk too much are boring. How are you doing in this area?

J. O. S. E. **P.** H.

A MAN OF SERVICE IS A MAN OF:

PRAYER

A man of Service, like Joseph, is a man of Prayer. Prayer is difficult for men for many reasons. We tend to be self-reliant and say, "Lord, tell me how to complete this task." While my mind is praying, I'm already figuring out the answer to my prayer. But prayer unlocks our relationship with God. It's more than just asking for His help.

Prayer can be difficult because you don't hear an audible response from God. Therefore, we need to know how God speaks to us today. Perhaps this little story might be useful in helping you feel more comfortable and at ease while praying.

> A man's daughter had asked the local pastor to come and pray with her father. When the pastor arrived, he found the man lying in bed with his head propped up on two pillows and an empty chair beside his bed.
>
> The pastor assumed that the old fellow had been informed of his visit.

"I guess you were expecting me," he said.

"No, who are you?"

"I'm the new associate at your local church," the pastor replied. "When I saw the empty chair, I figured you knew I was going to show up."

"Oh yeah, the chair," said the bedridden man. "Would you mind closing the door?"

Puzzled, the pastor shut the door.

"I've never told anyone this, not even my daughter," said the man. "But all of my life I have never known how to pray. At church I used to hear the pastor talk about prayer, but it always went right over my head. I abandoned any attempt at prayer," the old man continued, "until one day about four years ago my best friend said to me, 'Joe, prayer is just a simple matter of having a conversation with Jesus. Here's what I suggest. Sit down on a chair; place an empty chair in front of you, and in faith, see Jesus on the chair. It's not spooky because he promised, 'I'll be with you always.' Then just speak to him and listen in the same way you're doing with me right now.' So, I tried it, and I've liked it so much that I do it a couple hours every day. I'm careful though. If my daughter saw me talking to an empty chair, she'll think I'm either having a nervous breakdown or send me off to the funny farm."

The pastor was deeply moved by the story and encouraged the old guy to continue on the journey. Then he prayed with him and returned to the church.

> Two nights later, the daughter called to tell the pastor that her daddy had died that afternoon. "Did he seem to die in peace?" he asked.
>
> "Yes, when I left the house around two o'clock, he called me over to his bedside, told me one of his corny jokes, and kissed me on the cheek. When I got back from the store an hour later, I found him dead. But there was something strange, in fact, beyond strange, kind of weird. Apparently, just before Daddy died, he leaned over and rested his head on a chair beside the bed."[5]

In his book *How to Listen to God,* Dr. Charles Stanley gives us some helpful insights into prayer. To paraphrase, he says that God speaks to us today primarily in four ways. The first way is through the Word of God. When you have a problem and you pray for an answer, the Word of God is the number one place to look for answers. Many times, we pray and then we never read. So, how do we expect to find the answer? Often, I want an answer from God, but instead of going to God's letter to me, I just drive around all day thinking of my own solutions. Maybe they're from the Lord, maybe they're not. But the number one place to look for answers to prayer is the Word of God.

The number two place to look is the Holy Spirit. The Holy Spirit does convict us, move us, and draw us closer to answers. If we are Effective Listeners, God will perhaps use those around us to give us insights. The problem really arises when we know what to do and go a different direction because of our selfishness.

The third place to look is other people. God can use other people, even a non-Christian who doesn't know God. However, I will put a caveat on that and say that if I were asking for very serious advice about money or another critical life issue, I would go to a Christian for counseling. I would go to one

---

5 "The Empty Chair," JaredStory, n.d., http://www.jaredstory.com/empty_chair.html.

whom I believed to be "prayed up." Someone I believed to be living the Word of God—whom I believed would give me *God's best,* not their best.

And finally, God speaks to us through circumstances.[6] As I've told you before, I always worry a little bit about circumstances because I still think that open doors can be the open elevator shaft. I'm a believer in the test of time. I hear so many people tell me repeatedly, "God opened the door." How do you know God opened the door? Test your answer in the Word, by the Holy Spirit in prayer, and by wise counselors first.

Do your children see you pray? My dad told me that one of the most vivid memories he had was of his father falling asleep in the living room with his Bible on his chest. What a wonderful thing for a son to remember about his father. His father didn't do it to be remembered that way; he was remembered that way because it was his habit—the Habit of a Champion. Dr. Stanley also said, "If your child never sees his parents praying then he learns that fellowship with God is not required. That it's not necessary to ask God about the important matters of life. That trials and tribulations can be handled without any direction from God."[7] Prayer is critical; teaching prayer is critical. It is one thing that is both taught and caught.

Do you share answers to prayer with your children? We pray for things all the time, but do we talk to our children about when God answers prayers? Perhaps we do if the answer's obvious, but one of the ways a child's life can be enriched is in recognizing that the God of the universe cares enough to answer our individual prayers. I am always amazed at how He answers in such specific ways. I don't include this story to be sensational, but I include it to ask if you have ever dared to stretch your faith in God like Helen Rosevere, a missionary doctor from England to Zaire, Africa, who told this as it happened to her in Africa. She told her testimony one Wednesday night at Thomas Road Baptist Church:

---

6 Dr. Charles F. Stanley, *How to Listen to God* (Nashville: Thomas Nelson Publishing, 1985), 17.

7 Ibid.

"A LITTLE GIRL'S PRAYER"

One night, I had worked hard to help a mother in the labor ward; but in spite of all we could do, she died leaving us with a tiny, premature baby and a crying two-year-old daughter. We would have difficulty keeping the baby alive, as we had no incubator. (We had no electricity to run an incubator.) We also had no special feeding facilities. Although we lived on the equator, nights were often chilly with treacherous drafts.

One student midwife went for the box we had for such babies and the cotton blanket the baby would be wrapped in. Another went to stoke up the fire and fill a hot water bottle. She came back shortly in distress to tell me that in filling the bottle, it had burst. Rubber perishes easily in tropical climates. "And it is our last hot water bottle!" she exclaimed. As in the West, it is no good crying over spilled milk, so in Central Africa it might be considered no good crying over burst water bottles. They do not grow on trees, and there are no drugstores down forest pathways. "All right," I said, "Put the baby as near the fire as you safely can, and sleep between the baby and the door to keep it free from drafts. Your job is to keep the baby warm."

The following noon, as I did most days, I went to have prayers with any of the orphanage children who chose to gather with me. I gave the youngsters various suggestions of things to pray about and told them about the tiny baby. I explained our problem about keeping the baby warm enough, mentioning the hot water bottle. The baby could so easily die if it got chilled. I also told them of the two-year-old sister, crying because her mother had died. During the prayer time, one ten-year-old girl, Ruth, prayed with the usual blunt conciseness of our African children. "Please, God," she prayed, "Send us a water bottle. It'll be no good tomorrow, God, as the baby will be dead, so please send it this afternoon."

While I gasped inwardly at the audacity of the prayer, she added by way of a corollary, "And while You are about it, would You please send a dolly for the little girl, so she'll know You really love her?" As often with children's prayer, I was put on the spot. Could I honestly say, "Amen?" I just did not believe that God could do this. Oh yes, I know that He can do everything. The Bible says so. But there are limits, aren't there? The only way God could answer this particular prayer would be by sending me a parcel from the homeland. I had been in Africa for almost four years at that time, and I had never, ever received a parcel from home. Anyway, if anyone did send me a parcel, who would put in a hot water bottle? I lived on the equator!

Halfway through the afternoon, while I was teaching in the nurses' training school, a message was sent that there was a car at my front door. By the time I reached home, the car had gone, but there, on the verandah, was a large twenty-two-pound parcel. I felt tears prickling my eyes. I could not open the parcel alone, so I sent for the orphanage children. Together we pulled off the string, carefully undoing each knot. We folded the paper, taking care not to tear it unduly. Excitement was mounting. Some thirty or forty pairs of eyes were focused on the large cardboard box. From the top, I lifted out brightly colored, knitted jerseys. Eyes sparkled as I gave them out. Then there were the knitted bandages for the leprosy patients, and the children looked a little bored. Then came a box of mixed raisins and sultanas—they would make a nice batch of buns for the weekend. Then, as I put my hand in again, I felt the...could it really be? I grasped it and pulled it

> out…yes, a brand-new, rubber hot water bottle. I cried. I had not asked God to send it; I had not truly believed that He could. Ruth was in the front row of the children. She rushed forward, crying out, "If God has sent the bottle, He must have sent the dolly, too!" Rummaging down to the bottom of the box, she pulled out the small, beautifully dressed dolly. Her eyes shone! She had never doubted. Looking up at me, she asked: "Can I go over with you, Mummy, and give this dolly to that little girl, so she'll know that Jesus really loves her?"
>
> That parcel had been on the way for five whole months. Packed up by my former Sunday school class, whose leader had heard and obeyed God's prompting to send a hot water bottle, even to the equator. And one of the girls had put in a dolly for an African child—five months before—in answer to the believing prayer of a ten-year-old to bring it "that afternoon." "Before they call, I will answer!" (Isaiah 65:24)[8]

"There are also many hindrances to praying," as Dr. Stanley says.[9] Some of these hindrances are that we don't know God, we have a poor self-image, or maybe a false sense of guilt. (Remember that for the Christian, guilt is unnecessary. If you're feeling guilty and you think God is separated from you, go to God and confess your sins. You need to ask God for forgiveness and open the lines of communication.)

Busyness is another hindrance, as is anger directed at God and harboring sin. (If you have sin in your life, you need to deal with it.) Rejecting God's messenger is also a hindrance, as was the case of the man who prayed, "Lord, save me from the flood!"

---

8 Helen Roseveare. "The Hot Water Bottle," n.d., http://inspire21.com/stories/christianstories/thehotwaterbottle.

9 Charles F. Stanley, *How to Listen to God* (New York: Thomas Nelson, a division of HarperCollins, 2002).

> The rain was falling hard and the water was rising. The man was on the first floor of his house, and behold a rowboat came by. The man in the rowboat said, "Hey, you can come with us. Just get in the boat." The man in the house replied, "Oh no. God is going to save me."
>
> The water continued to rise so the man moved to the second floor. Along came a motorboat up to the second-floor window. The man in the motorboat invited the stranded man onto his boat. The man in the house again replied, "No, God is going to save me." And he continued to pray, "Lord save me!"
>
> Finally, the water rose to the top of the house. The man went out on the roof. While sitting on top of the house another boat came along with an offer of help. The man again replied, "No, no, no, God is going to save me." The water continued to rise, and the man drowned. As he stood before God he said, "I thought You were going to save me." And God said, "I sent three boats to save you, but you didn't take advantage of any of them."[10]

You see, sometimes we reject God's messenger instead of accepting the obvious way in which God has answered our prayer. He may answer in ways we do not expect. We need to be trained to listen.

The Moravian Church has been well known for its zeal and passion for missions. They recognize wonders can be done for God, but it all starts with prayer. Can you imagine this occurring today? In 1727, the Moravian community started a round-the-clock "prayer watch" that lasted *unbroken* for 100 years. There were about 300 persons in the community when the prayer watch began. Various people covenanted, or committed, to pray for one of the twenty-four hours. In 1792, *sixty-five years later*, with the lamp of prayer

10 Author unknown.

still alive, this small community had sent out 300 missionaries, a number sent equal to the entire group, sixty-five years earlier. The Moravians were utterly, radically committed to making Jesus known to the unsaved.[11]

When we truly *believe* God moves to His peoples' prayers, we will get serious about prayer. Remember that no one really believes something until they are willing to act on it. The wonderful thing about prayer is that you and I don't have to wait for anyone else in order to get started ourselves.

I believe in praying Scripture for your children by placing your children's names into the verse. In my case, I could paraphrase 1 Chronicles 29:19 for my youngest son like this: "Lord, give to my son Stephen a perfect heart to keep Your commandments, Your testimonies, and Your statutes." That is very powerful! Or Colossians 1:9–14 could be prayed for anyone you love by asking God to "fill them with the knowledge of His will." It asks Him "that they can walk in a manner worthy of the Lord." Who would not want to ask that for someone they love—perhaps your wife, son, daughter, or friend?

"Fill them with the knowledge of Your Will, Lord, so they can walk worthy of You. Bearing fruit in every good work; increasing in the knowledge of God; strengthened with power according to His might for the attaining of steadfastness and patience. Joyously giving thanks to the Father who qualifies as to share in the inheritance of the saints who delivered us from the domain of darkness, He transferred us to the kingdom of His beloved Son, in whom we have redemption, forgiveness of sins." Put your child's name in there, your wife's, your doctor's, or the President's name. You see, praying Scripture is always right; those are God's own words.

I read a book by Stormie Omartian called *The Power of the Praying Husband.* I really recommend it to you if you haven't read it. Oftentimes, we receive books like this from our wives and instead of reading it, we roll our eyes and put it aside. Please don't do that with this one. It is a magnificent book

---

11 "Herrnhut (The Lord's Watch) – 1727," The Hidden Ones, published July 30, 2012, http://hiddenonesmi.com/2012/07/30/herrnhut-the-lords-watch-1727.

filled with twenty different prayers you can pray for your wife that are filled with Scripture. It is full of insight on how to pray effectively for your wife.

One of the ways to begin to be proactive is to be a prayer warrior for your family. We need to cover our families, especially our wives, in prayer. Stormie said, "What you don't pray about in your life, you leave up to chance."[12] I don't believe in luck or chance, but what you don't pray about, you leave uncovered. That's not good enough for the heroic, warrior father God expects.

"WHAT YOU DON'T PRAY ABOUT IN YOUR LIFE, YOU LEAVE UP TO CHANCE."

One of America's great war heroes of World War II was General Douglas MacArthur. As fine a warrior as he was, he was also a warrior in prayer for his children. Let me share with you this inspiring prayer of his.

> Build me sons, O Lord, who will be strong enough to know when they are weak and brave enough to face themselves when they are afraid; sons who will be proud and unbending in honest defeat, humble and gentle in victory.
>
> Build me sons whose wishes will not take the place of deeds; who will know Thee—and that to know themselves is the foundation stone of knowledge.
>
> Lead them not in the path of ease and comfort, but under the stress and spur of difficulties and challenge. Here let them learn to stand up in the storm; here let them learn compassion for those who fail.

---

12 Stormie Omartian, *The Power of the Praying Husband* (Eugene, Harvest House Publishers, 2014), 25.

> Build me sons whose hearts will be clean, whose goals will be high; sons who will master themselves before they seek to master others; sons who will reach into the future, yet never forget the past.
>
> Give them, O Lord, a sense of humor so that they may be serious; yet never take themselves too seriously. Give them humility to always remember the simplicity of true greatness, the open mind of true wisdom, and the meekness of true strength.
>
> Then I, their dad, will dare to whisper: "I have not lived in vain."[13]

One of the greatest insights I got from Stormie's book was that 85 percent of women, when asked, "What is the most important thing that your husband could pray for?" responded that their husbands would pray that they would become the man, the husband, and the head of the home God wanted them to be. I would have thought that they would have wanted him to pray for good health, financial security, wisdom, understanding, or direction. But 85 percent of the women said what was most important for them to pray was that their husband would be the man God wants him to be. Please, Lord; make us the men You want us to be. I need to pray all the time; unceasingly, the Bible says (1 Thessalonians 5:16–18).

Imagine if we were prayer warriors like this next story illustrates:

> Some fathers deal with their sons eyeball-to-eyeball; others, nose-to-nose. My father dealt with me knee-to-knee.
>
> John Ashcroft had just moved from the governor's mansion in Jefferson City, Missouri to Washington, DC to become a United States senator.

---

13 BrainyQuote, "Douglas MacArthur Quotes," n.d., https://www.brainyquote.com/quotes/douglas_macarthur_115561.

"The night before I was sworn into the Senate in 1995, my father arranged for some close friends and family—maybe fifteen to twenty people—to gather for dinner. My father eyed a piano in the corner of the room and said, 'John, why don't you play the piano, and we'll sing?'"

"Okay, Dad, you name it, I'll play it."

"Let's sing, 'We Are Standing on Holy Ground.'"

It was one of his father's favorites, but he was not engaging in some sentimental ploy by suggesting it. He had a profound purpose in his request.

The family gathered the next morning at a house not far from the Capitol that was maintained by a group of friends for the express purpose of bringing members of Congress together for spiritual enlightenment. At the time, Ashcroft did not realize how weak his father was. He later learned that his father had told an acquaintance of his, "I'm hanging on by a thread, and it's a thin thread at that, but I'm going to see John sworn into the Senate."

As the family visited together, the earnestness of the senior Ashcroft's voice suddenly commanded everyone's attention. "John," he said, "please listen carefully." Everyone focused on John's dad.

"The spirit of Washington is arrogance," he said, "and the spirit of Christ is humility. Put on the spirit of Christ. Nothing of lasting value has ever been accomplished in arrogance. Someday, I hope that someone will come up to you as you're fulfilling your duties as a senator, tug on your sleeve, and say, 'Senator, your spirit is showing.'"

John then knelt in front of the sofa where his father was seated, and everyone gathered closer. When John realized his father was struggling unsuccessfully to lift himself off the couch, John said, "Dad, you don't have to struggle to stand and pray over me with these friends."

"John," his father answered, "I'm not struggling to stand. I'm struggling to kneel." John felt overwhelmed, humbled, and inspired all at the same time.

John was sworn into the Senate that afternoon. Early the next morning, on January 5, 1996, a friend awakened the Ashcrofts with the news that John's father had died. "John," the friend said, "There's something you ought to know. This was not a surprise to your dad. Yesterday your father pulled me aside and said, 'Dick, I want you to assure me that when John gets to his assigned offices, you will have prayer with him, inviting the presence of God into those rooms.'"

"I looked at your father and said, 'We'll do just that. And, as a matter of fact, we'll call you up in Springfield, put you on the speakerphone, and you can join us for the consecration.'"

"John, the next thing I knew, your father grabbed me by the arm and said, 'You don't understand. I'll be with you. But I won't be in Springfield.' He knew what was coming, John. He knew."

In 2001, Senator John Ashcroft left the Senate to become the Attorney General of the United States.

John Ashcroft is the product of a godly heritage. He would be the first to tell you that much of what he is today is due to his godly father. What heritage are you passing on to your children or to those whom God has placed in your life?[14]

---

14 E. Michael and Sharon Rusten, *The One Year Book of Christian History* (Carol Stream: Tyndale House Publishers, 2003), 10–11.

Personally, I have been challenged by this story to do a better job covering my family. Since we have not arrived, the key is improving. You can do it too, Dad. Remember, pray for yourself that you can be the leader your family needs and the man God wants.

FOUR PRIMARY WAYS GOD SPEAKS TO US:

- THE WORD OF GOD
- THE HOLY SPIRIT
- OTHER PEOPLE
- CIRCUMSTANCES

J. O. S. E. P. **H.**

A MAN OF SERVICE IS A MAN OF:

HOPE

A godly man of service is a man of Hope. Remember what faith is? Hebrews 11:1 tells us, "Faith is the assurance of things *hoped* for, the conviction of things not seen" (emphasis mine). What is hope? Hope is an unshakable confidence that things which haven't happened yet will. It's easy for us to become discouraged, but if you get discouraged, remember this story:

> The only survivor of a shipwreck was washed up on a small, uninhabited island. He prayed feverishly for God to rescue him,

> and every day he scanned the horizon for help, but none seemed forthcoming. Exhausted, he eventually managed to build a little hut out of driftwood to protect him from the elements, and to store his few possessions. But then one day, after scavenging for food, he arrived home to find his little hut in flames, the smoke rolling up high into the sky. The worst had happened; everything was lost. He was stunned with grief and anger, "God, how could you do this to me!" he cried.
>
> Early the next day, however, he was awakened by the sound of a ship that was approaching the island. It had come to rescue him. "How did you know I was here?" asked the weary man of his rescuers. "We saw your smoke signal," they replied.[15]

It is easy to get discouraged when things are going bad. But we shouldn't lose heart because God is at work in our lives, even in the midst of pain and suffering. The next time your little hut is burning to the ground, consider that it just may be a smoke signal summoning the grace of God.

Being a man can be wearisome. It is tiring, frustrating, and often we feel like throwing in the towel because no one appreciates us. Life is hard. Most guys I know wonder if it's worth keeping up the good fight. Being a husband is hard work. Being a father is *really* hard work. Being a grandfather is hard in a completely different way. We have all heard about how wonderful it is to be a grandparent; you get to play with the children, spoil them, and then give them back to the parents. But what if the parents decide to raise their child, your grandchild, in a way you don't agree with? That's really hard.

If we lose sight of the fact that we are men of hope, we might be inclined to give up the fight, walk away. We start to feel sorry for ourselves. We feel like no one appreciates us. Is it worth the effort? God knew we would feel this way and spoke to the issue in Scripture before the beginning of time. This is critical to know.

---

15 Ahmed Haroon. "The Only Survivor…" Ibearshad's Blog, published December 12, 2011, https://ibnearshad.wordpress.com/2011/12/06/.

In Galatians 6:7, God says, "Do not be deceived, God is not mocked. For whatever a man sows so shall he also reap." Some see this as a bad thing. If you do bad things, you will get bad things in return. The admonition is neither good nor bad; it's simply true. You will reap what you sow.

Galatians 6:8 says, "For the one who sows to his own flesh shall reap corruption, but the one who sows to the spirit shall from the spirit reap eternal life." It doesn't get any better than that. Hallelujah! Listen to this challenge from God in verse 9: "And do not let us lose heart in doing good, for in due time we shall reap if we do not grow weary." When you're feeling down, re-read this section of God's word.

Hebrews 10:23 says, "Let us hold fast the confession of our hope without wavering for He who promised is faithful." We've been given a job to do, a tough but fulfilling job by God Himself. The great news is that He chose us (Ephesians 1:4), He is faithful (Hebrews 10:23), and "He who began a good work in you will perfect it until the day of Christ Jesus" (Philippians 1:6). Those are promises. He chose you; He is faithful; He will finish the work He began in you. Be a man who finishes his life and can say, as Paul did in 2 Timothy 4:7, "I have fought the good fight, I finished the course, I kept the faith." For Manhood in Action, to stand before Jesus and have him say "well done" simply means that we ran the entire race without quitting. We ran with all the effort and enthusiasm we could.

I ask you to look for ways in which you can serve your wife and your children. I ask you to recognize that one of the most wonderful things we can do for your family is to care about them more than we care about ourselves. To do nothing from selfishness or empty conceit, but to regard them as more important than we are by listening to them and praying for their needs. And truly one of the most important things we can do for our family is to leave them with the greatest hope of all, as this story about Mikhail Kohre's father illustrates.

> He had grown up in Leningrad, where his father was a leader of a Baptist congregation. In 1938, church leaders were being arrested on a broad scale, and one day Mikhail had watched his father pack

his few possessions expecting to be jailed. In a backpack he put a shirt, a pair of thick, patched winter pants, boots he had soled himself, some underwear, a bowl, a spoon, and a mug. Then he sat down with his children at the kitchen table.

"Children," he said, "I am going on a long trip. I don't know if I will come home again. Only God knows the way and what difficulties will be on the path, or how long the journey will be. But as I begin this long journey, I want to agree where we will meet, so we will not lose each other." He explained that when people went to the train station or the market, they often agreed on a place to meet—perhaps at the entrance, or the information stand—in case they would get separated. He and his children should do the same thing in this situation, he explained. "We will be separated for a while. As soon as the heavenly Jerusalem comes, go to the white throne where Jesus will sit, and I will be there, too. We will see each other there and never be separated again." Then he took a pencil and began to draw the throne. Mikhail's father did all this without a trace of pathos. For him it was a certain thing, like making an appointment he was sure every member of the family would keep.

Four days later he was arrested. On that day, the "Black Raven," the wagon used to collect prisoners, stood outside the door of the house, waiting. The children watched as their father, his pack on his shoulder, got into the wagon looking back at them. Though he was guarded by soldiers, he smiled and raised his hand to say good-bye. Then the wagon door slammed shut, and he was gone. Eight months later he wrote his last letter and died perhaps an hour later. "When you hear that I have died," he said, "don't believe it, because whoever believes in Christ does not die but through death enters into life."[16]

16 Author unknown.

Thank you, Jesus, for You, Your Word, and Your People. God let us be flesh to the people You would want us to be. You tell us in your Word that people will know us by our love for one another. You also ask that we love one another as You have loved us. May we represent You, Lord, by being Your servants and "intentionally putting the needs of others first, expecting nothing in return." Let us become men of hope to a dying and lost world.

A MAN OF CHRIST

COMMITMENT = A PROMISE COMPLETED

HONOR = CHARACTER ABOVE REPROACH;
LIVING BY A BIBLICAL STANDARD

RESPONSIBILITY = TRUSTWORTHINESS DEMONSTRATED OVER TIME

INITIATIVE = BOLDNESS WITH INTEGRITY

SERVICE = INTENTIONALLY PUTTING THE NEEDS OF OTHERS FIRST, EXPECTING NOTHING IN RETURN

TRUTH = A STATEMENT OR PRINCIPLE THAT APPLIES TO ALL PEOPLE, IN ALL PLACES, AT ALL TIMES

C. H. R. I. S. **T.**

A MAN OF SERVICE

J. E. S. U. S.

JUSTIFIED

EXPECTS A HEAVENLY REWARD

STANDS FIRM AGAINST THE DEVIL

UNIQUE CALLING

SACRED MISSION

CHAPTER EIGHT

A MAN OF TRUTH

J.E.S.U.S.

COMMITMENT, HONOR, RESPONSIBILITY, Initiative, Service, and Truth. Of all of them, Truth is the most important quality of the biblical man. It is the trait that allows all the others to function.

When picking an acrostic for Truth, it was clear to me that no Bible character could be better than Jesus Himself. In John 14:6, Jesus said, "I am the way, *the truth*, and the life, no man comes to the Father, but through me" (emphasis mine). That is truth. When we talk about truth in Manhood in Action, we are talking about *the* Truth—that Jesus Christ is the one and only way to heaven. That may offend people; it may make them anxious; it may make them uncomfortable. But it is, in fact, the truth and foundation of Christianity.

Therefore, let's discuss the acrostic J. E. S. U. S. The letter J stands for Justified. First and foremost, a person must be Justified. The E tells us we should Expect a Heavenly Reward. The S is for Stands Firm against the Devil. It is important to know who the enemy is. The U is for Unique Calling. You and I have been given a unique calling by Christ. It is important for us to know what our calling is and to teach it to our children. And lastly, not only have we been given a Unique Calling, we have been given a Sacred Mission. If you want to be passionate about something in life, there can't be anything that is more worthy of your passion than knowing and telling the Truth.

This book will allow you to see the plan that Jesus has for the rest of your life regardless of your line of work, your personality, or your hobbies. Each of us is called by God to be His representative in a needy world. Friends, we are all called to the ministry of manhood.

J. E. S. U. S.

A MAN OF TRUTH IS:

JUSTIFIED

To be Justified is what's commonly known as being saved. Before we get too deeply into what this means, I want to make sure you really know how we are justified or saved. Perhaps you can identify with this man:

> A man dies and goes to heaven. Of course, St. Peter meets him at the Pearly Gates. St. Peter says, "Here's how it works. You need 100 points to make it into heaven. You tell me all the good things you've done, and I give you a certain number of points for each item, depending on how good it was. When you reach 100 points, you get in."
>
> "Okay," the man says, "I was married to the same woman for 50 years and never cheated on her, even in my heart."
>
> "That's wonderful," says St. Peter, "that's worth three points!"
>
> "Three points?" he says. "Well, I attended church all my life and supported its ministry with my time and service."
>
> "Terrific!" says St. Peter. "That's certainly worth a point."

"One point? I started a soup kitchen in my city and worked in a shelter for homeless veterans."

"Fantastic, that's good for two more points,"

"Two points!" the man cries. "At this rate the only way I get into heaven is by the grace of God."

"Exactly! 100 points! Come on in!"[1]

You see, we can't get to heaven on our own merits. It's impossible. We need God's grace—to receive His free gift given to us through Christ's death on the cross and His resurrection, which gave Him the right to be our personal Savior—the *way* into heaven. Given that, the question becomes, *"Will you accept God's free gift of salvation?"* Will the person who works next to you accept that free gift? Will they be justified? The next question might be, "How can a person become justified?" They need to receive Christ as Lord and Savior, and that's what I want to work through next.

There are hundreds of different ways to share the good news of Jesus Christ as Savior. One that I like very much is known as the "Roman Road," a series of verses in the book of Romans that lead us directly to an understanding of the truth. Romans 3:23 says, "All have sinned and fall short of the glory of God." All means all! There are people who really don't believe that this verse includes them. They compare themselves to those around them rather than to God and His perfect standard. God's standard for entry into heaven is to be perfect. Jesus Christ is the only person ever to live a perfectly sinless life. It is His sacrifice of shed blood on the cross that has paid the penalty for the sin of us all.

I heard a story about one of the great English preachers, who was giving a sermon outlining the sinfulness of man and God's provision for forgiveness.

---

1 "A Man Dies & Goes To Heaven. Of Course, St..." SermonCentral, December 8, 2005, https://www.sermoncentral.com/sermon-illustrations/22770/grace-by-sermoncentral?ref=TextIllustrationSerps.

He was approached by a woman in the congregation, who adamantly asserted her innocence, stating, "I have never sinned." The story goes that he then spit in her face and said, "What you are thinking right now is sin." Whether the story is true or not is debatable; however, the point remains that sin is insidious and permeates every area of our life. Sometimes we sin by what we do, and sometimes by what we don't do.

James 4:7 says, "Therefore, to one who knows the right thing to do and does not do it, to him it is sin." More difficult to address is that we also sin by what we think. "You have heard that it was said, 'You shall not commit adultery'; but I say to you that everyone who looks at a woman with lust for her has already committed adultery with her in his heart" (Matthew 5:27–28). Sin is not just what we do overtly, outside where people can see; it is also covert, what happens in our hearts. It includes what we think and what we believe. If it is not in concert with what Christ teaches us, it is sin. In our society today many people want to overlook sin as simply a mistake; no, a sin is a sin.

It has taken me a long time to understand that each of us has something in our life we don't want others to know. That is certainly true in my life. No matter how transparent we would like to believe we are, there are still things that we don't want others to know. There are thoughts that we have that we don't want others to know about. We each battle different battles and have problems we deal with—things that if left unchecked can easily become sin. The average person, however, confuses the true standard for heaven. They hold the attitude that they don't have to be perfect, just better than average. That is not the standard for entrance into heaven.

A pastor friend of mine once said, "There are two ways to heaven. One is that you can live a perfect life, the other is that you can accept Jesus as your savior." This may be theologically inaccurate, but he was trying to illustrate an important truth. He was trying to make the point of how ridiculous it was to believe that one can live a perfect life. You and I start out with what is termed "Adamic sin"; that is, sin inherited from Adam, the father of all mankind. Sometimes it is referred to as "original sin." The average person in our society believes that we start life as some sort of blank check, and we are either neutral or we are good. Most people think babies are good and innocent. Watch them for a while. They have a tremendous sin nature. It takes no effort to learn to sin, to be selfish, and to put our own needs first. No one has to teach a small child to lie.

There is only one way to heaven because no one can live a perfect life even if they tried with all their effort. The standard is perfection and you can't meet it. The standard is not, "Am I better than Ted Bundy, Adolf Hitler, or the Green River Killer, each of whom murdered countless humans?" That is not the standard. The standard is God Himself. Am I as pure as God? The answer, of course, is no.

One way to illustrate this fact is with a proposed swim based on good deeds people have done. You and three friends, whom you think are terrific people, are going to swim to Hawaii from California along with Billy Graham and Mother Teresa of Calcutta. You start off, get 100 yards offshore, and drown. Your friend, who is a great guy, manages to get 200 miles offshore and then he drowns. Your other friend, a really good man, takes off next and swims as much as 300 miles, but then he drowns. Billy Graham is a saint! He starts off next, gets 500 miles offshore and drowns. He and Mother Teresa go down at approximately the same place. If the swim represents your good deeds in life and Hawaii represents the goal of heaven, you can clearly see that you can never do enough good deeds to get there. So, if good deeds can't get us to heaven, how do we get there?

Romans 6:23 tells us, "The wages of sin is death," meaning that the consequence of falling short of God's standard, which is perfection, is death—both spiritual and physical. There are some in the world today teaching that after death there will be one more chance to accept Christ's sacrifice for your sin. That is not what the Bible says. Hebrews 9:27 says, "It is appointed for man to die once and after that comes the judgment." You do not get another chance after you die. This decision to accept or reject Christ comes here on earth. We need to know our Bibles well enough so we can gently correct a person who has been confused by this false teaching.

Romans 5:8 says, "But God demonstrated His love for us in that while we were yet sinners, Christ died for us." Christ didn't require us to clean up our act first. That is really good news. There's a tendency for us to believe that people must change certain traits and habits, especially if it is something we don't personally like, before they can come to Christ. Living a life pleasing to God the way we want to live is impossible without the indwelling Holy Spirit. We can't have the Holy Spirit dwell in us without recognizing who Jesus is: "In Him, you also, after listening to the message of truth, the gospel of your salvation, having also *believed*, you were sealed in Him with the Holy Spirit of promise" (Ephesians 1:13, emphasis mine).

In John 3:16, God tells of His love for us: "God so loved the world that He gave His only begotten son, that whoever *believes* in Him would not perish, but have eternal life." (Emphasis mine.) One of the most astonishing things for me is to believe that God would sacrifice His only son for me. With all due respect, there's no chance that I would have my kids die for you, no matter how much I love you. God, however, did that very thing. It is amazing to me the depth of the love that God shows to us to bring us into His Kingdom.

Romans 5:18 says, "So then as through one man's transgression there resulted condemnation to all men, even so, through one act of righteousness there resulted justification of life to all men." Adam's sin was the one transgression that the Bible is referring to, and because of that transgression, there was condemnation to all men born after Adam. But Christ's death and resurrection were the acts of righteousness that allow us to be able to be saved.

How shall we then be saved? Romans 10:9–10 actually uses the word "saved" as it pertains to salvation of our souls. The verses say, "If you confess with your mouth, Jesus is Lord, and *believe* in your heart that God raised him from the dead, you shall be saved. For with the heart man believes resulting in righteousness and with his mouth he confesses, resulting in salvation." In James 2:19 we are told, "Even the devil believes." So, there must be some specific kind of belief. We know the devil is not saved, so what does that tell us? It tells us that the devils (demons) believe in the historic Jesus Christ. Often, people will tell you, "I know that Jesus really lived and that he was a pretty good guy." The devil believes that, too. But that is not the belief that is necessary for entrance into heaven.

Jesus is also serious about a public confession of Him as your personal Lord and Savior. Matthew 10:33 says, "But whosoever shall deny me before men, I will also deny him before my father who is in heaven." Here, Jesus is straightforward. Romans 13:10 says, "Whoever shall call upon the name of the Lord shall be saved." While it is true that sometimes we require too much of a formula for the "right" words, Jesus does have clear instructions and expectations. I look at the thief on the cross and all the man did was say, "Jesus, let me be with you today in paradise" (Luke 23:42). It was simply, "Whoever shall call upon the Lord shall be saved."

Do you remember the story of John Newton? Even though his mother prayed for him faithfully for many years, he became a slave trader, led a life of debauchery, which included wine, women, and gambling. On one of his many sea crossings, a storm blew up and capsized his ship. While he was hanging on to a board in the middle of the ocean, he cried out to the Lord, "God, if you'll get me out of here, I will turn my life around." That was not a sophisticated, theological prayer; it was a heartfelt plea. "God, I know Who You are. You are the God of the universe and You can save my soul. Please save my soul!" John Newton was saved from that sea experience and became a pastor. He is best known as the writer of the well-known hymn "Amazing Grace," one of the greatest hymns in Christian history. His life was turned around and is a great illustration of repentance.

To repent is to turn around the other way. It is as if you are walking one way and you make a 180° turn and walk the other way. That was John Newton; that is Mike Stanley. My prayer was also simple and heartfelt: "Lord, if you're there, save me, because I've tried everything else. I have no other options. Please save me." Not a very sophisticated or theologically inspiring prayer, but God knew my heart.

The sincerity, the belief, the heart, that's what God is looking for. Jesus says, "I am the way, the truth, and the life" (John 14:6). So, justification, or salvation is not about religion, it is about a relationship with Jesus. You and I need to decide for ourselves what we will do.

This explanation is not original with me. St. Augustine explained it this way: Jesus was one of three things. He was either a liar, a lunatic, or he is, in fact, Lord. Those are your only options. If you say he was a liar, recognize that he taught against lying. He said lying was sin, which is wrongdoing. He would have to be teaching one thing and doing another. If you say he was a lunatic, his lifestyle did not indicate that. It would be strange to say that you are the Son of God, but there was nothing inconsistent in his behavior. He made a claim in the beginning and the same claim at the end of his earthly life. He never diverted from that claim. There was nothing mentally ill about the way he behaved. In fact, he cured people with mental illness. It doesn't make sense or match the facts to say he was mentally ill. Therefore, if he is not a liar or a lunatic, the only option you have left, if you are being honest and consistent, is that Jesus must be Lord, just as he claimed.

Have you asked Him to be your Savior? He is the only way. Some people resent that He is the *only* way. As human beings, we hate to be given only one choice. We may even feel there cannot be only one way because we wouldn't do it that way. The prophet Isaiah quoted God as saying, "My ways are higher than your ways" (Isaiah 55:9). We don't understand God. The best we can do is act on what God has clearly revealed to us.

Many people believe they are Christians and may not be. Going to church or being baptized doesn't make you a Christian any more than living in a barn makes you a horse. Jesus said in Matthew 7:21–23, "Not everyone who says to Me, 'Lord, Lord,' will enter the kingdom of heaven, but he who does the will of My Father who is in heaven will enter. Many will say to Me on that day, 'Lord, Lord, did we not prophesy in Your name, and in Your name cast out demons, and in Your name perform many miracles?' And then I will declare to them, 'I never knew you; depart from me, you who practice lawlessness.'"

I am truly sad that some churches who claim to be Christian churches are not teaching the truth about salvation. Why should that surprise us? Satan is a liar and the father of lies and he is shrewd. What better way to mislead people than by telling only part of the truth as he did to Eve in Genesis 3? Satan loves non-Bible-believing churches who teach a doctrine of "God is only love and will accept you into heaven no matter what you believe and practice." As Dr. Bridges points out, "God cannot express His mercy at the expense of His justice."

"TOLERANCE IN PERSONAL RELATIONSHIPS IS A VIRTUE, BUT TOLERANCE IN TRUTH IS A TRAVESTY."

Some people would tell us that Evangelical Christians are narrow-minded bigots because we don't tolerate any other way to heaven. We didn't set the rules, God did. In society today, many people worship at the altar of tolerance. The religion of tolerance is that anything a person does is all right and must be tolerated and embraced. The only sin in this religion is not tolerating another's position. I have often said, "Tolerance in personal relationships is a virtue, but tolerance in truth is a travesty." Governments must be willing to protect themselves and their people. To do so requires defining evil and sinful behavior and not tolerating such behavior. Our republic was built on the understanding that the Bible is God's Word and that the Bible defines acceptable and unacceptable behavior. There must be a basis for why killing is wrong.

My basis for why killing is wrong is because the Bible says it's wrong. When society allows all behaviors, nothing is wrong, and no action is to be condemned. Child molesters can behave as they wish because we no longer have an agreed upon set of moral values. As some have said, the Lord must punish us soon or He will have to apologize to Sodom and Gomorrah. And if there are no absolutes and no truth, why was Adolf Hitler wrong? We all know that Hitler was wrong, but just try to logically explain to an atheist why Hitler was wrong without using the Bible as a moral guide. They may say what he did was wrong because you shouldn't treat your fellow man that way. The problem is that their assertion is simply their opinion and has no more value than yours. Without God and His absolute truth, our society is doomed to fail.

Some claim Christianity is too narrow and restrictive. Being narrow or restrictive isn't bad unless it is narrow and wrong. For example, your pilot is told to fly at 35,000 feet. You don't want him at 34,000 or 36,000 because there are other planes flying at the other altitudes. You want your pilot to be very restrictive and very narrow about where he flies. Christianity is restrictive, that's true, but it is not exclusive. Don't let people fool you with terms. It is not an exclusive religion. It invites all who will to come. *All.* It doesn't matter what you look like, whether you are male or female, how much money you make—whosoever will, may come. It is restrictive but not exclusive.

Then perhaps someone will speak up and say, "But what about all the sincere people who sincerely believe in Allah?" Sincerity isn't enough. The nurse who sincerely believes she is hooking a patient up to oxygen when it is really nitrogen truly believes she is right. She is sincerely wrong.

Belief isn't enough. I don't care how strong your belief is. The key is the object of your belief. When I was a McDonald's owner, I had an employee who told me his power came from a stainless-steel ball that hung around his neck. He believed in that stainless-steel ball. We laugh at that, but he was sincere. It is not the sincerity of your belief or the strength of your belief; it is the object of your belief. What you believe in must be truth or your belief is worthless. Hopefully this story will illustrate why the object of your faith is the only real issue.

> Two men were hiking in Colorado in January. When dusk came upon them quickly, their only hope for getting back to the lodge before dark was to cut across the lake. One of the men was afraid the ice would not support him and hesitated. His friend reminded him that it was the middle of January, the ice had to be at least six feet thick, and they had no reason to worry. The frightened man had little faith and so he inched his way back to the lodge. The ice supported him; *his faith was weak, but the object of his faith was strong.*
>
> Later that year the two men were again hiking, and dusk came upon them suddenly. The once fearful man now suggested they cut across the lake. The first man, however, told his now brave friend that it was late May and the ice was not thicker than a quarter of an inch. But he could not be dissuaded, for his faith was great. So, he ventured a few feet from shore and crashed through the ice. *His faith was much stronger and more sincere the second time, but the object of this faith was very weak.* Our faith is only as justified as the object of our faith is able.[2] (emphasis mine)

Let me digress for a moment and ask you to examine the position of an atheist. It requires incredible faith to believe as atheists do. They contend that "no one

---

2 Ken Boa and Larry Moody, *I'm Glad You Asked* (Wheaton: Victor Books/SP Publications Inc., 1982/1994), 81.

created something from nothing." Now, that requires an immense amount of faith. Where did the stuff come from to bang in the Big Bang Theory? If you go back to when history began, something or someone had to create the first things. Either God created things, or material just appeared from nothing—not darkness—nothing. For me personally, this reality was one of the big steps in my coming to accept Christ. It just doesn't make sense to me that if there was nothing, something could come from that. It just isn't logical.

> One day a group of scientists got together and decided that humans had come a long way and no longer needed God. So, they picked one scientist to go and tell God so.
>
> The scientist walked up to God and said, "God, we've decided that we no longer need you; we're to the point that we can clone people and do many miraculous things, so why don't You just go on and get lost."
>
> God listened very patiently and kindly to the man. After the scientist was done talking, God said, "Very well, how about this? Let's say we have a man-making contest." To which the scientist replied, "Okay, great!"
>
> "But," God added, "We're going to do this just like I did back in the old days with Adam."
>
> The scientist said, "Sure, no problem" and bent down and grabbed himself a handful of dirt.
>
> God looked at him and said, "No, no, no. You go get your own dirt."[3]

---

3 Shaun, "Get Your Own Dirt," The Collection, June 2, 2012, https://cbclawrence.wordpress.com/2012/06/02/get-your-own-dirt.

Let's go a step further. How did we get eyes? Do you think an amoeba was swimming around in a muddy pool and ran into a rock and said, "I think I need an eye?" The eye is unbelievably complex, but evolutionists want us to believe it just happened; that there was no designer. Why aren't our noses upside down so we drown in the rain? How can people truly believe as atheists do that chaos produces order and design; that lifeless matter produces life; that chance produced intelligence?

The second law of thermodynamics is critical to understanding how our world is changing. On Earth, things go from order to disorder, as the second law of thermodynamics postulates. So things are becoming more volatile, more disorganized as the earth ages. Evolutionists contend that our world is changing from disorder to order randomly. They contend that everything is pure accident. That position is neither logical nor good science.

Evolutionists and atheists also believe the world is billions of years old because the theory of evolution requires millions of years to make it work. People begin to believe that with time, anything is possible. Our public schools continue to teach evolution as truth, not theory. To be an evolutionist requires far more faith than believing in an almighty God who designed, created, and still oversees our well-ordered, well-designed, logical physical world.

As we continue to review God's plan of salvation, we read in John 1:12, "For as many as *received* Him, to them He gave the right to become the children of God, even to those who *believe* in His name." (Emphasis mine.) So how do we receive Him? We just ask Him to be our personal savior. Romans 10:9 says, "Believe in our heart." So, what does believe mean? Practical belief is illustrated like this: When I flip on the light switch, I believe the light will come on. When I stand on a chair, I believe it's going to hold me. My friend Tom Smith says that you only believe something when you are willing to act on it. The following story proves just that.

> Charles Blondin, a Frenchman, was one of the world's finest tightrope walkers. In 1860, he successfully crossed the treacherous Niagara Falls (approximately a 1,000-foot span, 160 feet above the raging waters) on a tightrope. He then turned to the gathered crowd that was awestruck by this incredible feat and asked how many believed he could traverse the tightrope a second time pushing a wheelbarrow. The enthusiastic crowd cheered, acknowledging their belief in Blondin. Blondin succeeded, and then addressed the astonished crowd again, "Does anyone believe enough in me to get in the wheelbarrow and cross Niagara Falls with me?" No one volunteered! Finally, Blondin's manager climbed on Blondin's back, and they crossed the great chasm together. The crowd claimed with enthusiasm that they believed in Blondin, but they wouldn't get in the wheelbarrow. Jesus wants us to get in the wheelbarrow and He will do the rest.[4]

You should be able to point to a specific time or setting in your life where you acknowledged and accepted Christ as your personal Savior. Jesus holds out his hand and says, "Here is salvation." All you need to do is open your hand and accept it. Jesus has the cure for death, not just cancer, heart disease, and old age. He offers you the cure, but we must open our hand and accept it. The people in hell kept their hand closed and shook their fist at Jesus. Jesus loves you and me and "is patient toward you, not wishing for any to perish but for all to come to repentance" (2 Peter 3:9). All who will may come!

Keep this in mind when you have doubts about your faith and belief. "Faith is not the absence of doubt, it is a decision based on the evidence at hand."[5] Our lives have hardships and produce doubt from time to time, but

---

4 Boa & Moody, *I'm Glad You Asked,* 240.

5 Boa & Moody, *I'm Glad You Asked,* 242.

our salvation is based on Jesus's word, not our emotions. You may have doubt that flying is safe. But you still get on the plane believing that it will get you there safely. Remember also that Jesus said, "This is the will of him who sent Me, that of all that He has given Me, *I will lose nothing,* but raise it up on the last day. For this is the will of My Father that everyone who beholds the Son and believes in Him will have eternal life and I myself will raise him up on the last day" (John 6:39–40, emphasis mine). I don't believe that you can lose your salvation. You and I are weak and unstable at times, but Jesus is our rock. It is like a father holding the hand of his child. If the child stumbles, Dad doesn't let go. He hangs on. And that's just what Jesus would do. Day by day, your life is being transformed to be more like Christ.

Jude 1:24–25 says, "Now to Him who is able to keep you from stumbling and to make you stand in the presence of His Glory blameless with great joy, to the only God our Savior, through Jesus Christ our Lord, be glory, majesty, dominion, and authority before all time now and forever." Who is it that keeps us from stumbling? Clearly, Jesus Christ!

Perhaps this illustration will help you better understand my point. When doubts arise, they do not put a Christian salvation in jeopardy. Larry Moody and Kim Boas have written a tremendous book that addresses this issue called *I'm Glad You Asked.* It is one of the finest books on evangelism I have ever read. It lays out in a logical manner why faith makes so much sense. Their contention is that faith is not some sort of naïve, blind act, but is the natural reaction to the facts. The author of *Ben-Hur* and former governor of Arizona, Lou Wallace, came to know Jesus in a personal way after setting out to prove Jesus wasn't God.

> When doubts arise, they do not put a Christian's salvation in jeopardy. A visitor in Manhattan may decide to take the elevator up to the observation floor of the Empire State Building. When he steps on and the elevator begins to move, he has made an irrevocable decision that commits him to the whole vertical

journey. He may be gripped with a sudden panic after 15 seconds, fully convinced that the cable will break. But this does not change the fact that he will safely arrive at the observation deck. Similarly, coming to Christ does not involve intellectual assent alone but a willful choice to place one's eternal destiny in the hands of the Savior. This choice needs to be made only once; then regardless of how we feel, He will bring us safely to our destination."[6]

"A WILLFUL CHOICE TO PLACE ONE'S ETERNAL DESTINY IN THE HANDS OF THE SAVIOR."

—LOU WALLACE

Ephesians 1:13 gives us an amazing promise: "In Him you also after listening to the message of truth, the gospel of your salvation—having also *believed* you were sealed in Him with the Holy Spirit of promise" (emphasis mine).

What an incredible promise. The Holy Spirit will live inside followers of Christ and teach us and guide our lives.

My personal faith journey was impacted by three things:

The first was St. Augustine's explanation of the fact that the world could not have started when no one created something out of nothing. The second was the fulfilled prophecies in the Bible. They revealed to me that God was so powerful and completely in control, He was outside of time, able to see the end and the beginning at the same time. The third thing was changed lives, including my own, after trusting Jesus to save and protect me.

I had an uncle who was a psychiatrist at the Mansfield Reformatory in Ohio. Knowing he was an atheist, I asked him one time if he had ever seen anyone truly change while in prison who hadn't become a Christian. He thought about that for some time and then replied, "No." I found that

6 Ibid.

remarkable. I believe he remained an atheist until the day he died even though he saw the hand of God at work. He was a psychiatrist, trained to help people change their lives for the better, and yet, he never saw lasting change apart from Christ. The only lasting change occurs when the Holy Spirit came into a person's life. He knew it but refused to accept it.

"The evidence may be powerful, but one must choose to respond. This is where faith comes in, not against the evidence but as a response to it. Belief in God is not a leap into the dark but a step into the light."[7]

I would like to make two more points about being justified. Some people call religion a crutch. Crutches are good in the right circumstances. However, a relationship with Christ is not a crutch, it's a cure. It is a cure for what ails us—sin. The other objection and criticism I hear often is, "There are hypocrites in that church." Yes, that is true in some cases, but sometimes people feel this way because they don't understand what a hypocrite is. A hypocrite is someone who claims he is one thing and behaves in another way. I am not a hypocrite because I know I am a sinner saved by God's grace. True Christians understand what God has done for them. They realize they aren't perfect, but that they are, in fact, forgiven.

Churches should be hospitals for sinners, not museums for saints. Sometimes churches seem to want all the unhealthy people to stay out of their church. Where else should they be? They came for the cure, but too often those who have had the cure for a long time begin to look down their noses at those in need. What a tragedy. Justification is by faith, not by any amount of good works we do. This is Truth.

Sometimes people reject Jesus because the world has so much suffering. It reminds me of the story about a minister and a barber who boasted of being an atheist. One day they walked through a disreputable part of the city. As they looked around the barber said, "This why I can't believe in a God of love. If He is as kind as they say why does He permit all this poverty, disease,

---

7 Boa & Moody, *I'm Glad You Asked,* 26.

and squalor? How can He allow all this drug dealing and vandalism?" The minister said nothing until they came across an unkempt and filthy man with hair down his back and a half inch of stubble on his face. Then he said to the atheist, "You can't be a very good barber, or you wouldn't let people like this live around here without a haircut and a shave." Indignantly the barber answered, "Why do you blame me for that man's condition? I can't help it if he looks like that; he's never given me a chance! If he would only come to my shop, I could fix him up and make him look like a gentleman." With a penetrating look the minister said, "Then don't blame God for allowing people to continue in their evil ways. He constantly invites them to come to Him and be changed. The reason they are slaves to sin and evil habits is because they refuse to accept the One who died to save and deliver them."[8]

Now is the time. Have you asked God to save and justify you?

Lord Jesus, I know I am a sinner and that sin keeps me from heaven. I know that You died to pay the penalty for my sin. I ask You, Jesus, to be my Savior and friend because I trust You alone to save me and give me an abundant life. Thank You, Jesus!

J. **E.** S. U. S.

A MAN OF TRUTH:
EXPECTS A HEAVENLY REWARD

The E in Jesus stands for Expect a Heavenly Reward. This is so critical, Dad, that you and I understand we are not working for the here and now only. We're working for a reward that comes much later in heaven. As men, we should live our lives as Hebrews 12:2 says to: "Fixing our eyes on Jesus, the

---

8 Boa & Moody, *I'm Glad You Asked,* 137–38.

author and perfecter of our faith." We should look at the time when we could go to our true home and see what Jesus has prepared for us there.

As our lives near completion, I hope that we have lived with the perspective that this missionary couple had.

> A large ocean liner pulled into the dock at New York harbor. Aboard were many people including a famous general returning home after a great military victory. Also, on board were an old missionary and his wife, who had stood tall with her husband all the many years they had served their Lord overseas.
>
> Thousands met the huge ocean liner to help welcome home this famous general. A parade had been arranged, army troops were to parade in his honor and a very festive occasion was in the offing.
>
> No one was there to meet the missionary and his wife. They looked through the large crowd for a familiar face; however, their family all lived far away out west, and no one they knew lived close by. They felt alone and somewhat neglected. They had served so faithfully for so many years, yet their many efforts and their long life of sharing the Gospel of the Lord Jesus seemed to have been overlooked.
>
> The couple needed to get to the nearest bus station so they could start their long trip to their home and family. They hired a taxicab and started down the boulevard. How thrilled they were, as was everyone in the street that day, with the great pomp and ceremony of the general's homecoming. People lined the streets. Banners, flags and balloons helped make this a very jubilant occasion.
>
> As they rode in a taxi to the bus terminal, the old missionary looked out the window at the great crowds and the festive decorations.

> He mused over all this and asked his wife, "This isn't much of a homecoming for us, is it?"
>
> His wife took his arm, as she had done so many times when his ministry seemed to be going nowhere, and uttered these words of encouragement, "Don't worry about all this, my dear. You must remember, we are *not home yet*!"[9] (emphasis mine)

We must realize the important distinction of who receives the warm welcome here, or when we arrive at the gates of God's Kingdom when we *really* return home. Those who will receive the greatest rewards will be those who, like this missionary, have been faithful in their service to the Lord. Military victories, political landslides, athletic awards, and all those achievements that we attach so much significance to here will not be noticed at all up there. Those who have been faithful will be welcomed with open arms. The Scriptures tell us that those who have laid up treasures in heaven will find them *all there.*

The following story entitled "Keep your Fork" should give us all a wonderful sense of the joy that awaits us.

> There was a woman who had been diagnosed with a terminal illness and had been given three months to live. So, as she was getting her things "in order" she contacted her pastor and had him come to her house to discuss certain aspects of their final wishes.
>
> She told him which songs she wanted sung at the service, what scriptures she would like read, and what outfit she wanted to be buried in. The woman also requested to be buried with her favorite Bible.

---

9 222 Men's Fellowship, "2-21-2018 Greetings Men of 222, Billy Graham died today! If you are a Christian…" Facebook, February 21, 2018, https://www.facebook.com/222MensFellowship/posts/2-21-2018greetings-men-of-222billy-graham-died-today-if-you-are-a-christian-you-/1798558286883366/.

Everything was in order and the pastor was preparing to leave when the woman suddenly remembered something very important to her. "There's one more thing," she said excitedly.

"What's that?" came the pastor's reply.

"This is very important," the woman continued. "I want to be buried with a fork in my right hand."

The pastor stood looking at the woman, not knowing quite what to say.

"That surprises you, doesn't it?" The woman asked.

"Well, to be honest, I'm puzzled by the request," said the pastor.

The woman explained, "In all my years of attending church socials and potluck dinners, I always remember that when the dishes of the main course were being cleared, someone would inevitably lean over and say, 'keep your fork.' It was my favorite part because I knew that something better was coming...like velvety chocolate cake or deep-dish apple pie. Something wonderful, and with substance! So, I just want people to see me there in that casket with a fork in my hand and I want them to wonder 'What's with the fork?' Then I want you to tell them: 'Keep your fork...the best is yet to come.'"

The pastor's eyes welled up with tears of joy as he hugged the woman goodbye. He knew this would be one of the last times he would see her before her death. But he also knew that the woman had a better grasp of heaven than he did. She *knew* that something better was coming.

At the funeral people were walking by the woman's casket and

> they saw the pretty dress she was wearing, her favorite Bible, and the fork placed in her right hand.
>
> Over and over, the pastor heard the question, "What's with the fork?" and over and over he smiled. During his message, the pastor told the people of the conversation he had with the woman shortly before she died. He also told them about the fork and about what it symbolized to her. The pastor told them that they probably would not be able to stop thinking about it either.
>
> He was right.
>
> So, the next time you reach down for your fork, let it remind you oh so gently, that the best is yet to come.[10]

The greatest thrill here or in the life to come will be that moment when we see Jesus and He welcomes us *home* with the greeting, "Well done, thou good and faithful servant! Well done!" If your goal is as mine, to stand before Jesus and have Him say "well done," we need to live our day-to-day lives working to please Him.

Some people are described as being so heavenly minded they are no earthly good. If they are, they are missing a huge part of God's plan. We have a significant role to perform on earth before we get to heaven. Ephesians 2:8–10 gives us insight into this role: "For by grace you have been saved through faith; and that not of yourselves, it is the gift of God not as a result of works to that no one may boast." But keep reading, because verse 10 says, "For we are His workmanship, created in Christ Jesus for good works which God prepared beforehand for us to do."

You and I are here to be servants of Jesus Christ to those around us. We tend to lose our focus at times. The present world is our playing field. Play

---

10 Guideposts, "Why Do People Say Keep Your Fork?" Guideposts.org, last modified November 23, 2010, https://www.guideposts.org/inspiration/life-after-death/why-do-people-say-keep-your-fork.

smart. Play hard. Play to win. Be God's ambassador out there. 1 Corinthians 3:10–15 encourages us to do good works intentionally so when we get to heaven we can expect heavenly rewards. Take God at His Word.

J. E. **S.** U. S.

A MAN OF TRUTH:
STANDS FIRM AGAINST THE DEVIL

To win this critical battle, we must live the S in Jesus—Stand Firm against the Devil. In any struggle, we need to know as much about our opponent as possible and never underestimate him. However, we must never overestimate him either.

When I was a young man, I used to wrestle. One of my opponents was known as a real stud. He was bigger than me, taller than me, and a really good athlete. I was a first-year wrestler when we had our first match together. Even though everyone said he was going to "kill me," I beat him the first three times we wrestled. The next meeting was at a big invitational tournament at his home school. I was to meet him in the first round of this tourney. I began to rehearse to myself the other wrestler's attributes; how he was so tall, so big, so athletic, and how even though I had beaten him, our matches were close. So I wrestled him, and he absolutely walloped me.

I learned a great lesson from that defeat. I had made my opponent larger than life in my mind. I wrestled him twice more that year and never lost to him again. I respected him, but I also respected myself and didn't make him out to be better than he was.

We don't want to underestimate Satan, but we don't want to overestimate him either. Satan isn't like Jesus Christ who is God. God is omnipresent (present everywhere) whereas Satan can only be in one place at a time, and most of his time is spent in Washington DC!

1 John 4:4 says, "Greater is He that is in you than He who is in the world." Satan is an equal with angels like Michael and Gabriel, but not with Jesus. Satan is described in the Bible as "a murderer from the beginning, a liar and the father of lies; He does not stand in the truth." John 8:44 tells us he is an evil being. Don't forget that. We must respect him, but we must not fear him. Jesus can protect us quite well.

We must never lose sight of the fact that the Devil tries to distort everything. Christians need to stand on the risen Savior Himself because He is greater than he who is in the world. In his book *Wild at Heart*, John Eldredge says men need a battle to fight. There is no bigger battle than fighting Satan day in and day out during our earthly lives. There is no more important battle either, and we need to teach our children that we must keep up the good fight and expect a heavenly reward. Jesus did!

Paul warned us in Ephesians 6:11 to "Put on the whole armor of God that you may be able to stand firm against the schemes of the devil." The devil is smart. I quoted the Bible to say that he is a murderer and a liar; nowhere in the Scripture does it describe Satan as dumb. He is not. He is very smart, and he has a lot of experience—since the beginning of earth's history.

The same temptations work now that worked in David's time; it's human nature. Pray or pray and fast to prepare for the battle, but we must stand firm. You've got to stand firm and pray. What a noble cause we, the believers, have been entrusted with. We have been given the opportunity by God to stand for Him here and to spread the good news about Jesus. What an honor. But we must stay connected to Christ so that we have the power to overcome. John 15:5 says, "I am the vine and you are the branches; he who abides in Me and I in him, he bears much fruit, *for apart from me you can do nothing*" (emphasis mine).

As Oswald Chambers said, "When the crisis comes and courage is required, God expects His men to have such confidence in Him that they will be the dependable ones." The way we can be able to Stand Firm Against the Devil is by having a close trusting relationship with God through the Holy Spirit.

EPHESIANS 6:10–18 (NASB)

10 FINALLY, BE STRONG IN THE LORD AND IN THE STRENGTH OF HIS MIGHT.

11 PUT ON THE FULL ARMOR OF GOD, SO THAT YOU WILL BE ABLE TO STAND FIRM AGAINST THE SCHEMES OF THE DEVIL.

12 FOR OUR STRUGGLE IS NOT AGAINST FLESH AND BLOOD, BUT AGAINST THE RULERS, AGAINST THE POWERS, AGAINST THE WORLD FORCES OF THIS DARKNESS, AGAINST THE SPIRITUAL FORCES OF WICKEDNESS IN THE HEAVENLY PLACES.

13 THEREFORE, TAKE UP THE FULL ARMOR OF GOD, SO THAT YOU WILL BE ABLE TO RESIST IN THE EVIL DAY, AND HAVING DONE EVERYTHING, TO STAND FIRM.

14 STAND FIRM THEREFORE, HAVING GIRDED YOUR LOINS WITH TRUTH, AND HAVING PUT ON THE BREASTPLATE OF RIGHTEOUSNESS,

15 AND HAVING SHOD YOUR FEET WITH THE PREPARATION OF THE GOSPEL OF PEACE;

16 IN ADDITION TO ALL, TAKING UP THE SHIELD OF FAITH WITH WHICH YOU WILL BE ABLE TO EXTINGUISH ALL THE FLAMING ARROWS OF THE EVIL ONE.

17 AND TAKE THE HELMET OF SALVATION, AND THE SWORD OF THE SPIRIT, WHICH IS THE WORD OF GOD.

18 WITH ALL PRAYER AND PETITION PRAY AT ALL TIMES IN THE SPIRIT, AND WITH THIS IN VIEW, BE ON THE ALERT WITH ALL PERSEVERANCE AND PETITION FOR ALL THE SAINTS.

J. E. S. **U.** S.

A MAN OF TRUTH HAS A:

UNIQUE CALLING

Now if we are Justified and we Expect a Heavenly Reward and we Stand Firm against the Devil, then the U stands for Unique Calling. We are called personally by Christ according to Mark 12:31–32 when He says, "You shall love the Lord your God with all your heart, all your soul, all your mind and all your strength. And the second is, You shall love your neighbor as yourself. There is no greater commandment than these." We are called to love God and to love one another. Some folks just aren't very lovable. Nevertheless, God's call to us is very clear. It is simple but not easy.

Could you see yourself as the hero of this story? To love our neighbor, we must see them, care for them, and be committed to loving them as this lady was.

> This story starts out where she, Beth, is sitting at an airport terminal, waiting to board a plane. She was sitting there with several other people who were also waiting, whom she did not know.
>
> As she waited, she pulled out her Bible and started reading. Suddenly, she felt as if the people sitting there around her were looking at her. She looked up but realized that they were looking just over her head, in the direction right behind her.
>
> She turned around to see what everyone was looking at, and when she did, she saw a stewardess pushing a wheelchair, with the ugliest old man sitting in it, that she has ever seen before. She said he had this long, white hair that was all tangled and such a mess. His face was really, really wrinkled, and he didn't look friendly at all.

She said she didn't know why, but she felt drawn to the man, and thought at first that God wanted her to witness to him. In her mind she said she was thinking, "Oh, God, please, not now, not here."

No matter what she did, she couldn't get the man off of her mind, and all of a sudden, she knew what God wanted her to do. She was supposed to brush this old man's hair.

She went and knelt down in front of the old man, and said, "Sir, may I have the honor of brushing your hair for you?"

He said, "What?"

She thought, "Oh great, he's hard of hearing." Again, a little louder, she said, "Sir, may I have the honor of brushing your hair for you?"

He answered, "If you are going to talk to me, you are going to have to speak up, I am practically deaf."

So, this time, she was almost yelling, "Sir, may I please have the honor of brushing your hair for you?"

Everyone was watching to see what his response would be. The old man just looked at her confused, and said, "Well, I guess if you really want to."

She said, "I don't even have a brush, but I thought I would ask anyway."

He said, "Look in the bag hanging on the back of my chair; there is a brush in there."

So, she got the brush out and started brushing his hair. (She had a little girl with long hair, so she had lots of practice getting tangles out, and knew how to be gentle with him.) She worked for a long time, until every last tangle was out.

Just as she was finishing up, she heard the old man crying, and she went and put her hands on his knees, kneeling in from of him again looking directly into his eyes, and said, "Sir, do you know Jesus?"

He answered, "Yes, of course I know Jesus. You see, my bride told me she couldn't marry me unless I knew Jesus, so I learned all about Jesus, and asked Him to come into my heart many years ago, before I married my bride."

He continued, "You know, I am on my way home to go see my wife. I have been in the hospital for a long time and had to have a special surgery in this town far from my home. My wife couldn't come with me, because she is so frail herself." He said, "I was so worried about how terrible my hair looked, and I didn't want her to see me looking so awful, but I couldn't brush my hair, all by myself."

Tears were rolling down his cheeks as he thanked Beth for brushing his hair. He thanked her over and over again.

She was crying, people all around witnessing this were crying, and as they were all boarding the plane, the stewardess, who was also crying, stopped her and asked, "Why did you do that?"

And right there was the opportunity, the door that has been opened to share with someone else, the love of God. We don't always understand God's ways, but be ready; He may use us to meet the need of someone else, like He met the need of this old man, and in that moment, also calling out to a lost soul who needed to know about his love.[11]

11 Skywriting.Net, "Tangled Hair – Caring Heart," www.skywriting.net/inspirational/messages/tangled_hair-caring_heart.html.

In Romans 12:17–18, we are given some practical advice on how to love men and women, especially those we don't like. Paul says, "Never pay back evil to anyone. Respect what is right in the sight of all men and if possible, so far as it depends on you be at peace with all men." Are you up to the challenge?

Let me tell you a life-changing experience of one of the finest men I have ever known. His name was Ed Jackson, a former Ohio State Highway Patrolman, and pastor in the fellowship of Grace Brethren Churches. Ed had served his country in the military and was a patriot's patriot. When he saw the flag, he recognized that freedom isn't free. So the Vietnam protests in the early `70s really bothered him.

In 1972, The Ohio State University campus was in tremendous upheaval, as were many other college campuses during that part of the Vietnam War. The student body was in great unrest. Many were sincerely anti-war, others just wanted to get out of class, and still others just wanted to be destructive. One day, Ed and some other patrolmen were protecting the administration building while protestors were outside throwing rocks and other things and burning the American flag. Ed had been given an undercover assignment as a photographer so that students and others on campus would think he was with a newspaper company.

As the riots broke out, the students laid siege to the administration building. The police and the highway patrol responded with tear gas. The tear gas permeated the air, burning the eyes of all who were in the vicinity. The patrolmen radioed to those on the outside requesting gas masks as the tear gas was getting thick inside the building as well. Ed and two or three others brought the gas masks in by way of underground heating and ventilation tunnels large enough to walk through. There were now six or seven highway patrolmen inside the building.

As the situation intensified, Ed became more and more disgusted by the behavior of the mob. At one point a young man threw a brick at the window from close proximity. As he turned to retreat to the relative safety of the crowd, he was hit in the eye by another brick that had been thrown by someone in the mob. He fell to the ground screaming for help with his orbital bones crushed and the eye hanging precariously from the socket. He lay there screaming for someone, anyone to help him.

Ed and the other men had a dilemma. No one in the crowd was going to help this fellow and the patrolmen didn't really want to either. To help this young man would require them to sacrifice their personal safety. But, putting their personal feelings aside, they did rush out to give aid to this person, dragging him back to safety and giving him the help he needed. Ed remembers looking at this still-screaming boy and thinking to himself how unlovely this guy was. Ed felt as if the Lord said to him, "He sure is unlovely, isn't he, Ed?" Ed answered the Lord, "He sure is, Lord. He burns my flag, throws rocks and bricks at public property, throws urine on fellow officers. He sure is unlovely, Lord." Then Ed says the Lord simply said to him, "So were you, Ed. So were you!"

Ed's life changed that day as he realized that God had seen him just as he saw this unworthy student. We must never become so high and mighty that we forget our own sin and believe we are righteous in our own right. Ephesians 4:32 makes it very clear why we should care about one another: "Be kind to one another, tender-hearted, forgiving each other, just as God in Christ also has forgiven you."

Pastor Ed's story reminds me that I often feel other people don't measure up to my standard and then I realize how far I am from God's standard. In spite of my failings, idiosyncrasies, and shortcomings, God loves me and expects me to love others. In fact, He commands us to love others: "A new commandment I give to you, that you love one another, even as I have loved you, that you also love one another" (John 13:34). We forgive and love not because someone deserves it, but because Christ forgave and loves us even though we don't deserve it, either.

The Golden Rule in Luke 6:31 (NKJV) says, "And as ye would that men should do to you, do ye also to them likewise." That is, do unto others as you would have them do unto you. This is not just great advice to live by; this is what God calls us to do. Love God and those whom God loves, which is everyone. If you and I can live that way and teach our children that they have a unique calling, our world would be a better place where God is honored. As Christians, we are called to a much higher standard than the rest of society.

However, sometimes Christians study the Bible but never apply what we learn. If we don't love others, we are in danger of becoming like the Dead Sea. A few miles south of Jerusalem, the Dead Sea is the lowest place on earth—1,476 feet below sea level. Six and a half million tons of water flow into it every day from the Jordan River. But the Dead Sea has no outlet. Everything flows in, nothing flows out. Because of that, the water had become incredibly salty and absolutely nothing can live there. No plant life can exist. If a fish flows into the Dead Sea, it dies almost immediately. The whole thing is completely dead. A lot of Christians are just like the Dead Sea—stuff flows into them like crazy, but nothing flows out.

As Christians, we are God's chosen people on earth to represent Him. We have a calling unlike any other people. We should be overwhelmed with appreciation to serve Him in a dark and dreary world. How are you doing with that? Change intentionally if need be. As my friend Mike Hassey always says, "It's either day one or one day." Let's make today day one.

J. E. S. U. **S.**

A MAN OF TRUTH HAS A:

SACRED MISSION

Lastly, the final S in Jesus stands for Sacred Mission. If there ever was an adventure to live, it is the Sacred Mission God has called us to as we represent Him. Isn't it amazing that the God of the universe has given you and me The

Truth? He has given us the mission to act as ambassadors to those who don't know Him. If you want to feel that your life has true meaning and be filled with a passion for each day, dedicate your life to telling the good news of Jesus Christ, the sacred mission for all Christians.

You and I have been entrusted to take the Word of God to the world. Matthew 28:18–20 tells us, "All authority has been given to Me in heaven and on earth. Go therefore and make disciples of all the nations, baptizing them in the name of the Father and the Son and the Holy Spirit, teaching them to observe all that I commanded you; and lo, I am with you always, even to the end of the age." If you know what God has done for you, you will love Him. If you love Him, you will serve Him. We serve Him by telling people about Jesus and teaching them who Jesus is.

Are you committed to sharing the gospel? Do you remember the Moravian Church and their 100-year prayer vigil? They didn't just pray, they acted. They knew the secret of loving the souls of men was found in loving the Savior of men.

On October 8, 1732, a Dutch ship left Copenhagen harbor bound for the Dutch West Indies. On board were the first two Moravian missionaries—John Duber, a potter, and David Nitschman, a carpenter. Both were skilled speakers and *ready to sell themselves into slavery to reach the slaves of the West Indies*. As their ship slipped away from the dock, they lifted up the cry that would one day become the rallying cry of all Moravian missionaries, "May the Lamb that was slain receive the reward of His suffering." The Moravians' passion for souls was surpassed only by their passion for the Lamb of God, Jesus Christ!

Could you present the gospel to someone? According to statistics only 10 percent of the Evangelical church has ever presented the gospel to someone! I can't believe that. What a privilege to have someone come to know the Lord as you share the gospel. It's not you or me who brings the person to an understanding of the truth. It's the Holy Spirit.

So if you get turned down, you need to remember it's not you they are rejecting, it's God.

Penn Jillette the atheist illusionist made this point: "I don't respect people who don't proselytize. I don't respect that at all. If you believe there is a heaven and hell, and people could be going to hell or not getting eternal life or whatever, and you think it's not really worth telling them this because it would make it socially awkward. How much do you have to hate somebody to not proselytize? How much do you have to hate someone to believe everlasting life is possible and not tell them that?"[12]

Have you ever gotten up in the morning and prayed, "Holy Spirit, please put someone in my life today with whom I can share the truth about you"? It amazes me how often opportunities to share the gospel come my way when I take the time to make that request. As a father, I need to teach my children how to share their faith. That's part of my job as a father. What could be more important than teaching your children how to be used by the Holy Spirit to keep someone from eternal torment in hell?

We never know when God may call us home. We need to be ready right now. Many stories have come out about 9/11. This is just one by Dan Goldsmith that points out God's sovereignty and what can happen when we are yielded to the Spirit of God.

> Bill Faye, an evangelist who was a guest speaker at our church on Sunday, September 9, 2001, returned to his home in Denver on Monday, September 10. On his American Airlines flight, he saw a stewardess breaking up ice with a wine bottle. He got up from his seat and asked her if there wasn't another way she could more safely do it. He said he was afraid she would hurt herself. She was

12 Brian Kelly. "Atheist Magician Penn Jillette Says Christians Have Obligation to Proselytize," Catholicism.org, January 22, 2016, https://catholicism.org/atheist-magician-penn-jillette-says-christians-have-obligation-to-prosyletize.html.

> moved that he would be so concerned. He then gave her a gospel tract to read when she had a spare moment.
>
> A short time later she found Bill and told him that this was the sixth gospel tract she had received from someone. "What does God want from me?" she asked.
>
> Bill responded, "Your life." A few minutes later he was praying with her to accept Jesus Christ as her personal Lord and Savior.
>
> After the 9/11 attack on America, Bill looked up the names of those on American Airlines Flight 11, the first plane that crashed into the World Trade Center. The stewardess's name was listed. On Tuesday, 9/11, she entered into the eternal presence of her Lord and Savior—after being a Christian for less than 24 hours!
>
> God knows the times! He had led six people into this young lady's life in the weeks preceding her untimely death. If God leads you to witness to someone, *do it*! You never know when someone is living their final hours. And never hold back because someone else has already witnessed—this person received *six* tracts before one finally got through![13] (emphasis mine)

A friend of mine was asked by his grandson when the Rapture would occur. Dave's reply was wonderful! He said, "It's not important when the Rapture is coming. What is important is that when it comes, will you be ready? Are you?" It's amazing how God will use people who will believe Him and step out in simple, obedient faith!

---

13 Truth or Fiction.com, "The 9/11 Flight Attendant Who Found God Before Her Fatal Flight - Unproven!" published December 8, 2013, https://www.truthorfiction.com/billfay.

We live in a world of cast-off appliances, shallow friendships, and very little personal warmth and caring. Often this leads us to believe no one cares, no one loves us, and we have no real value. The following story recognizes that we may be tossed and torn, beaten and battered, but we are still of incredible worth to God.

> A speaker started off his seminar by holding up a $20 bill. In the room of 200, he asked, who would like this $20 bill? Hands started going up. He said, I am going to give this to one of you, but first, let me do this. He proceeded to crumple the bill up. He then asked, "Who still wants it?" Still the hands were up in the air. "Well," he replied, "what if I do this?" He dropped it on the ground and started to grind it into the floor with his shoe. He picked it up, now crumpled and dirty. "Now, who still wants it?" Still hands went into the air. "My friends, you all have learned a very valuable lesson. No matter what I did to the money, you still wanted it, because, it did not decrease in value. It was still worth 20 dollars. Many times, in our lives, we are dropped, crumpled and ground into the dirt by the decisions we make and the circumstances that come our way. We feel that we are worthless, but no matter what has happened or what will happen, you will never lose your value, dirty or clean, crumpled or finely creased, you are still priceless to Jesus. The worth of our lives comes not in what we do, or whom we know, but by Whose we are. You are special, don't ever forget it! [*sic*] May God bless you!"[14]

Truth is truth for all people, in all places, at all times. God says that we are fallen, sinful human beings, and therefore, we need a way to be cleansed of that sin or

---

14 "Twenty Dollars," InspirationPeak.com, published 1997-2008, www.inspirationpeak.com/cgi-bin/stories.cgi?record=33.

we cannot be in heaven with a Holy God. Jesus came to earth of His own volition to save His people, as many as would receive His free gift of salvation. Not all will choose to do so but the gift is there if they do respond to His call. As Christians, we can live Expecting a Heavenly Reward by Standing Firm Against the Devil. But it's about more than just our salvation. We are given a Unique Calling to go into all the world and tell others the good news; that is our Sacred Mission.

In this book, I have given you a strategy for living "intentionally" as a man. It's like anything else you learn; it won't work if you don't apply it. While I appreciate you reading the book, my real goal is to help you live a better life in view of honoring Jesus! To do so requires you to be a Man of Commitment, Honor, Responsibility, Initiative, Service, and Truth. Live as a child of Truth so you are indwelt with the Holy Spirit. It is from the Holy Spirit that we get the power to follow C. H. R. I. S. T.

In Ephesians 1:13, we discover that the Holy Spirit comes to live within us. "In Him, you also, after listening to the message of truth, the gospel of your salvation—*having also believed, you were sealed in Him with the Holy Spirit of promise*" (emphasis mine). It is the Holy Spirit that serves as our Teacher, *"But the Helper, the Holy Spirit, whom the Father will send in My name, He will teach you all things, and bring to your remembrance all that I said to you"* (John 14:26, emphasis mine).

In Acts 1:8, the Bible clearly tells us that we receive power from the Holy Spirit: "But *you will receive power when the Holy Spirit has come upon you;* and you shall be My witnesses both in Jerusalem, and in all Judea and Samaria, and even to the remotest part of the earth" (emphasis mine). When Jesus was on earth, He was 100 percent man and 100 percent God, but do you realize that it was in the power of the Holy Spirit that Jesus was able to live a sinless life? He was the only person to ever be able to do that. "How much more will the blood of Christ, *who through the eternal Spirit offered Himself without blemish to God,* cleanse your conscience from dead works to serve the living God?" (Hebrews 9:14, emphasis mine).

I am stunned at how many of us realize we are saved by faith but then believe we must work our way to heaven in our own strength, which isn't enough. We must turn to the Holy Spirit humbly knowing we need Him more than we need air and water to survive.

Let me pray for you:

> *Father, I ask that You bless everyone who reads this book. Let them live their lives realizing that You are worthy, and we are needy. Life can be so empty and hard without Your very presence in our lives. May the readers of this book Glorify God with their lives, Honor Jesus and Obey the Holy Spirit. It is from appreciation not obligation that we serve You and seek to advance Your cause. In the mighty and precious name of Jesus I pray,*
>
> *Amen!*

ABOUT THE AUTHOR

MIKE STANLEY has been a coach, mentor, and business owner for over fifty years. In his career he has coached seven State Champions, an All-American, a team state championship, as well as owning four McDonald's restaurants. Despite all these accomplishments, something was missing in Mike's life.

Yet, through a personal relationship with Jesus, he found peace. Now he shares with other men what he has experienced and learned through his writing and speaking.

Before Mike knew Jesus his primary motivation for coaching was self-serving. Now he seeks to honor Jesus in every way, both on and off the field. His mission in life is to model and teach biblical manhood. As such, he is most proud of his family and his time coaching the Columbus Crusaders, where Jesus is honored and manhood is taught.

God has graciously used Mike to lead men of all ages to Jesus and help them become what God has called them to be.

To learn more about Coach Mike Stanley and keep up with his weekly newsletters, visit his website, **WWW.MANHOODINACTION.ORG**, or contact him directly at Mike@ManhoodinAction.org.

INTENTIONAL MANHOOD, TAUGHT BY COACH STANLEY

COACH MIKE STANLEY is a seasoned speaker and teacher, available for consulting, speaking, and mentorship.

Intentional Manhood was designed with men's groups in mind, and is available at a bulk, discounted rate for churches and other organizations. For more information on booking Mike to teach Intentional Manhood in your church or small group, please contact Mike directly at:

MIKE@MANHOODINACTION.ORG

WWW.MANHOODINACTION.ORG

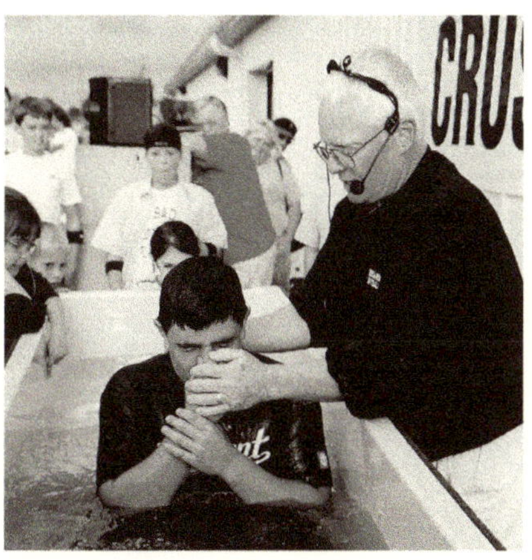

www.ingramcontent.com/pod-product-compliance
Lightning Source LLC
Chambersburg PA
CBHW030916090426
42737CB00007B/208

* 9 7 8 1 6 3 3 3 7 3 8 9 1 *